A SCHOOL FOR OTHERS

A SCHOOL FOR OTHERS

The History of the
Belize High School of Agriculture

A Memoir by George LeBard

To order additional copies of this book, contact:
Xlibris Corporation
1-888-795-4274
www.Xlibris.com
Orders@Xlibris.com
83136

CONTENTS

INTRODUCTION

When I first arrived in Belize, March 17, 1981, as a peace corps volunteer, I was thirty-one years old and struggling to survive. My life consisted of drinking, drugs, and one-night stands. I had no formal education and had low self-esteem.

During my time as a volunteer, I discovered empowerment. I also discovered an abandoned school in the jungle. That discovery was the beginning of a vision for the Belize High School of Agriculture, an institution of higher learning that would accept at-risk youth. These were students who would not otherwise have the opportunity to attend high school. My belief at the time was that these students were academically challenged and teaching them how to be entrepreneurs with their land offered the best option for them to succeed in life.

I requested funding to make the school a reality. The United States Agency for International Development and the United States Peace Corps agreed to provide the funds on the condition that I stay for another two years as a volunteer to manage the project. I agreed, and so the Belize High School of Agriculture began.

The years I worked on the school, 1984-1986, was an intense period for the country as Belize was introduced to the culture of drugs and drug-trafficking. As drug lords and their gangs jockeyed for position, the competition became deadly. The drug wars where I lived were so vicious and common that the local newspapers labeled the district "Rambo Town."

This is a true story that chronicles the history of how the Belize High School of Agriculture came into being. It's about empowerment, adventure, some unintentional altruism, and finding true love. In the end, we created something good and lasting in an environment that had been turned upside down by the greed and lust for drug money.

Everything in this book is true only the names have been changed to protect the innocent.

ACKNOWLEDGMENTS

There are a handful of people who helped make this book possible with their encouragement, editing, and occasional nudging. I would like to thank Katrina, Ann, Beth, Margie, Colleen, Emily, Andy, Deedie, Gwen, Linden, Elyse, Shai, Karli, and Julia. I also want to thank all the people who made the school a possibility. The first class of twenty-five students and teachers. Ces and Pedro, you took a leap of faith and made it happen. Margo and Steve for all their hard work. Arlen Johnson, for taking the school to the next level. John Masson, Father Wright, Ernest Raymond, David Eck, the Orange Walk REAP District Council, the United States Peace Corps, United States Agency for International Development, the Roman Catholic Mission of Belize, Orange Walk Rotary Club, the Belize Ministry of Education, Honorable Guadalupe Pech, Honorable Said Musa, Honorable Ruben Campos, Rosendo Urbina, Louis Lindo, Lou Miller. Bill Perrin and Neb, who believed I could do it when I wasn't even sure I could. The current Belize High School of Agriculture students and staff, especially Cecilio Pech, Pedro Baki, and Ben Ramos, whose dedication to teaching is inspirational. Last, but not least, my wife and kids who inspire me every day with their unconditional love and acceptance.

> *Man, despite his artistic pretensions, his sophistication, and his many accomplishments owes his existence to a six inch layer of top soil and the fact that it rains.*
>
> *—Anonymous*

Prologue

The Kings

There were three bikes in our motorcycle gang, but we did an awful lot of walking. That was because our parents did not allow us out on the motorcycles after dark. At least not at first. It was 1963 and I belonged to the Kings IV in Reno, Nevada. At thirteen years old, I was the youngest so I didn't have a motorcycle. I was a member because my friends had their motorcycles, and I was number four in the gang. The other gang members had two Honda Dreams and a Harley. We designed our own "colors" on the back of a Levi jacket with the sleeves cut off. Then we had the king of hearts, spades, clubs, and diamonds with the words Kings IV printed underneath. You were extra cool if you put your colors underneath your motorcycle overnight to catch any oil leaks. My colors took turns under all three bikes. The "Hell's Angels," the "Outlaws," and any other motorcycle gang that happened to roll through town were our heroes, and we envied the life they led—freedom on a Harley. We had big dreams for the Kings IV. We were going to control our own destiny and accomplish something with our lives. We were going to be modern-day Robin Hoods, taking from the powerful and rich to give to the poor.

The other three kings were Fred, Hugh, and Teddy. Other members were considered from time to time, but we were the originals. It was not that easy to become one of the Kings. I mean, we did not let just anybody into our gang. You had to pass a test or kind of an initiation. One of the first requirements was you had to participate in a "gang bang." That was when everyone in the gang screwed the same girl, one after the other. Or at least pretended to. Other requirements were smoking cigarettes, drinking, and doing anything against the law. You also had to have a switchblade in your pocket and be willing to use it if necessary.

For recreation, we used to cut school and hang out at the bowling alley playing the pinball machines. We did this for free by melting the end of a fishing line to a quarter and pulling our quarter back after it racked up a few games. We also used to walk down the main drag in town and watch all the tourists playing the slot machines. Sometimes, if it was cold, we went to a Sambo's restaurant and drank coffee for a nickel with all the free refills we wanted. There we talked about all the things we would do if we could. Then we usually ended up walking down the railroad tracks. If we were lucky, once in a while, we got to watch drunken Indians from the local reservation in a knife fight cutting each other up. We had to hide because if they spotted us, they would try to catch us. There were times we had to run for our lives.

It seems like we were always running from something. We were rebelling against the system, against being put in a box like our parents and everyone else. We thought our way was the way to a good life. We were determined not to become like everyone else. We felt the immortality of youth, and our rebellion was a badge of honor to us. It was better to become an outlaw than to become part of the system. We would spend our lives fighting the bad guys that represented the "establishment." In a fair world, we would win and become the heroes we wanted to be. Four young boys ready to take on the world. There was power in our ignorance, and there was power in knowing what we wanted.

Somewhere during the sixties, as I staggered along the path to adulthood, I lost contact with the other three kings. I also lost my way; I forgot who I was and all I wanted to be. There was always something there, nagging me in the back of my mind, telling me there was more to life, that my existence had meaning. I knew that in order to be successful and make something out of my life, I would have to change everything. The problem was that every time I thought about taking charge, I did what I always did—drank, did more drugs, and got laid. It didn't help me find what I was looking for, but it helped me forget that there might be something better.

ACT BY CONGRESS

Declaration of Purpose

The purpose of this Act (is) to promote world peace and friendship through a Peace Corps, which shall make available to interested countries and areas men and women of the United States . . .

(1). to help the peoples of such countries and areas in meeting their needs for trained manpower, and

(2). to help promote a better understanding of the American people on the part of the people served and

(3). a better understanding of other peoples on the part of the American people.

The Peace Corps Act,
United States Congress
September 22, 1961

1

Learning How to Walk, Talk, and Eat, 1981

It was an epiphany that shook me to my core. It happened during one of my crazy drug and alcohol binges, with bizarre behavior and blackouts, and then the appropriate apologies the following day. I realized, saw it clear as day, that if I didn't change my lifestyle quickly, I wouldn't live much longer.

The intensity of that truth hangs over me like a death sentence, and now here I am on a plane headed for a new life. A second chance—I'm running away from my old life and I know I've got to make it work.

The TACA 737 makes a sharp bank to the right as we come in over the Caribbean Sea, and then left and we're over a mangrove swamp. I can see a long, brown river winding around like a snake toward the sea. We come in low over coconut and palm trees, onto a runway flanked by camouflaged tanks, antiaircraft guns, jeeps, and helicopters. Soldiers in camouflage uniforms stand along the runway and around a small building that I'm guessing is the airport terminal. In the distance, I see two Harrier jets lined up for takeoff. Our pilot settles down easy and makes a smooth landing. Everyone on the overcrowded plane gives a big applause for the pilot's skill, inspired in part because of TACA's generosity with free liquor. It is 3:45 p.m. Belize time.

I step off the plane and I'm immediately hit with a wall of tropical heat and heavy humidity. A small group of people are waving their hands and pointing in the direction of an octagon-shaped building separate from the airport terminal. Our group of thirteen new Peace Corps trainees touches the ground for the first time in our new home. We're checking out all the sights and sounds along the way, trying to get a feel for the country and people we'll be living with for the next two years.

Even with sunglasses on, everything's a glare. The Caribbean sun is intense and the airport looks barren. It's just a big cement landscape with clumps of weeds growing in between the cracks. The only contrast is the Belize flag—bright blue, red, and white, flying on a small flagpole on top of the airport terminal. In the background is a panoramic blue sky with towering white clouds floating across. There are soldiers scattered strategically around the airport. They're tall, black, sturdy-looking men in freshly pressed, slightly worn green uniforms. They look very serious with tight grips on their automatic weapons. The octagon building looks like the only friendly shade around.

One week earlier, when I was saying my good-byes, people were telling me that they admired my courage. They couldn't understand how I could leave everything I knew and loved to join the Peace Corps and go live in a foreign country for two years. In a way, I felt guilty for accepting their praise because for me, it was easy to leave. I knew that if I stayed where I was and continued living the way I was, I was going to die. I was not afraid to leave; I was afraid to stay.

The twelve others in our group will be my friends for the next two years. In my world back home, these are not people I would choose to hang out with. There are five older people: Alfred, in his early seventies; Alan, a real estate salesman in his sixties; Betty, a woman in her late sixties, who takes to bossing Alfred around right away; another guy, Joe, in his late thirties; and then Doc who's in his late fifties. Joe's a mercenary type who likes to read *Soldier of Fortune* and see what he can get for nothing. Doc's not really a doc at all; he just likes to be called that. He had started out to be an optometrist, but somewhere along the way, he let his drinking get the better of him. Doc's partner is Charlie or Carlos, as he likes to be called. Carlos and Doc are partners only in the sense that they were in a Peace Corps program in Guatemala together. They had to be pulled out because of the escalating violence brought on by the civil war there. Peace Corps Belize has an opening for them, but they have to go through preservice training again. That's something they're not too excited about. They complain that it's like repeating fourth grade all over again.

The rest of our group is younger and fresh out of college. Ryan and Olivia from Minnesota are twenty-four years old and the only married couple. Sabrina from Los Angeles, twenty years old; she's a big girl, about six feet two inches and around 190 pounds. She has dark eyes and an exotic look about her that makes her attractive. Linda from Louisiana is a twenty-one year-old, brown-eyed brunette, a little chunky and a real southern belle. She's looking for romance and a man to take care of her. John from Michigan is twenty-two, five feet seven inches, a little chunky and looking for a woman to take care of. Alex, who is a six-foot, 190-pound, twenty-two-year-old jock with a habit of grabbing his balls while you're talking to him, is from Boston.

Then there's me: thirty-one years old, six feet tall, and a skinny 155 pounds on a good day, with reddish-blond hair and fair skin that burns at the thought of going into the sun. The difference between me and the rest of the group is education. They've all been to college and have degrees. I had a hard time finishing high school, but I know people and have a knack for getting along with just about anyone.

The staff of Peace Corps Belize meets us in the octagonal building. We're given an official welcome and introductions are made. A beautiful brown-skinned woman with green eyes and a seductive smile collects our government-issued passports and we're out the door and into a van. The Belize International Airport is about fifteen miles north of Belize City on the Northern Highway. We drive about eight miles south to the Rio Haul Motel situated next to where the Rio Haul River empties into the Caribbean Sea. The rooms are shabby with paint peeling off, dirt smudges around the doorknobs, torn window screens, dirty floors and mattresses, cobwebs and a single uncovered neon light in the middle of the room. Not having enough rooms, they put all the single men into one room and single women into another, with Ryan and Olivia getting their own room. There are only two beds to a room, so we take mattresses and spread them on the floor.

Once we get settled, I dig out my swimsuit.

"Hey John, I'm going to take a swim. You want to come?"

"Naw, I'm going to rest."

Everyone else has already gone in search of the bar, so I look for a place to get in the water. There's a small rickety pier on the river and I walk over to check it out. The river looks dangerous, dark, and deep with strong currents and undertows swirling in every direction. It's not like the clear mountain rivers I'm used to around Lake Tahoe. I look over at the sea and up both sides of the river for something that resembles a beach. There's a lot of mangrove and swamp but no beaches.

In the five minutes I've been standing here in my swimsuit, the mosquitoes, sandflies, and every other type of flesh-eating insect known to man has managed to find me. Here I am, my first day in the tropics of the Caribbean and not only is there no place to swim, but I'm also getting eaten alive. I make a beeline back to my room and get into the shower to cool off with warm, rusty water. It's so hot and humid that before I can dry off, I'm sweating again.

I'm ready to find the bar and everyone else when Linda shows up. "Hi, George, I thought you might be here. Everyone else is in the bar." She comes in the room and closes the door behind her. I know what she wants and I want no part of it.

"Yeah, I'm just heading there myself. Can I buy you a beer?"

"I think I want to rest for a minute first."

Dressed in a short cotton skirt and a low-cut top that leaves nothing to the imagination, she sits down on one of the mattresses. She's an attractive, sexy woman and she knows it.

"So tell me about yourself. What's Tahoe like?" She leans back on her elbows, looking even more seductive. The thought of locking the door and joining her on the bed is getting stronger, along with the rise in my pants. I have to admit at home I would have taken her to bed in a second and not worried about following up with any kind of relationship. The difference between then and now is the fact that we're going to be in close quarters for the next three months. I don't need or want to start anything that will distract me from this new adventure, no matter how horny I am. That's the old me. The new me, using all my will power and discipline, walks over to the door and opens it. "Come on, I'll tell you about it over a beer."

Turns out the bar is two rusty refrigerators behind the desk in the motel office. I buy two warm beers and give one to Linda. Then we go to join everyone sitting in a small patio area.

"Hey, where were you two?"

John is the only one who seems to notice we were missing, and I pick up a tinge of jealousy from his remark. Linda, being the charmer that she is, doesn't miss a beat. "We were looking for the bar and you guys." Smiling her best down-home southern smile, she heads directly to where the women have congregated. They seem to be addressing some concern that Sabrina has. I sit down next to John who, again, asks me where we were.

"We were talking about you." I make a quick decision to play matchmaker.

"You were? What about me?" I can see right away that he's completely smitten with Linda.

"I think she likes you. She's definitely interested in you."

"Really, how do you know?"

"She asked me a couple of questions, like where you're from—what you're like.

"What'd you tell her?"

"I said you're a nice guy and that's all I know about you. I think you ought to talk to her when you get the chance."

"You think so?"

"Yeah, why not? She's a pretty lady and it might be worth your time." I leave John to ponder the possibilities of him and Linda and get into a conversation with Doc and Carlos about Guatemala. After a few more beers, someone breaks out the rum, and we start drinking rum and Coke. There's some reggae music coming from a radio someplace, and that, plus the rum and Coke, makes me finally feel like I'm in the Caribbean.

The men's room doesn't get much sleep that night because it's so hot. If we open the one window we have, mosquitoes storm the room. It's either hot or mosquitoes so we take turns opening the window until the mosquitoes become unbearable, and then we close it until the heat's making us suffocate. Once we get to sleep, either sandflies (also known as "no-see-ums") biting us or mouse-sized cockroaches running across our faces or down our legs wake us. Ryan and Olivia have a bad infestation of sand flies in their mattress, and they get infections from all the bites on their legs that last for weeks.

I remember when I first discovered that Belize is on the Caribbean Sea. I imagined myself in a hammock on the beach, with coconut trees, beautiful brown-skinned women, and a pina colada in my hand. Now I'm having a dream that I'm in a white room with bright lights and a heater that I can't find the off switch for. Every time I try to turn it off, I get attacked by a swarm of mosquitoes. Then I wake up, wipe the sweat off my face, and try to swat some of the mosquitoes buzzing around my ears. Welcome to the tropics.

We find out later that we're the only Peace Corps group to stay at this particular motel. Every other new group to Belize spends their first few days at the luxurious San Ignacio Hotel in the Cayo District. The Cayo District is a popular spot with Americans because of its cool mountainous terrain, with rushing rivers and beautiful waterfalls all set in a background of tropical vegetation. The San Ignacio Hotel itself is first class with air-conditioned rooms, hot and cold water, and a swimming pool.

Eventually, we discover the reason we're denied these luxurious accommodations. Recently, there's been rioting in the district towns, and there was a big riot in Belize City the night before our arrival. To get to the Cayo District means passing through Belize City. The Peace Corps staff did not want to take us through the city because we would see all the signs of the riot. They were justly worried that some of us might get scared and go home. As a result, we're the first group to stay at the beautiful Rio Haul motel, for three fun-filled days, fighting mosquitoes and sandflies. The whole time thinking this is the same treatment all new Peace Corps trainees received.

The motel does have semicold beer, and the Peace Corps staff donates a few bottles of good Belizean rum. Happily, all of our meals are catered from outside. The whole purpose of three days together in a hotel is to give the training staff an opportunity to provide us with an orientation to Belizean culture and customs. This is in preparation for meeting our Belizean host families, whom we'll be living with for the next three months of preservice training.

We can't even call ourselves Peace Corps volunteers until we're sworn in at the end of our thirteen-week training period. Until then, we're known as Peace Corps "trainees." Another purpose for the three days alone at the motel is to get familiar with the people in our group and begin that bonding process that lasts forever, no matter how diverse your fellow trainees are.

The training staff, all Belizeans, give us a list of do's and don'ts. "Do" listen to your host mother, father, brothers, and sisters and ask for advice when you're not sure what to do in a particular situation. "Don't," if you're female, give your underwear to your host mother to clean. "Ladies clean their own underwear." Women are told to wear bras and slips. "Do" communicate your needs, likes, and dislikes and learn to work out problems or miscommunication. "Don't" spend a lot of time hanging out with other Peace Corps trainees or volunteers. "Do" spend time with your host family. "Don't" get involved in Belizean politics. "Do" keep your eyes and ears open and learn as much as possible about Belize.

We do an exercise on our second day where we all sit around in a circle and share different things about ourselves. "What do you consider your greatest accomplishment in life?" Mr. York is leading the session.

Everyone thinks for a minute, and all the answers are very positive: "Getting my master's degree," "Getting married," "Raising my children." Then it's my turn and I say the first thing that comes to mind: "Staying alive." I say it without even thinking of the impact it might have. Immediately, everyone becomes silent and looks at me. "What do you mean, George?" It's Denise and I know I've raised a warning flag across her radar.

"Just kidding." I smile. "My greatest accomplishment was finishing my apprenticeship as a chef." It works. Everyone nods approvingly and we move on.

We continue probing each other after we're done with our little bonding session and having a few beers. I don't tell them about the time I was sixteen and died in the backseat of a car inhaling gasoline fumes through the pour spout of a gas can because someone said it was a good high. Or the time I overdosed on a particularly strong batch of heroin. I also don't mention my recent cocaine and alcohol problem. There are a number of things I feel best to keep to myself. None of them are anything I'm very proud of except for the fact that I'm still around. I know I have a long way to go. It's the beginning of a healing process that I'll have to keep to myself.

I make a mental note to watch what I say and who I say it to. I'm being scrutinized and tested like all the other trainees, and I don't want to give them a reason to send me home.

We're entering a new culture where values and priorities are different, not good or bad, but different. Basically, we're learning how to walk, talk, and eat all over again. It doesn't matter if you had a PhD or had been a chief executive officer of a huge corporation just three days earlier. We're all equal in starting over, and I figure that gives me an advantage. Our status here depends on our ability to adapt and survive. That's something I know how to do. I've made it so far, despite a few bad decisions.

The training staff is our first contact with Belizean culture. The training director is a very distinguished Creole man in his early seventies, who has the ultimate respect of the training and Peace Corps staff. He has his own driver and people rush to open doors for him. He speaks in crisp, precise words with an accent that sounds both Caribbean and British. It's called "the Queen's English," just enough to remind you that Belize is a British colony. His name is Edward York. He's assured of himself and his position. When he appears, it's as if we're in the presence of a king. He's someone who has aged with distinction. His gray hair is always trimmed and his eyes sparkle. He moves a little slow because of his age, but he always has a smile and he speaks with humility. I can't help but like the man. The respect for him is genuine.

The majority of the Peace Corps Belize staff are Belizean. Denise, the programming and training officer (PTO), is our closest American contact. She's an attractive woman in her midthirties, slender build and short dark hair. Denise (Mr. York pronounces her name Dennis) lets us know she's available if we need her. Otherwise, the Belizean training staff is in charge.

It's time to move on to our next stage of training in Belize City. We've been at the motel for three days now, consuming mass quantities of beer and rum and getting to know each other while retaining a wealth of knowledge about the "do's" and "don'ts" of Belizean culture. It's time for a change, time to meet our host families.

2

The Mosquito Coast and
My New Family

Belize City literally sits upon the Caribbean Sea, one foot above sea level. Some historians say it was built on top of mangrove swamps and the rum bottles left there by the pirates and loggers that called the Mosquito Coast home. At one time, it was the capital of the country, but in 1961, Hurricane Hattie did so much damage that the government offices were moved about fifty miles inland. The new capital, Belmopan, became the seat of the nation's government.

Belize City is considered the "business capital" of Belize and the hub of activity, with the international airport, deep-water port, and the beginnings of all roads leading to the rest of the country. With a population of forty-five thousand, it is the largest city in Belize. The majority of residents are Creole, descendants from African slaves brought to British Honduras to cut logwood in the 1800s.

My first impression of the city is similar to the airport with cement, heat, high humidity, and the sun's glare. We see signs of the riot that had kept us out for the first few days, a few cars that were burned and overturned and small patrols of soldiers in camouflage uniforms on the streets.

The downtown area is a maze of narrow one-way streets with parked cars on both sides. Traffic's thick with vehicles, bicyclists, and pedestrians all scrambling to avoid each other. Buses and trucks rumble through the streets, seemingly oblivious to the fact that they barely miss parked cars and bicyclists.

Taxicabs stop wherever and whenever they want, holding up traffic while they pick up or let off passengers while everyone blows their horns at them. Sidewalks are overflowing with a steady stream of pedestrians going in both directions. From watching people on the street, I can see that Creole comes in all shades, from black to light brown.

The city is divided in the middle by the Belize River and the famous swing bridge. The bridge opens sideways twice each day at 8:00 a.m. and 5:00 p.m. to allow boat traffic between the river and the sea. Buildings along the main street contrast between modern two- and four-story professional cement structures to older single-story wood-house dwellings that are converted into commercial shops or restaurants.

There are deep canals fed by smaller canals crisscrossing the city and eventually emptying into the sea. They look like thick, stagnant rivers of raw sewage. People's homes line both sides of the canals, and their plumbing empties directly into it. In the evening and early morning, children and women empty "night soil" from five-gallon plastic buckets into the canals or directly into the sea.

Once we leave the downtown area, the streets became wider and quiet, with little or no traffic. Some areas have traditional colonial homes—remnants of British influence. Other neighborhoods have tall wooden houses carefully balanced on stilts in between cement block houses. There's more color here with the bright colors of the homes contrasted by the tropical vegetation and the blue sea.

We drive from street to street, dropping off members of our group one by one to their host families. John and I are going to share a family, and we get dropped off last on Douglas Jones Street.

Our new home is on the second floor of a wooden two-story building. Downstairs is a carpet store. Our level has three bedrooms, two baths, a kitchen, dining room, and a living room with a veranda that overlooks the street. John and I join our three new brothers in a room that's very clean and organized. Five metal-framed single beds are lined up in a row resembling army barracks. The south wall facing the street has three windows with glass louvers and clean, white curtains blowing lightly in a sea breeze that carries the smell of the canal with it. The east wall has two windows, with the morning sun reflecting off clean windows. A bathroom adjoins our room, complete with a bathtub with a shower. The west wall has a large closet with shelves to put away our belongings and hang up our clothes. The only other furniture in the room is a small desk in the corner by the bathroom. After three days in a mosquito- and cockroach-infested motel, this looks pretty good.

My host mother, Miria, is "Mestizo" (a mixture of Maya and Spanish). My new father, John, is Creole with dark brown skin. The rest of the family includes two beautiful host sisters, Andrea and Maria, and three host brothers, Hubert, Miguel and David. Miria (who has the same birth date as my real mother) is a housewife, and my host father works at one of the better-known businesses in town as a sales manager. Besides their children at home, they have a daughter living in Chicago and a son living in Belmopan.

Hubert, twenty-two and Miguel, nineteen, work full time for a framing shop right around the corner. Andrea, eighteen, is in her last year of high school. Maria, sixteen, is in her sophomore year of high school and is a real dark-eyed beauty. David, at thirteen, is the baby of the house in middle school. All of my host brothers and sisters are light brown skinned and can pass for either Spanish or Creole. Because they've grown up in the Creole culture of Belize City, Creole is their first language and what they consider themselves to be.

Right away, I notice the close relationship of the family. Everyone is respectful to each other, especially the children to the parents. The father is waited on to the extreme. His food is brought to him. Even his bath is prepared for him. His work clothes and casual clothes are always laid out for him. When they speak to him, they address him as "papa" and answer him with a "yes, sir" or a "no, sir." Whenever he's mentioned in absence by my host mother, she refers to him as "Mr. Johnson." The children refer to him as "father" in his absence.

My new mother is small and stout, about five feet tall with short black hair peppered with gray. She's wearing a sack dress that makes her look wider than she really is and big thick glasses that make her eyes look big and a little comical. She's very talkative and wants to know all about us and what we're going to do in Belize. From some part of the house, I can hear a reggae beat and Bob Marley on the radio singing "No Woman, No Cry." At first, it's difficult to understand what Miria's saying, and I have to concentrate on listening carefully to her words. Her accent is Creole and Spanish, with Spanish being her first language. The background music adds rhythm to the Creole. She ended most of her sentences with "yes mon," "no mon," or "no true."

"Where are you from? Where is your home?"

"I come from Lake Tahoe, Nevada."

"Where is Nevada?"

"It's close to California and Lake Tahoe is in the mountains. From where I lived, I could walk to California."

"Oh yes, mon. I know di place. Mi daughter Sylvia lives in Chicago."

I really like my new mother. She seems genuine and interested in learning more about us. Our host brothers and sisters are very polite and quiet.

I'm witnessing a family life that I've only imagined before. I grew up afraid of my stepfather. I disliked being around him and, as a result, avoided any kind of home life. I respected him, but it was respect born out of fear. My mother's allegiance was to my stepfather, so she was never a big part of my life. Here in Belize, I'm seeing a family that has mutual respect for each other, has daily communication, and is very open about their feelings and needs.

In the early evening, the family goes out on the veranda over the street to watch kids playing and the people taking a walk or riding their bikes past. People going by sometimes shout out a greeting or stop to talk for a while. Mr. John, my host father, usually arrives home late in the evening, and I can tell he likes his scotch. He "drinks tea," bathes, and goes to bed. Some days, we only see him for a few minutes. Once in a while, one of his buddies comes over for a visit, and they sit on the veranda drinking scotch. They like to tell jokes and stories. At first, they're very hard to understand since they only speak Creole. I have to ask them to repeat the story until I understand.

I learn to take some of my questions to my host brothers. Others I take to my mother, who's always ready to talk about things. Miria (mom), Andrea, and Hubert are the most helpful to me when I have questions. Overall, I feel they're interested in me and want to help me adapt to their culture. It's very obvious that they're proud of their country and proud to be Belizeans.

As I get to know them better, I'm impressed with their insight and concern about the future of their country. They're on the verge of gaining independence from Great Britain, a move they have some grave concerns about including national security and economic factors. This is a decision that everyone, old and young, is involved with. Some Belizeans are for it, and others are against it.

My host family and the political party they belong to happen to be against it. They say Belize isn't ready to be independent. Some say that the government is making secret negotiations called the "Heads of Agreement" to cede some of Belize's territory to Guatemala. They suspect it's being done as part of a security pact to settle a long-standing claim by Guatemala that Belize belongs to them. There are other issues, but this one fuels the most passion and the recent riots. All Belizeans are opposed to any negotiations with Guatemala. They don't trust Guatemalans and considered them violent and racist. I can see Belizeans are knowledgeable and passionate when it comes to the future of their country. This is a level of thinking and awareness that has been absent from my life since the sixties and the Vietnam War.

This is my new family, whom I'll be living with for the next thirteen weeks while I go through preservice training. It feels good to unpack my bags and have a home.

3

Exploring the City

Every morning, we have to be at the training center by 8:00 a.m. For me, that means a twenty-minute walk that includes crossing one busy street, Free Town Boulevard, and a cab/bus stop area with the story-book name of Cinderella Plaza. The rest of my walk is through a fairly quiet residential neighborhood on Bayman Avenue. About halfway there, the Caribbean Sea comes into view and, along with it, a refreshing breeze that cools down my sweaty body.

I love seeing the children passing me on their way to school, looking shiny and clean in their freshly pressed school uniforms of white shirts and navy blue pants or skirts. You can see the wonder and eagerness in their bright faces as they make their way through the streets, trying to keep their uniforms clean. Most of them are Creole, and they're always polite, responding to my "Good morning" with "Mawning, suh."

Our training takes place in a large room below the director's house. It consists of cultural orientation along with the history and geography of Belize. There are lots of safety, health, and medical orientations we have to go through too. Most of it is boring, sitting on hard chairs while we listen to our trainer's lecture.

Training also involves a lot of drinking. A few of us like to get together and drink a few beers after class each day. We also host or go to parties on the weekends. It's like first aid for culture shock and helps everyone get used to our new environment. For me, it's a fix to help me through the withdrawal of my other addictions. I figure if I can stay away from the hard booze and cocaine, I'm making progress.

There are no real bars, or at least not any that we feel comfortable going into. Instead, we go to Chinese restaurants when we want to drink. There's one on every corner, and it seems to be the culturally appropriate thing to do. We feel safe sitting at a table in a restaurant drinking beer as compared to going into one of the dark places we've seen that resemble nightclubs.

I don't see much of John, and when I do, he seems preoccupied. He's completely infatuated with Linda and thinks about nothing else. He leaves before me in the mornings so he can meet her, and they walk together to the training center. Ever since the motel, they've been joined together at the hip. It's one of those relationships where one person is clearly in charge, and it's not John.

A pattern develops with the Belizean adults I meet on my walks. Some are leaving for work, some are working in their yards, and others are taking a walk. Always friendly, they stop to say "hallo," or "how da mawning?" or "good day, sir." Some speak the Queen's English while others speak Creole and are harder to understand. I shake hands with them, introduce myself, and learn their names. I also learn that in Creole, to say hello to someone is to "hail" them. "I am going to hail you when you pass by" means I'm going to call out to you and say hello whenever I see you. I also noticed that they don't conjugate their contractions, which has the effect of making what they say more meaningful in a way. Instead of "I'll say hello," it's "I will hail you." It's become part of my daily routine to "hail" these people every morning.

The first few days of training, I go out exploring with the rest of our group after classes. Everything's new and exciting to us, and we want to check out the city. We try not to stand out too much by going in smaller groups of twos and threes, but we still feel like we're in a fishbowl. In between the Chinese restaurants are the small shops with names like Mona Lisa, New Morning, and the Glory Store. They all sell an amazing variety of things from tennis shoes to bicycles to underarm deodorant. The "Hindu" community owns all these small shops. Belizeans call all East Indians "Hindu," regardless of their religion or birth country.

Further downtown and across the swing bridge is the "market"—an outdoor farmer's market alongside the Belize River. It's about half the size of a football field, covered with a rusty zinc roof for protection from the sun and the rain. Inside, it's filled with open stalls and vendors selling just about anything you might desire. Belizeans go there to buy fresh fruits, vegetables, meat, and seafood.

Every time I walk into the market, my senses are overwhelmed with a barrage of colors, smells and, noises. On a typical day, it's crowded with men and women bargaining for the best deal. Children are dashing around playing or being towed in tears by their ears behind their mothers. Beggars have their hand out; a vendor chasing a thief; hungry, mangy dogs hanging back just out of kicking range waiting for a scrap to be thrown or dropped. In the meat section, bloody, fly-covered quarters of beef and pork swing from large rusty hooks hanging down from cross beams. Every so often, the butcher waves a bloody towel in their direction and the flies lift off, like a small black cloud. The cloud hovers just out of reach for a moment before settling back down to their feast. The fish vendors work alongside the river, gutting and filleting fish and throwing the guts right back into the chocolate-colored water (which is also where the same fish are being cleaned). Large sea turtles trapped on their backs are unmercifully cut up alive. They're selling fresh, "undersized" lobsters and conch; the biggest and the best go to the fish co-op for sale abroad. "The market" is where people go, and it's full of commotion, connections, and activity. Everyone's yelling, bargaining, arguing, hustling, fighting, and laughing all at the same time. This is a good place to start the day.

Past the market are the banks and a couple of modern supermarkets. Brodie's and Romac's sell just about anything you'd find in a supermarket in the USA. But you have to pay high prices since practically everything is imported from the UK or the United States. The Belize dollar is tied to the U.S. dollar; two Belize dollars equal one American dollar. Our Peace Corps allowance is equal to about sixty-five U.S. dollars per week, not enough to shop in Brodie's or Romac's. But we're into checking things out and window-shopping. I buy a few postcards to send back home to family and friends.

Belizeans on the street are, for the most part, friendly. Little boys on the street come up to us holding out their hands. "Plees, mista, gimme shilling (quarter), mista." There are a few older and sometimes crippled beggars on the streets, in corners or doorways, holding their hands out. People seem to ignore them. A scammer approaches us thinking we're tourists.

"Hey, white man. I got sumting fo yu." I hear him calling me, but I keep walking, hoping he'll go away. He catches up with me and, holding out his hand, he introduces himself. "My name is John." I shake his hand but keep walking.

"Hi, John." I don't want to talk to this guy, but I don't want to be rude either.

"What is your name, mon?" He hustles to keep up with me.

"George. I'm a Peace Corps volunteer."

"George, yes mon. I have a cousin named George. Eh all right, mon. You want to see Belize, no true?"

"No, thanks. I live here. I'm a Peace Corps volunteer." Maybe he didn't hear me the first time.

"George, you have a dollar you can give me? I want to get some bread."

"No, I don't have a dollar." I hear him cussing as he trails off and I keep walking.

We've been warned about "street scammers"—bad guys that prey on tourists, offering to take them to the best places Belize has to offer. Once they get a victim somewhere out of sight, they rob them.

After a couple of weeks, the newness wears off, and unless we have a training assignment that requires us to go downtown, I usually go home at three o'clock. The heat and humidity are too much for me by late afternoon. It feels good to take a short nap and work on any Peace Corps homework assignment I might have before heading back at 5:00 for Creole classes.

After Creole class and a few beers, it's time to go home for dinner or "tea," as the evening meal is called even though there's usually no tea involved. Most Belizeans substitute instant coffee for the traditional tea time.

The average Belizean doesn't have TV. There are a few of the wealthier families with satellite dishes, and the nicest hotel in town has a dish, but the rest of Belize listens to the "stories" on Radio Belize. The stories are British soap operas, and they come on every day at noon. If you walk down the streets at 12:00 p.m., the radios are turned up, and you hear the stories coming from everywhere. People eat lunch in their cars so they can listen to the stories on their car radios. Businesses and shops have their radios blaring into the streets. Everyone—big burly men, mothers, students, young, and old—listens as if the stories are a real life drama they're all involved in.

It's nice not to have a TV around to distract me. If I want to hear news, I listen to Radio Belize, the one and only (government controlled) radio station popularly known by the political opposition party as "Radio Disease." The regular Belize news is on every hour, and the British Broadcasting Corporation (BBC) is on twice a day for world news.

To hear about U.S. news, we rely on our free weekly *Newsweek*, which I always read cover to cover, hungry for news from home.

The first topic in training is "hot spots"—places in the city you don't want to go because there's danger of being mugged, beaten, or raped. There are also new hot spots because of the recent riots and the political situation. They use a map of the city to show us different areas that are "off-limits." For political purposes, the city is divided into electoral divisions that represent different residential and business areas. Each division has a political representative that's voted in by the constituents for that particular area. The divisions each have their own names like "New Town Barracks," "Pickstock," or "Kings Park." That's how you identify where you are or where you're going.

Throughout the city, they have "base boys." These are young men and boys who pick out corners next to various downtown neighborhoods as their base. Bases are used to hang out, make connections, sell drugs, and sometimes just to harass and intimidate people who walk by. Belizeans know where the bases are and can point them out on a map.

There's anywhere from four to eight boys to a base, hanging out bare-chested with unbuttoned pants hanging down around their underwear. Most of them are fairly big, muscular, and intimidating. Sometimes they try to sell me pot, telling me they have something that will make me "smile and hop like a frog."

The base boys in Cinderella Plaza are usually in a pickup game of soccer at a small park close to the plaza when I walk through in the mornings. In the afternoons, they're hanging out in the shade looking for action. Since we're new and don't understand Creole, we're not always sure what they're saying to us. Sometimes it's "Hey, white boy," said in a challenging tone. I'm a minority here, so I figured its best I don't always know what they're saying.

It's harder for girls to walk past bases. As soon as they see a girl, any girl, white or Creole, they start with the *pssst pssst* hissing noise that most Belizeans use to get someone's attention. When they get closer, they start with comments like, "Hey, white gial. Yu jes mi size. Want to feel sum pressuur." If a girl happens to be with a guy, that doesn't even slow them down. They still have rude comments unless it's a Belizean man who understands what they're saying and has the muscle to stand up to them. Base boys only respect those that can hurt or intimidate them, and unfortunately, I can't do either.

By keeping my eyes open, I learn to avoid these guys. Sometimes if I'm going downtown and I see a base, I cross the street and act like I know where I'm going. Base boys only pay attention to the first ten feet directly in front of them. There are some loners on the street that might go after you, asking for money or trying to pull a scam. They're harder to avoid.

Mugging is part of life in the city. Every time a Peace Corps volunteer gets mugged, it's reported to the Peace Corps office. Then an official complaint is lodged with the U.S. Consulate, who makes an official complaint to the commissioner of police. The police then feel they have to make a show of force and come out just like in the old movies of the *Keystone Kops*. They all pile into the two or three old Land Rovers they own and pick up as many base boys as they can catch. They take them back to the station house, beat the crap out of them, and keep them locked up for a day or two before releasing them back on the streets. You always know when something's up because the bases are empty for a few days.

Because of mugging and other crimes, Belize occasionally makes it on the embassy's "travel advisory" list. The advisory makes it clear that Belize is considered a "high-crime" location and that you're taking a risk if you come here.

On weekends, we all try to plan trips outside the city. Peace Corps staff encourages us to check out the rest of the country. Just getting around is a lesson in itself. It takes me a while to learn which buses go where and that Belizean time is different than American time. I get into a cab one time hoping to catch a 3:00 p.m. bus to the districts. I notice the driver's clock on the dash says 3:10.

"Is that the right time?"

"Yes, mon. Di clock correct."

"Well, I've already missed the three o'clock bus to Corozal then."

"No, mon," he said wagging his finger, "bus no leave yet."

He gets me to the bus in time, and I end up sitting in it for another ten minutes before we pull out. I eventually learn that everything's on Belize time and can run as much as thirty minutes late. Sometimes meetings start even later, unless it's a government agency.

4

Riot

Today, I skip the usual after-class get-together for a beer and go home early, about 3:00 p.m. The house is empty; in fact, it seems strangely quiet. It's the first time no one's been home since my arrival eight weeks ago. I have an uneasy feeling, like something's wrong. Trying to ignore the silence, I get settled in my room to do some homework.

I'm sitting at my desk letting the fan blow full speed in my face when I hear the unmistakable sound of the power going off. I know right away it's not just at our house; the whole neighborhood has lost power. When there's no electricity, all the background noises become louder. I'm waiting for it to come back on when I hear a faraway buzzing noise that's getting louder and louder. Now I recognize it as voices, thousands of voices blended together into one loud drone. I look out the second floor window and see the streets filled with people for as far as I can see. Many of them are students in their school uniforms. There must be a thousand people on our little street alone, and I see hundreds more going past on the side streets, all surging forward to merge together like one big animal. No one is shouting or chanting. They seem to be talking to each other, having normal conversations.

Not sure what's going on, I stay out of sight on the balcony and watch. From the direction of downtown, I hear someone on a loudspeaker shouting words I can't clearly understand. After about twenty minutes, my street and the side streets are completely empty, like no one was ever there. I see the tail end of the animal moving closer to downtown. The voices once again become a faraway drone, now joined by the voice on the loudspeaker. After another thirty minutes, sirens begin to wail, and I see smoke coming from the downtown area.

I go back into the house and turn my boom box to batteries. Tuning into Radio Belize, I get a regular program with absolutely no indication of what's happening downtown. Frustrated, I curse the government-controlled radio station out loud. Twenty minutes later, the station goes to dead air.

Since no one's home, I assume that they're in the big animal that just passed by. I feel left out and a little threatened. I'm not sure what to do. I suspect this has to do with the "Heads of Agreement." I don't feel like I'm in any kind of real danger, but I don't feel safe enough to go follow the crowd either.

Thirty minutes later, Denise and some of the trainees are in front of my house blowing their horn. They gather us all at the training center to make sure we stay out of trouble. Someone thoughtfully brought along a few bottles of rum, so we make rum and Cokes and sit on the veranda watching the smoke from the fire burning downtown. We're close to the sea, and we can see the fire across the bay about a mile away. The whole thing's a little scary but kind of exciting too.

Sabrina joins the party late and is crying. It seems that what had started as a peaceful demonstration against the government's Heads of Agreement turned into a rioting, looting mob. A fire was started to burn down the income tax building right around the corner from Sabrina's host family. There was a big mob in front of her house, and the fire had spread dangerously close. Because of the mob, she had to be rescued by Belizean Peace Corps staff members. Grabbing what she could carry of her personal possessions, she followed them as they pushed their way through the angry crowd to the car. No one had harmed her, but being that close to the fire and the protesting mob had scared the hell out of her. After a few rum and Cokes, she calms down and watches the fire with us.

Around 8:30 p.m., five hours after it went off the air, Radio Belize comes back on and Prime Minister George Price is speaking to the country. He officially declares a state of emergency, announcing a 9:00 p.m. to 6:00 a.m. curfew effective immediately. Soldiers will be out patrolling the streets, arresting anyone caught out after the curfew. That means our little party is over, and we all get rides back to our host families, except for Sabrina. She goes home with Denise.

My family is home and pumped up with excitement. They had all been downtown and part of the action, and they're enthusiastically filling me in with all the details. First, they tell me that the whole thing had been carefully coordinated for all public servants and students to walk out at the same time. The public servants turned off the city's power and water when they left. When the fire started at the income tax building, the fire department showed up to do their job, but the mob cut their fire hoses with machetes. At some point, a bad element of the crowd had decided to take advantage of all the chaos and started breaking shop windows to do a little looting on the side. Those in the more organized part of the demonstration had managed to take over Radio Belize and barricade themselves inside. Their goal had been to let the rest of Belize know what was happening in Belize City in the hopes of sparking off similar demonstrations planned for the district towns. They were unsuccessful, however, because the staff ran away, and no one else knew how to operate the equipment or get on the air.

The British army eventually arrived with their fire trucks and the Belize Defense Force to break up the demonstration and put out the fire. By this time, a few houses next to the income tax building had burned down as well. The whole riot was put down in a little over three hours with a few minor injuries, some shop damage, and one less income tax building. The rest of the country had no idea of what was happening. We find out the next day that there were some demonstrations in the district towns, and in Corozal town, a member of the United Democratic Party (UDP) had been shot and killed by a member of the People's United Party (PUP). But there were no demonstrations as big and determined as the one in Belize City. It takes several days to a week for the rest of Belize to find out what happened in the city and the district towns. The government-controlled radio station plays down the riot as much as possible, calling it a small demonstration of UDP supporters. But it was not small, and it was not just UDP—it was all Belizeans concerned about the "Heads of Agreement."

The state of emergency stays in effect for two weeks throughout the country. In addition to the curfew, groups of three or more are not allowed to gather on the streets. Heavily armed Belize Defense Force soldiers are everywhere throughout the city, patrolling day and night. Anyone caught out after curfew is put in jail. It becomes entertainment to go out on the veranda after 9:00 p.m. It's better than watching TV as young boys and men try to make it home without getting caught.

Our training schedule hasn't changed. We still start class at 8:00 a.m. and still walk everywhere. The only difference for us is we can't be in groups of more than two. The Belizean staff doesn't talk much about it. We pick up little things here and there, mostly from our host families. My family is happy. They feel like they accomplished something. Life is back to normal except for the curfew and all the soldiers.

It's interesting to witness the growing pains of a country working toward independence. The riot sent a strong message to the government, particularly in regards to the Heads of Agreement negotiations. Belizeans will not tolerate it, and they want no deals with Guatemala that affect the sovereignty of Belize.

If there really were secret negotiations happening with Guatemala, they were no longer a reality.

As a result of the protest, Prime Minister George Price shuffles the portfolios of his cabinet members. According to Hubert, he did this to show the people he was still in charge. The government is still moving ahead with plans for independence but at a slower pace and with more active input from the opposition party. The people have shown that they have a voice. The demonstration was a test of democracy. Were there secret negotiations? I strongly suspect there were and that they were dropped after this bipartisan show of force.

I have a conversation with Hubert, my host brother, about the whole political scene. I'm having trouble understanding what they were trying to accomplish and why they thought they had a chance.

"What got you involved in politics?" As usual, I hear Bob Marley on the radio in the background. *Sit up, Stand up.*

"You see, our country is young. *Get up, stand up.* We received self-rule in 1964. That makes us seventeen years old, and we are still learning how to govern ourselves. *Stand up for your rights.* There are many bad influences, and there are people who want to run the government for their own benefit. We have to speak up for our rights so our country will develop correctly as a democratic nation." He uses English instead of Creole when speaking with me. *Get up, stand up.*

I ask him, "Do you really think one party is better than the other?"

"The PUP has been in power from the beginning, and we see how they treat people. Most of them do not care about our country. They only care about themselves and how they can profit. I believe in the UDP leadership. I want to believe that they will treat everyone fair and lead us in the right direction." *Don't give up the fight.*

"What do you think the PUP will do if they stay in power?"

"The prime minister, Mr. George Price, is a good man. He is honest and he cares about our country. But the rest of the government is corrupt, and they will steal our money, our land, and tell us lies. There are two ministers more powerful than the prime minister and he cannot control them."

"Who are they?"

"The minister of health and the minister of education. They are communist with strong ties to the Cuban government."

"Do you think Belize is ready for independence?"

"We are not ready yet. There are too many things we disagree on. I am worried for our small country. I am worried we will give it up to Guatemala, or we will become a country that does not progress or become a better place for our people to grow and prosper." *Get up, stand up.*

Once again, I'm impressed with Hubert's clarity and sincerity. I can see that all Belizeans, whether they are UDP or PUP, passionately care for the future of their country. I have never seen patriotism demonstrated like this before.

I thought about the sixties when I was growing up. Everywhere, there were Vietnam War demonstrations and groups against the government. We read about the Black Panthers, the Weathermen, the Chicago Seven, the Seattle Seven, Patty Hearst and the SLA, Kent State, Jerry Rubin, Abby Hoffman, Timothy Leary, the civil rights movement, Haight-Ashbury, and *Rolling Stone* magazine. These people were saying the system is wrong. "America is going to the 'fascist pigs' if we don't do something about it."

The message we were hearing was that there had to be more to life than going to school, getting a career, getting married, having kids, paying taxes, being a consumer, and dying. We had been put into a box, and we did not want to be there. That was our culture as we saw it. The government planned our lives for us. There had to be something better, other views on life, other values, and another way of living life. We didn't know what it was, but we knew there had to be something. That was our patriotism; we saw something we didn't like and we changed it. We also demanded freedom of expression in our music, our art, and our lifestyles. During the sixties, it was like we went from a black-and-white world to one with color. In a way, our rebellion reminded me of what Hubert and other Belizeans were going through. The difference was that we rebelled, or many of us did, with sex, drugs, and rock and roll. The rebellion here seems a little more levelheaded.

5

Empowerment

I'm assigned to the ministry of education to assist in the development of new curriculum materials for primary schools. I find it amusing and ironic that I've come all this way to work with schools and education. I hated school as a student, and I never did well as far as grades. Now I'm back at school? How is this happening to me? But I also see some beauty in it. This could be my opportunity to take revenge on the institution that tortured me so much.

The ministry of education is developing new curriculum because Belizeans want to get rid of all reminders of colonialism. Likewise, I want to get rid of all reminders of the life I just fled from. This is a new life for both of us. The amusing part is that they are looking to me to help make change happen. I don't even know if I can change myself.

My training to be a Peace Corps volunteer is over, and now it's time to get to work. The new program I'll be working with is designed to integrate all subject areas around the garden, the natural environment, and cultures of Belize. It includes studies in agriculture, health and nutrition, environment, weather, village life, flora and fauna. My first job is to get school gardens up and growing. Once the gardens are established, I'll help teachers create "learning activity packets" (LAPs) in math, science, and language arts. We're going to create these LAPs using the school garden and the surrounding environment. I'll be working with one district. All the other districts will have volunteers and teachers working simultaneously on their LAPs. After a year, we'll gather everyone together and develop a curriculum guide with all the LAPs we've created.

During my training, I met different people that I'll be working with, including education officers, teachers, and principals. I've met so many people, I can't remember all their names. They're from all the different cultures of Belize: Creole, Mestizo (mixture of Maya and Spanish), Garifuna, and Mayan. I visit them in their offices, and I see their college diplomas on the wall. From talking with them, I learn that the majority have received their degrees on scholarships to the United States and the UK. They've traveled, lived, and studied in other countries with foreign cultures. Some of them have two degrees, some have masters, and a few have PhDs. All of them have more experience, education, and training than I've ever dreamed of having. They're also very humble men and women, serious and dedicated to improving the education system of their country.

Now that I'm a volunteer and no longer a trainee, I am officially under the supervision of Belizeans. My direct supervisor, Mr. Puk, is with the curriculum development unit under the ministry of education. Until I move to my assigned site, I report to him every day. He's friendly but I sense he's a little skeptical about my true intentions as a Peace Corps volunteer.

"Mr. Jorge (hore-hey), do you feel prepared to begin your new assignment?"

"Yes, I think I'm ready."

"What about your other volunteer friends, Ms. Linda and Ms. Sabrina?"

"I think they're ready."

"They are quite a bit younger than you, no true?"

"Yes, but I wouldn't hold that against them. They're ambitious."

"I can tell you have some experience over them, what do you say?"

"Yes, that's true, but I'm not sure all my experience is necessarily good."

"Why do you say that?"

"Well, they're young, right out of school. They have a good education and most of my experience is from working with people."

"I think that is the best kind of experience. I know you Americans get around, no true?"

"Have you ever been to the States?"

"Yes, I went to the University of Minnesota for my bachelor's degree in education."

"How long were you there?"

"I was there for two years."

"How did you like living there?"

"Oh, it was very nice. You Americans have a very good life."

"You think so?"

"I will tell you the truth. There are many opportunities for young people in your country. It's not like here where our choices are limited. But I know that by coming back, I can do something for my country. Belize is very small and offers few opportunities but it is my home."

"Do you think you'll ever go back?"

"Yes, I want to go back for my master's degree, but I will have to wait until I can get some help or a scholarship, no true?"

"Do you think you'll ever go there to live?"

"No, my family is here and I prefer to stay close to them. But many of our youngest and brightest are going to live in your country because they know they have no future in Belize, no true?"

"Yes, I think you're right." I remembered hearing about the "brain drain" during training.

"But together we are going to make a difference with the way things are, no true?

"I hope so."

I felt a new sense of respect and understanding for Mr. E. and all the other Belizeans like him who came home to make a difference. I hope he's right. I hope they can make a difference.

Anytime I get a feeling that I might be able to accomplish something or "make a difference," I hear voices from my childhood. They're the voices of my teachers and my stepfather telling me I'm stupid, I'm slow, and I'll never accomplish anything. I convince myself that they're right, that anything I do will turn out negative, so I don't even try.

At the same time, I sense something is happening to me as I begin working and spending time with my Belizean counterparts. It takes me a few days to figure it out, but then I understand it, and it's a life-changing experience for me. It has to do with the way people see me. Because I'm white, because I'm American, because I'm a Peace Corps volunteer, people automatically assume that I am the best of the best here to help them. Even though it's never mentioned, it's understood that I have a university degree, experience in the field of education, and more knowledge than the average person. I'm given instant celebrity status. The Belizeans I work with are professionals and address me as a professional too, calling me "Mister" or "Maestro" (teacher). For the first time in my life, people are deferring to me as an educated, knowledgeable person whose opinion matters. I mean *everyone*, not just Belizeans, but Peace Corps volunteers and staff as well.

My first reaction is surprise. Then I feel like I'm being deceptive, but it's not me who's doing the deceiving. I can keep my mouth shut and enjoy my new status, or I can tell everyone the truth. Instead, I decide to be honest without putting myself down. I make a vow to never try to hide my educational background or lack thereof. Despite my bad habits and lack of education, I know who I am and I'm not ashamed of it. But I can't help but notice that, somehow, being recognized as the teacher makes me feel empowered. I feel like my mind has opened up to realize endless possibilities, and I don't know if I've just been miraculously cured of a mysterious brain illness that's kept me from learning my whole life or if I've finally flipped on the learning switch in my head. The most likely explanation is that I have everybody fooled and that this somehow empowers me to use my brain for the first time in my life. Whatever the cause, it has profound effects on me.

I feel empowered and confident. A whole new world has just opened up to me. The license it gives me is intoxicating, and I feel like there's nothing I can't do or learn. For the first time in my life, I understand what it means to grow and develop myself as a human being. It's like I've just woken up from a dream and I can learn and retain anything with immediate understanding. Whether it's from a book or a teacher. This freedom to learn makes me thirsty for more knowledge.

I've also found a new compassion for myself. I'm willing to move forward, take risks, and learn from my mistakes. My job in this new country is to guide Belizeans through the stages of developing their learning process by using their natural environment and educational resources. Even though I know I'm only one piece of a very large puzzle, the realization that everyone I'm working with is expecting me to show them how it's done, is scary. Intuitively, I know that I can do it and do it well.

I step back and look at what I'm doing with my life in a new land and a foreign culture. How do I do this? For starters, I have to establish myself as a person beyond the assumed white American with a college education. I have to gain the respect of the Belizeans around me for who I am, not for who they presume I am.

In my own culture, people who have education and degrees are rewarded with higher-paying jobs and a certain level of respect. People who don't are not. I'm a volunteer, so I'm not doing this for money. I'm doing it to get my life back on track. Not getting paid also helps take away any guilt I might occasionally feel for my lack of education and experience. My reward for taking the first step to change my life is a clean slate to start over.

With my new freedom, I know I can be a teacher, a chef, a Peace Corps volunteer, or anything else I want to be, but I know I have to be me first. I have to get in touch with my values and put them in front of everything else. I have to focus on characteristics like honesty, respect, and hard work. I know from being a restaurant manager that if you give respect, you get respect. After that, everything else falls into place. The difference now is that I feel empowered to go beyond anything I've ever done or experienced before.

With my new discovery, I feel an abundance of curiosity, enthusiasm, and energy. Much of the skill required for my new job involves organization and planning, and I gained those skills from my career as a chef. Peace Corps and my host agency gave me some training and direction. I also recognize that I have at least one advantage over many of the young volunteers. Even though they have college degrees, they have very little experience living in the real world.

In a way, I feel like I'm going back to school, to a university for the degree I never got. I feel confident that I can do it. This is the kind of culture that I can thrive in. It's so different from the life I'm used to and the oppressive environment I grew up in.

6

Orange Walk Town

Once again, I'm packing my bags and moving on, this time to my new home in the Orange Walk District in Northern Belize. I say good-bye to my host family.

"Okay, I wish you luck in your new home."

"Thanks, Ms. J. I think it will be fine."

"No, forget us. Remember yu always have fi home here."

"I won't forget. Thanks for everything."

"Da mi pleasure."

"Say good-bye to everyone for me."

"Okay, I wan tell dehn you done gone fi find one Spanish gial." I laugh knowing I'm going to miss that Creole humor. I walk to Cinderella Plaza with my backpack and hop on the bus for a three-hour-plus ride to my new home.

The Orange Walk District is located right below the Corozal District and Mexico's Yucatan Peninsula. Parts of the Orange Walk District border Mexico and Guatemala. Orange Walk Town itself is about thirty miles inland from the sea and fifty miles from Chetumal, the capital of Quintana Roo, Mexico.

Both the Corozal and Orange Walk districts have factories to process the sugar before shipping it out. I'm told this is the heart of sugarcane country, and this is the most thriving economy in Belize. The majority of the people who live in the Orange Walk District have work that involves sugarcane. There are cane farmers, cane cutters, truck drivers who take the cane from the fields to the factory, or they work in one of the factories.

Alex, the twenty-two-year-old jock from Boston, is also assigned to Orange Walk Town. His job is to work with the local veterinarian. He makes a decision that we're going to be roommates and manages to find a house on the outskirts of town in an area called San Francisco. To go anywhere from here means at least a one-mile walk into town or to a bus stop.

Alex is a college graduate from an Ivy League school. He's a nice guy, but we don't have anything in common. He assumes we've bonded to a degree beyond my true feelings; part of the problem is he still thinks he's in a fraternity.

Our home is a small, two-story wooden house on stilts located directly across the street from the San Francisco Bar and Restaurant. The bar plays loud music every single night of the week. About the time the music stops and I start to get some sleep (usually around one or two in the morning), the drunks leaving the bar start arguing and fighting right outside our house. Once we fall back to sleep, the neighborhood pigs wake us up fighting and squealing and rooting through neighborhood garbage. Then the dogs start barking until the sun comes up, and then the roosters start crowing. I don't know how anyone in this neighborhood ever gets a good night's sleep.

The town has a population of around ten thousand. There's a central park in the middle of town surrounded by Hindu shops, Chinese restaurants, and one bank. In the whole town, there's one small supermarket about the size of a 7-Eleven, a couple of gas stations, an outdoor market selling fruits and vegetables, and numerous churches of different denominations.

Everywhere we go, we have to walk or take public transportation, which is slow and unreliable. To go to Belize City, just sixty miles away, sometimes takes four hours driving down a half-paved single-lane road that wanders through small villages. Sometimes the bus stops let's someone off, goes another fifty feet, and stops again. Plus, it seems like we get a flat tire on every trip. When that happens, everyone gets off and finds some shade while a few of the men take turns changing the tire. I'm learning to pace myself and to take something to read whenever I travel.

The majority of the schools I work with are in villages, which are accessed only by dirt roads. Transportation to the villages is unreliable because there are no buses. There are covered transport trucks with benches that sell rides for one dollar, but they only run three days out of the week. They come into town in the morning and go back in the afternoon. The only way that will work is if I go to the villages in the afternoon, stay the night, and then come back in the morning. That would do me absolutely no good at all unless I stayed for two days.

I'm learning "Belize time," which somehow means a 3:00 p.m. meeting is really held sometime between 3:30 and 4:00. The amazing thing is that everyone (except me) knows this and shows up at the same late time. The exception is government business, which is, for the most part, on time.

I'm having a hard time with the heat and humidity. I feel lethargic most of the time, and I'm not used to so much walking. At home in Lake Tahoe, I always hopped into my air-conditioned car when I needed to go someplace. The only time I got exercise was on the job as a chef. Other occasional exercise included swimming in the lake or, in the winter, cross-country skiing. I notice that compared to most Belizeans I meet, I'm in very bad shape. Anytime I do anything physical, I feel weak and physically inadequate.

After two months of living in Orange Walk Town, I reevaluate my situation. I'm spending too much money eating in restaurants and drinking beer. Our house is hot. It's like living in an oven, not to mention all the noise from the San Francisco Bar at night. We have electricity for only twelve hours a day, which in some ways is almost worse than having none. I buy things that need refrigeration, but after twelve hours, when the power goes out, my food goes bad. I'm always throwing stuff away. Much of my time is spent with the other volunteers stationed in town, and I'm not meeting or hanging out with Belizeans. We know a few people like our next-door neighbor and our landlord, but it seems like it's hard to meet Belizeans; everyone's working and busy. I know I don't want to live like this for the next two years. Plus, Alex is getting on my nerves just being Alex. Once again, I need a change, a big change.

The majority of my work is in the villages, and village life looks good to me. Mainly, it's quiet and peaceful; people are friendly, and they always seem to have time to talk. It's more of a "real" Peace Corps experience—no electricity, no running water, and no bars or restaurants. Most of the villages are named after saints: San Esteban, San Roman, San Felipe, and San Luis. For over a month, I've been working with four villages in particular: San Jose, San Lazaro, Trinidad, and Yo Creek.

When I visit a school, I work with the students to get a garden started. First, we have to identify an area that has good soil and access to water. Then we clear out all the weeds and vegetation. Once we have it cleaned, we measure for our raised garden beds and start digging and turning over the hard black earth. They call this type of soil Louisville clay, and when it's wet, it sticks to everything. To get a garden established is hot, hard work. The students turn out to be good workers, and they handle most of the machete work while I work with the shovel.

I'm often invited to students' homes for lunch. This is something the teachers or principals arrange by asking the students to talk to their parents about taking turns to feed me. The students, whose parents agree, are proud to offer me lunch at their home.

The kitchen is usually a thatched hut separate from the main house. With every meal, I'm served a warm bottle of Coca-Cola, and I learn that this is considered a treat reserved for special guest. I always drink my Coke and do my best to eat everything on my plate so I don't insult my host.

I start looking for a new home, exploring the villages I work with plus a few others. The people living in these villages are all Spanish, in contrast to town, where they're mostly Creole. I notice that many of the people have an Oriental look about them. Some of the women and girls could easily pass for Asians. It gives them an exotic look that I find very attractive. I learn that these people are Yucatan Mayan or Mestizo, a mixture of Maya and Spanish, and make up the majority of villages in Northern Belize.

They say that Belize was home to a large Mayan population at one time. I know that we're surrounded by thousands of ruins because every time we dig a hole in the ground to start a garden, we find chards of Mayan pottery. Other than that and the pretty Mayan girls, I know nothing about them. I'm about to learn.

THE MAYAN ARE ALIVE AND WELL IN BELIZE

Key Historical Dates

AD	300-900	Height of the Maya civilization
	1638	First European settlement
	1798	Battle of St. George's Caye: Spanish forces defeated.
	1832	Main Garifuna settlement
	1838	Freedom for African slaves in Belize
	1840s	Mestizo and Maya settlers flee Caste War in Yucatan, Mexico
	1871	Declared a British colony—British Honduras
	1935	Limited adult suffrage
	1954	Universal adult suffrage
	1964	Attainment of self-government
	1974	Name changed to Belize
	1981	Full independence gained

7

The Storyteller

One of the great mysteries of history is what happened to the Mayan civilization. There are many theories including famine, sickness, war, and possibly a combination of all three. The good news is that the Maya of Belize are alive and well. They have their own history that is passed down from generation to generation through storytellers. Every village has them; they are also known as "the old people." Some, maybe all, have a reputation for embellishing the truth a little. I have chosen to share history from some storytellers whom, for reasons that will become apparent later, I have the most access to. This is their story, most likely with a few embellishments.

The old man was lying in his hammock when he heard the kids come into his yard, and he knew they were sent by the school. They're coming to ask him the history of Yo Creek and how his family and others settled here. Tiburcio Novelo, Don Tib, is ninety-three years old and the oldest man in a village of twelve hundred souls. He is one of the few oracles left to tell stories of the "old Mayan ways." He shared his memory with many generations of students and always appreciates the attention, but today, he's annoyed by it. He opens his door to a small group of six students.

"Tatito (grandfather), we have come to ask you questions about the village." The little girl speaking is his great-granddaughter, Irmita.

"Go away. I don't have time. I am tired of telling stories."

"Tatito, I am your granddaughter and I have come to hear your stories."

"Who is your mother, little girl?"

"My mother is Bernadina, daughter of Anatascia. My name is Irma."

"I will not do this again so listen good the first time." The children come inside and gather around the old man as he lay in his hammock and told them the story of how his family and others escaped the Great War and made Yo Creek their home. These are stories that Don Tib's grandfather and father have passed down to him.

"The Caste War" (war of the races) in Mexico was long and brutal. Fifty-four years in total, from 1847 to 1901. My family escaped from the Yucatan Peninsula during the early 1850s. We were running from the Icaiche Maya leader, Marcos Canul. He wanted to kill anyone who was not "pure" Mayan. Our family was considered Mestizo (mixed race). One of our ancestors mixed with Spaniards, and from then, our heritage was no longer pure Maya. That made us and thousands of others fair game for killing.

The Icaiche Maya were ruthless in their attacks. Sometimes, a village knew when they were coming and everyone would hide. If they did not have time to hide, the men were chopped to death with machetes or taken captive to be sold as slaves. They raped the girls and women, kidnapping the pretty ones and stealing all the food they could find.

My family, like many others, was tired of the constant threat of violence. They moved regularly to avoid surprise raids. It was heard from talking to others that many families and sometimes whole villages were fleeing south to Belize. They knew the journey was a long and dangerous one on the Rio Bravo (angry river). Fearing that Marcos Canul was getting near, they moved close to the river, and after choosing the best trees, they began working on their dugouts.

After a month of hand-shaping their riverboats, they were finally ready to begin their move to the safety of a new country. They left just as Marcus Canul was on their trail. Scouts going out every day had seen signs of his army and knew they were getting closer. It was time to go.

There were many dangers on the trip. The biggest threat was in the water. They could only travel on the Rio Bravo when the sun was high and the crocodiles were sunning themselves on the sides of the river. They passed by large herds of the huge reptiles. It was not unusual to see up to forty at a time, some as long as twenty feet, lounging lazily in the sun by the riverside. Sometimes, one of the big beasts slipped into the river and disappeared under the dark swirling water. When that happened, everyone paddled faster, hoping they would not be turned over into the deep, swift current and eaten alive in a feeding frenzy.

Every day, they had to begin searching early for a place to camp for the night. Using their machetes, they first had to clear away the thick bush lining the river and pull their dugouts out of the water. They had to make camp far from the shore to avoid the crocodiles coming out at night looking for food. Fighting back the snakes and insects, they took turns resting so that someone was always on lookout for wild animals and Marcus Canul. For food, they brought *maize* (corn) with them. They also fished and hunted, sometimes killing a wild pig or Gibnut (large rodent).

It took them three days of traveling on the river before they felt safe from Marcos Canul and his army. They stopped at a small settlement called Santa Cruz (Holy Cross). The Mayans there told them that there was a larger settlement further inland. Worried that Marcos Canul might follow them on the river, they traveled through the jungle for five miles and came here to the village of Tres Cruzes (Three Crosses), which is now known as Yo Creek (on the creek). The first families escaping the caste wars had arrived and settled the village. They were the Blancos, Garcias, and Esquivels—these were their baptized names. They had given up their Mayan names for the Catholic religion that the Spanish introduced.

Soon, more families arrived including Don Tib's grandfather. Other villages began and grew as more and more Maya escaped the Caste War. Yo Creek, San Antonio, San Lazaro, Trinidad, Santa Cruz, Santa Rita, August Pine Ridge, San Victor, and Chan Pine Ridge were just a few of the Maya villages established along the Mexican-Belize border.

Don Tib heard the stories from the old storytellers of his time. At one time, Belize had over three hundred thousand Mayans and a vibrant civilization. Yo Creek had been a thriving community. The only evidences left of the previous inhabitants were the Mayan temples scattered around the area.

Then came drought and famine, then plagues of locust that caused mass starvation. Tens of thousands of Mayans starved to death as four seasonal crops in a row were destroyed. Some tribes survived the famine by fleeing to the bush and eating wild roots. The only evidences left of their prosperous civilization were the temples that now laid in ruin across the country.

Marcos Canul and his army of "pure" Mayans were still after those escaping the Caste War, and in 1871, he crossed the border and occupied the town of Corozal in northern Belize. In 1872, he moved further south and attacked Orange Walk Town just five miles from the village of Tres Cruzes. There, he was defeated by the British army. In that battle, Marcos Canul was mortally wounded, and the Maya of Mexico and Belize no longer had to fear him.

After the children left his home, Don Tib reflected on his life. He felt as if he had lived many lifetimes and seen many things. Now he felt tired, tired and sick. It was becoming hard for him to breathe, and every time he took a deep breath, his chest hurt. He was dying and he knew it. He had been healthy his whole life, even in his nineties he could still read without glasses. Now this thing had a hold of him, and he couldn't get rid of it. It made him angry that it was getting the best of him, but he had not given up yet. He had not reached ninety by giving up.

His third wife had died long ago and left him alone, just like the first two. He lived by himself in a one-room "bush house" made out of pimento sticks and bay leaves from the jungle. The only furniture in the room was a stick bed with a grass mattress, his hammock, and a table with two chairs set in a corner on a limestone floor. In his backyard, he had a small thatch-roofed kitchen with a *fogon* (standing fireplace made out of wood and filled with limestone), where his daughter-in-law cooked his beans and tortillas. He had a well for water in his front yard.

Directly across the street was the Catholic church. Don Tib was a religious man and a good Catholic. His job was to ring the church bell whenever the priest came for mass or when someone in the village died. The bell was an old, gigantic flywheel left over from some ancient piece of British machinery. He used an iron rod to hit it with, and he always beat the same tune—*tinga, tani, tani, tani; tinga, tani, tani, tani*—over and over. It was the oldest communication tool in the village, and when he played his song, people came to the church to attend mass and share news. It was a volunteer job, to be in charge of the bell, but it was not a job they would give to just anyone. He was proud that he was the one.

Don Tib's first language was Yucatan Mayan, but he also spoke Spanish. He had been a farmer his whole life, practicing slash-and-burn farming growing corn, a crop sacred to the Maya. He lay in his hammock now thinking about his village and his past. His granddaughter and the other students spoke Spanish. There was a time when everyone in the village spoke Mayan. Now Spanish was the popular language. Even his language was dying.

Don Tib had seen the village progress from traditional bush huts to modern homes made out of cement with zinc roofs. Recently, people in the village were being promised electricity that would go directly to their homes, thanks to the Belizean politicians and the parliamentary government set up by the British. There were no roads in the old days. If you went someplace, you went by foot, horse, or canoe. There were no medical services, only bush doctors, unless you hiked the five miles through a jungle path to Orange Walk Town. Trade happened on the Rio Hondo River, which was a three-mile hike to meet a cargo boat that came once a month with general goods to trade for maize or wild game.

In Don Tib's eyes, the old ways were gone. It was up to him and a few others to keep the stories passed down. Very few people still taught their children the Maya language or practiced subsistence farming. Even the wild animals had moved out. He hardly ever saw a jaguar or a large crocodile like the twenty-footers he used to see by the scores. At one time, he provided his family with food he grew on his *milpa* (farm), fish from the river, and wild game he killed with his rifle in the bush. Now people paid for their food at the corner shop with money they made from working for other people. They still grew food on their milpa, but mostly they grew sugarcane for the money they could make from it. They used the money to build fancy cement homes and fill them with things they didn't need.

When the British came, everything changed. First, they built a sugarcane factory and then feeder roads to all the villages that connected them to the District Town of Orange Walk and the factory. Farmers now had tractors and trucks to move their cane to the factories, where it was made into sugar and molasses and shipped away.

The great Maya temples of Tres Cruzes were gone now. They had been torn down and used to build limestone roads in the village. When they escaped the war, they brought gold coins stored in pottery jars with them. Now all the gold was gone. Most of it had been traded with the British for trinkets. Some of it had been buried, and the owners died without revealing the secret location, believing it would help them in the afterlife. Sometimes, the young boys of the village asked Don Tib if he knew where the gold was. He knew it was there, but he did not know where. Some of these boys went out with shovels to look in places they thought it might be. He smiled at the number of empty holes they left looking for buried treasure.

Don Tib's first wife was Beatrice Bacab. She gave him four daughters before dying during the Spanish influenza of 1921. The influenza had killed many people. He heard from the boat traders that whole villages were wiped out with only a few families surviving. In some villages, no one came out to meet the boat as it came on its monthly visit for trade and news from the outside world.

One of his daughters from Beatrice was Anatascia. She married and had four daughters and four sons. She was also a storyteller, passing down the stories she had heard from her father and others. One of her granddaughters was Irmita, the same little girl Don Tib did not recognize.

Don Tib died from respiratory failure when he was ninety-three years old. He was one of the last who still lived the Mayan way.

8

San Lazaro

San Lazaro is a village of approximately six hundred souls, mostly Mestizo sugarcane farmers. There is one elementary school managed by the Catholic mission and one smaller school managed by the Methodist mission. Church is a very big part of village life, and every village has several religions, with Catholic being prominent. This village has at least six different churches, some in modern cement buildings, others outdoors under thatched *ramadas* (a shelter with no walls, only a roof made out of sticks and palm leaves).

One of the teachers I work with, Jose, knows I'm looking for a village to live in. He introduces me to the chairman of the San Lazaro village council. Don Salus is a burly man, big and strong. He has a friendly smile that makes me feel welcome, and right away, I respect him. He invites me into his home, and as soon as I sit down, his wife brings me a warm bottle of Coca-Cola. *My teeth will go rotten here if everyone keeps giving me Coke.* The furniture in his home is sparse but sufficient. The living room and dining room are joined as one long room. A table and chairs are at one end, and a sofa and love seat are at the other end. His wife and four daughters stay at the dining room end and watch Don Salus and I sit across from each other at the other end. After a few uncomfortable minutes on my part, I begin speaking in my best Spanish, which is not very good. His English is also not good, but with some body language and help from one of his daughters, I finally get it communicated that I want to live in his village. I ask him if he knows of any houses available for rent. He does, and after I finish my Coke, he takes me to see Don Pablo.

Don Pablo lives with one of his daughters, and he's swinging in his hammock on the front porch when we walk up. Like Don Salus and most people in this region of Belize, he is Mayan. He has a healthy head of thick white hair with cowlicks that he never combs and a big round stomach. He has an oriental look about him, especially in the eyes, which are slanted below thick, white eyebrows. He reminds me of pictures I've seen of Buddha. When he sees we're coming to visit him, he gets out of his hammock with the help of a wooden staff. After an introduction, I shake his hand and, in my best Spanish, say I'm happy to meet him. That or my poor Spanish puts a big smile on his face that he has for the rest of our visit. Don Salus explains to him in a mixture of Mayan and Spanish that I need a place to live. Don Pablo says he has a house I can use and has his daughter bring me a key. Then we walk over to see my new house. It's a two-story wooden house with a big mango tree in front, and it sits directly across the street from the school I work with. It has one front door with a big padlock and lots of windows with wooden louvers. It's a mess inside from being used for storage, but I see its potential and decide it will do just fine.

Don Pablo says I can pay him whatever I want. I offer forty Belize dollars a month since that's my Peace Corps budget allowance for living in a village. He nods his head smiling and says something agreeable in Spanish. He hands me the key, and I count out BZ$40. We shake hands.

"I have to get back to work at the school," I tell them. As I'm leaving, I hear Don Pablo says something to Don Salus. In broken English and Spanish, Don Salus explains. "He said you need to find a good Spanish woman to take care of you. He says it's not healthy for a man to live by himself."

9

Home

Anxious to get out of Orange Walk and to my new house, I hire a taxi. The cab gets me as far as the first village, which is Yo Creek, but then the road gets bad, and his car sits too low to go any further. I remember that Jose, the teacher I work with at San Lazaro School, lives in Yo Creek. I find his house just by saying his name and asking people where he lives. His mother says he's working on his father's cattle ranch and gives me permission to unload my stuff on their porch so the cab can leave.

Jose arrives a few hours later, and he's very understanding as I explain my situation. He borrows his father's truck to get me the next five miles up the road to San Lazaro. I've been up since six this morning, and it's late afternoon when I finally arrive at my new home.

My new neighbor, who lives directly across the yard about seventy-five feet from my front door, comes out to greet me. He's short and well built with a neatly trimmed mustache and short black hair. Samuel (pronounced Sam-well) is Don Pablo's youngest son, and he lives there with his family. As I walk up, I hear the familiar sound of Radio Belize, and once again, Mr. Bob Marley is on.

"Hello, I am Samuel," he greets me with a firm handshake.

"Hi. I'm George. Nice to meet you, Samuel."

"Jorge, your name is Jorge in Spanish. That is what I will call you."

"Okay, sure. You can call me just about anything." His English is very good. About this time, I notice his wife who's standing behind him smiling shyly. She's shorter and a little chubby with long black hair. Close by her side, holding onto her legs, are two kids—a little boy around three and a girl around six years old.

"This is my wife, Chabby, and these are my children Olga and Pedro." The wife smiles and timidly shakes my hand when I offer it. Samuel says something in Spanish, and Olga and Pedro step up to shake my hand as well.

"You are welcome here, Jorge," Samuel said this very matter-of-factly, as if now that it was spoken it's true no matter what.

"Thank you, Samuel. I appreciate that." I feel I have to be as sincere as he was in accepting his proclamation. His wife, Chabby, says something in Spanish and then shyly covers her face with her hands.

"She said to tell you that you are welcome to use the bathhouse and the latrine." He points behind him to the location for each of these accommodations.

"You will get your drinking water from our rain tank, Jorge." He points to the galvanized aluminum water tank by the side of his house set up to catch rain water and anything else that may happen to be on the roof.

"Thank you, Samuel, but I don't want to take your water. Maybe I can figure something out."

"No, Jorge, do not worry. There is plenty of water to share." I can tell by the way he says it that I might insult him if I don't accept his offer, so I gladly accept.

"Thank you, Samuel. Again, I appreciate it."

"That is no problem, Jorge. If you need anything, just let us know."

Jose and Samuel start speaking to each other in Spanish, and it's obvious that they know each other. I begin grabbing my belongings.

"Can we help you, Jorge?" Samuel very politely asks me.

"Yeah, sure. There's nothing delicate here so grab whatever you want."

The whole family follows me into my new home, and I notice right away that someone has scrubbed the place down.

"Wow, who cleaned it?"

"Oh, that was my wife." Chabby smiles and says, "I hope it is okay, Mr. Jorge."

"Wow, are you kidding? It looks great! Thank you, Chabby."

"You are welcome, Mr. Jorge." She blushes and puts her hand over her mouth.

"Oh yes, she does a good job, no true?" Samuel is obviously proud of his wife.

"I have to go, Jorge, but you are home now, no true?"

"Yes, I'm home now. Thank you, Jose."

Samuel then gives me a tour of the house with his wife and kids following closely behind us every step of the way. Yes, I'm home now.

10

Dogs and Snakes

My new house is called a "Mennonite house" after the Mennonites that built it. They constructed it in their community about twelve miles away and then moved it to the village on trailers pulled by horses. They set it on a foundation of strategically placed cement blocks stacked two high. It doesn't have running water or electricity. There's one large room upstairs that I make into a bedroom because it has a nice breeze at night that cools things off enough to sleep. Plus, it's high enough off the ground to cut down on the number of mosquitoes that come out at night.

There are two rooms downstairs. I make one into a living room and the smaller one into a kitchen with a little two-burner butane stove. To wash dishes, I use two basins, one to wash and one to rinse. To get water for cleaning, I have to go a little less than a quarter mile to a water pump with a handle that you work manually. Most people in the village prefer not to drink pump water. They say that rain water is sweeter for drinking and pump water is good for cleaning. They're right—rain water does taste better.

The family bathhouse is about the same size as the family outhouse. The difference is a cement floor and a stool to sit on. The outhouse just has a dirt floor and a wooden bench with holes cut in it. Whenever I want to take a bath, I fill my five-gallon plastic "pigtail" bucket about half full with cold water. Then I add a tea kettle full of hot water heated up on my butane stove. A pigtail bucket is a five-gallon plastic bucket that comes with pigtails in brine (pigtail is a popular Creole dish shared by most Belizeans). If it's dark, I take a candle or flashlight and sit on the stool with my bucket of warm water in front of me. I use a little plastic cup to scoop up the water and pour it over my body. Whenever I need to use the outhouse, I take matches and a candle because, day or night, it's always dark in there.

Samuel is a sugarcane farmer who also drives a cane truck and delivers to the factory during the harvest season (crop). He's a friendly guy and is always helpful if I have questions. Chabby's also friendly but a little more guarded. Her English isn't as good as Samuel's, but we can communicate. Pedro and Olga are friendly and playful. They all make me feel welcome in my new home.

The first thing I do is work on getting settled in my home. I need to make it livable so I start a list of supplies to get from town. Sitting in the front yard, there is a small kitchen made out of bush sticks and bay leaves. Since the house is already clean, I decide to clean the bush house. I sweep some leaves out of a corner, and right there, rolled up under the leaves, is a snake. I've heard stories during training about Belize having some of the deadliest snakes in the world—two steps and you're dead, the stories said. I automatically jump back, but the snake stays still, coiled-up and watching me. It's not a big snake, but it doesn't matter; the venom from a small snake can kill just as fast as the venom from a big one.

With my hand shaking and not taking my eye off the snake, I grab an old machete leaning against the wall. Then, gauging the distance by the length of my machete, I get as close as I dare, take careful aim, and swing as hard as I can. Then I jump back to see if I got him. He's hurt but still alive. He's angry now, striking and flinging his body around in every direction. Feeling a little braver, I move closer and chop him into pieces. Once I'm sure it's dead (sixteen pieces ought to do it), I scoop him up in a shovel. Samuel had shown me a trailer earlier and told me to dump any trash I had there so I threw him in. Feeling a certain amount of pride for claiming victory in my life and death battle, I go back to my cleaning and soon forget all about him.

About an hour later, I go to dump more garbage in the trailer and scare myself all over again when I see the head of the same dead snake. This time, I cover him with some cardboard so I won't keep scaring myself. Later, I see Samuel come home and call him over.

"Samuel, I have something to show you. Come and see this." I notice I'm still a little shaky.

"What do you have, Jorge?" I pull the cardboard back and show him the part of the snake with the head still attached. He looks and gives a low whistle.

"Where did you find this snake, Jorge?"

"Right here in the kitchen." I point to the corner where he was under the leaves.

"You are lucky, Jorge. This is a bad snake. If he bites you it is very bad."

"Do you know what kind of snake it is?"

"We call it tommygoff."

"Are there a lot of these around?"

"Oh yes, mon. They like to live in the cane fields. That's why I keep my yard cut low because they like high grass."

I look around and do a quick calculation. I have a cane field about twenty-five feet directly behind my house. The village soccer field is on one side, which is surrounded by high grass. Samuel's house is directly in line with my front door. The main street of the village is on the other side.

"What do people do if they get bit by one of these guys?"

"They go to the bush doctor, but there is no bush doctor here in San Lazaro. Mr. Blanco, he is the nearest one and he lives in Trinidad."

"Does that work? Can the bush doctor heal people that get bit? Do they survive?"

"Yes, but you have to get there in time." He did not seem too sure and was not giving me much confidence in the bush doctor.

"How much time is *in time*?"

"You have to get there fast, Jorge, as soon as you can."

"What if the bush doctor is not home?"

"There is another one in Yo Creek. Oh yes, they have two bush doctors there."

"Does anyone go to the hospital in Orange Walk for a snake bite?"

"No, mon. The hospital does not know what to do. You have to go to the bush doctor."

"What exactly does he do?"

"You have to stay at his house. He has bush medicine."

"Does anyone ever die from snake bite?"

"Oh yes, mon."

"Great." Samuel's enthusiastic honesty is not making me feel too safe.

After working around my house all morning, I'm hungry and realize I don't have anything to eat. I decide to see what I can find in the village. I walk down the main road, which is partially paved. The unpaved part is full of big potholes. Everyone already knows who I am and, for the most part, make me feel welcome.

There are a lot of dogs, and they're aggressive and come out barking and growling at me. Some of them come too close for comfort, and I'm not sure what to do. Then some kids come to my rescue. They walk toward the dogs like they have rocks in their hands and the dogs back down. I've always been taught to stand still and show no fear, but it wasn't working. I try the rock trick the next time a dog comes after me, and it works, much to my relief. Now I won't have to walk around the village facing down dogs all day.

There are "shops," little stores run out of people's homes where you can buy essentials like warm Coke, sweets, cookies, rice, and beans. I'm looking for something healthy like fruit, but almost everything is canned foods or sweets. I give up and buy a Coke and some cookies. Later on, I find some bananas for sale and eat those. I'm going to have to do something about my food situation.

The next day, bright and early, I decide to go to town and buy some of the things on my list. As usual, I'm short on money, so I have to figure out my priorities. Food is high on the list. Getting to town is a challenge and a learning experience, and I quickly discover that's true of everything I do in this new environment.

11

New Volunteers and a Minister

The only transportation in the village are cane trucks and tractors. I find out that many cane farmers only license their trucks during crop season when they're transporting sugarcane to the factory. The rest of the time they sit parked in their yards or are just used within the village. Samuel told me that on Mondays, Wednesdays, and Saturdays, there's a regular "transport truck," which is a large truck with a canopy and wooden benches to sit on. But it's coming from two villages up the road and is almost always full by the time it reaches our village. The only other option is to hitchhike and wait for someone with a personal vehicle to come along. But personal vehicles are rare and far in-between.

It's a Wednesday and I stand on the side of the road waiting for "passage." The transport truck stops and it looks full, but someone points to a spot that has just enough room for me. I climb on and squeeze in between two fat-bottomed women, who both look the other way as I get personal and wedge myself in-between them. After a slow thirty-minute ride with plenty of stops, we reach town. I make sure I know when the truck is leaving and where to catch it.

The first thing I do is stop at a little stand that sells chicken tacos and eat until I'm full. They're not like the tacos I'm used to in the United States—this is a mixture of chicken and spices rolled up in a fresh, hot corn tortilla. They're delicious and cheap—four for a dollar.

After eating my fill, I walk over to visit some new Peace Corps volunteers in town. Matt is assigned to the local high school as a biology teacher. Tim and

Susan are married and assigned to the hospital. Peace Corps volunteers tend to stick together, and I know I can always count on these three when I need a place to stay or someone to party with.

Susan's working, but Matt and Jim are home and just getting out of bed. They walk downtown with me while I do my shopping. This is my first time shopping for my kitchen, and I'm having a hard time figuring out what to buy. I always felt I could cook under any circumstance or situation. I'm wrong. Without a refrigerator, I don't know what to buy or how to store it. The types of food that I'm used to cooking are nowhere in sight or too expensive. The main diet in the village is rice and beans with chicken and tortillas in different combinations. They also add to that whatever fresh vegetables or fruit may be in season. *But how am I going to store chicken without a refrigerator? How do I get enough fruits and vegetables for the week with no place to store it? How do they do it? The hot, humid climate will rot anything within a day.* In the end, I buy some peanut butter (expensive) and "bun," a local sweet bread that's the only alternative for white bread. There are several outdoor markets that I buy some fruit at, but even that seems expensive. I don't know what else to buy. Being someone who likes to cook, I feel frustrated by my lack of options.

The three of us are walking around the main street checking out shops and the outdoor market. I notice that kids keep coming up and asking me if I'm selling "cacahuates," Spanish for peanuts. Then a couple of adults ask me the same thing. I can't figure out what the hell's going on. No one's asking Tim or Matt for peanuts.

"Why is everyone asking me for peanuts and giving me strange looks when I tell them I don't have any? I feel like I have a sign on me that says, "Peanuts for sale."

Tim says, "I don't know but maybe you should buy some and double the price." We walk another block, and I see some Mennonites up close for the first time. They're parked on the side of the road with a horse and buggy. As we walk past, they ask if we want to buy peanuts. They're white with a similar complexion to mine, and they're all wearing overalls, same as mine. I make a mental note not to wear my overalls into town again.

By the end of the day, Matt and Tim have invited me for dinner and talked me into staying the night. We wait for Susan to get off work then go out to eat at a Chinese restaurant. There are no TVs or any other types of entertainment so we talk, tell jokes, and get to know each other better. Tim's a natural comedian, and it really comes out when he has an audience. He has us all doubled over laughing with his imitations of other volunteers and Belizeans he's met.

The next day, I go out on the road to wait for a ride to San Lazaro. I don't have to wait long before getting a ride with someone who has a pickup truck.

I'm even invited to sit in the front seat. The driver is obviously a Belizean. Everyone seems to know him and his truck because every time we drive past someone, he honks his horn and waves.

At first, I think he's a little too nosy asking me questions about myself and what I'm doing. He's not the typical friendly Belizean I'm used to, and I feel like I'm being interviewed or investigated. When I get in the truck he ignores me by looking in his rearview mirror.

"What are you doing in Belize?" His tone's not entirely friendly, and he speaks like a man in a position of authority. He's also physically bigger than most Belizeans, and he looks strong.

"I'm a Peace Corps volunteer working with the schools."

"Where are you going?"

"I live in San Lazaro." This response seems to soften him up a little.

"Tell me about your assignment here."

"I visit the schools and work with the REAP program, helping the teachers establish school gardens and developing curriculum materials."

"What schools do you visit?" I'm beginning to feel like I'm being tested.

"I work with San Lazaro, Trinidad, Yo Creek, San Jose, and Chan Pine Ridge." This seems to satisfy him and we don't talk much after that. I don't feel comfortable asking what he does, and he doesn't offer any information about himself. When we pass through the village of Yo Creek, everyone seems to know his truck and waves at him. He stops a couple of times to talk with people. They speak in Spanish so I don't understand what they're saying. It seems like the people he talks to are presenting some kind of problem and he's supposed to solve it. Finally, we reach San Lazaro.

"I can get off here. Thank you for the ride."

"Good luck with your assignment."

"Thanks, I appreciate that." That's the only nice thing he said the whole ride.

Samuel's in the yard and sees me get dropped off. "Jorge, what were you doing with the minister?"

"What minister?"

"That was the minister of energy and communication."

"Oh, I didn't know who he was. He picked me up hitchhiking."

"Well, you got a good ride then."

"Is he a popular politician?" I remembered that he had not seemed very friendly. On the other hand, he had given me a ride.

"He's okay."

"Just okay?" I could tell he had more to say but wasn't saying it.

"Yes, Jorge. It's politics and he is a politician."

I let it go, and after talking for a while, I went in to organize my cooking situation. It would not be the last time I would see this particular minister.

During my Peace Corps training in Belize City, I had gained some knowledge about Belizean politics. I learned you were either hard-core People's United Party (PUP) or hard-core United Democratic Party (UDP). There was no middle road. You either took the party line or you didn't. If a politician belongs to "your" party then he or she can do no wrong. If they are in the opposing party then they are corrupt and no good.

There are a lot of different groups in the village—youth groups, religious groups, women's groups, sports groups, and political groups. All of them are doing good things. As a Peace Corps volunteer, I quickly learn that I can never align myself with any one group because there will always be another group against that group. With village politics, it can be tricky to stay out of trouble. I have to be very careful not to appear as if I favor any one particular group. There's only one place in the village where politics are left at the door, and that's the school.

12

Victor

Victor is a leader; I sense it the first time I meet him. It happens one day after soccer practice on the field beside my house. I'm walking away when I hear someone behind me say my name. "Yes, Jorge, how are you?" I turn around to see him standing there with some other men, and I can tell right away they are "his" men. Physically, he stands out from the crowd. He's tall for a Mestizo, over six feet and about 190 pounds with dark eyes that look intelligent but hard. His hair is black, and he has acne scars on his upper cheeks and forehead. The combination of the latter makes the top half of his face look dark and sinister. I'm not surprised he knows my name. Being the only white guy around, I stand out like a full moon. I say hello and "nice to meet you" in my best Spanish and we shake hands. Right away, I feel respect for him, partly for being friendly and partly because he looks like he could have me shot. As if reading my mind, he looks me directly in the eyes and says, "Don't worry. You are welcome here. You have friends." And then he smiles and proclaims, "We will be friends." He then introduces me to the men with him. Each one of them stands out on his own as intelligent and respected. I'm impressed with these guys.

After assuring me that we'll be friends, we go our separate ways. It's not unusual for him to want to be my friend. I've discovered that most people appreciated the fact that I'm living here far from my own home to work in the schools with their children. They feel proud that out of all the villages I could have chosen to live in I chose theirs. Being friendly is their way of welcoming me to the village.

Like many Mestizos in the village, Victor has a way of speaking English that's like a literal translation. It's as if he's reading from a book of poetry in a very passionate and direct manner. His vocabulary is good, and he's not shy about using it. Like the Creole in Belize City, the Mestizo doesn't use contractions when speaking English.

He made me a little nervous with his command that we "will" be friends. But on the other hand, I'm going to live in this small village for two years, and I'm in no position to turn down friends.

Later, when I see Samuel, I ask him who Victor is.

"He is in charge of the cane cutters, Jorge."

"How does that work?"

"Each cane season, we (farmers) get together and decide when the fields will get cut and when we will deliver our cane to the factory. Victor is in charge of this schedule and the *caneros*"

"Who are the caneros?"

"They cut the cane with machetes, Jorge."

"That sounds like hard work."

"Oh yes, mon, it is very hard work."

"If everyone is a farmer, who cuts the cane?"

"Everyone has to cut cane, Jorge. I cut cane too, but Victor has a group of men that come here every year to work. They are aliens from Guatemala, El Salvador, and Honduras. Victor's job is to take them to the fields and make sure they have a place to sleep and food."

I learn that once you burn your cane field, you have three days to get the sugarcane into the factory before it will spoil. If your field is burned by accident and you need to jump your scheduled turn, Victor's the man you talk to. If for some reason you don't get it to the factory in time, you lose everything that you've worked the whole year for. I ask Samuel if he ever said no to anyone. He said he didn't and shouldn't, but he can cut it pretty close sometimes. My first impression of Victor as a strong leader contributes to my image of the job he has. It seems like an important position that takes someone who knows how to handle people.

13

Softball

After making friends with Victor, I feel a new level of acceptance. It's like I've passed my first initiation and I'm ready for the next one. I don't have to wait long.

Every village has a soccer field. It's as much a part of the village as the school is. On weekends, during soccer season, teams travel for competitive games. I can always count on seeing at least one day of games a week on our village field.

I've never played soccer before, and I have no idea what the rules are. But the first time I stop by to watch the village team practice, I'm hooked. It's intense and exciting. To see close-up the skills these players have is very impressive. They can do things with the ball and their feet that I never thought possible. During games, I can literally stand right on the sidelines and feel like I'm part of the action. In fact, if I'm not on my toes, ready to move, I may be part of the action.

One day, I notice a man at practice with a small group of young women. They seem to be interested in me because they keep motioning toward me as they're talking. After a few minutes of this, I'm approached by the man while the girls stay back a good distance.

"Hello, Jorge. My name is Arnufo, but most people call me Junior." We shake hands. Junior is short and skinny. His movements are quick and furtive, and he reminds me of an Italian gangster.

"Nice to meet you, Junior." He seems like a nice guy.

"You see those girls over there?" He points at the girls who all, except one, turn away when I look at them.

"Yes, I see them."

"Well, they say they want you to be the coach for their softball team." Junior takes a step back with one foot forward nervously tapping while waiting for my response.

"They want me to be their softball coach? But I'm not a softball coach."

"Yes, they said you are the one they want." One of the older girls had moved closer, with the other younger girls following behind her.

"But I've never coached softball."

"You are the one we want." It's an older woman speaking now, and I can see she's determined. She's a heavyset woman, bigger than Junior.

"This is my wife, Jorge. Her name is Fatima." She moves closer, and Junior stands to the side.

"We want you to be our coach," she says this with a smile and sets her jaw firm.

"I was just telling Junior that I've never coached softball before."

"But you are an American. You know how to play it," she said this as matter-of- fact.

"Yes, I know how to play."

"Then we want you to coach us." She sets her jaw as if the decision is final.

"I know how to play, but I've never coached."

"You are the one we want." I start thinking there may be some benefits to this job. Besides, how hard can it be.

"Well, I'm willing to give it a try if Junior will be the assistant coach."

"Oh yes, mon. I will help you." He shuffles his feet, nervously nodding his head and looking at his wife who smiles approvingly.

"Where do we play?"

"We practice every afternoon after the boys leave the soccer field."

"When do you want to start?"

"My husband will contact you."

"Yes, mon, I will contact you."

"Okay, it's a deal." We shake hands.

I can tell right away that Junior does pretty much whatever his wife tells him to do. This is an unusual example of Spanish role reversal.

I see an opportunity here to get my foot in the door and make some female friends. I have not had any problem meeting men in the village, but the women barely acknowledge me.

Once again, this is a case of instant empowerment. I don't tell them I've never even played before. I played a little baseball as a kid, but it really wasn't my sport. I agreed to do it on the condition that Junior helps me as assistant coach mainly because I know I'll need help with the language and because I like him.

After our little meeting, I go see Matt in Orange Walk Town to get a quick lesson in coaching. He's coaching a team in town, and he knows what he's doing. He gives me an official rule book and a crash course in softball.

14

Making Friends

Making friends is high on my list of priorities, but I still don't have my living situation in order. I make another shopping list of supplies I need from town. Things like a lantern, kerosene, something cockroach-proof to store food in, wash basin, cooking utensils, and household stuff in general.

Early Saturday morning, I go with my list to stand on the road and wait for the transport truck. I've just gotten paid and figure I better buy these things before I spend my money in restaurants or on beer. I wait thirty minutes in the hot sun before the transport truck from Trinidad reaches me. The driver stops just long enough to politely tell me he's too full to make any room for me. I look for my last two traveling companions but don't see them or any space I can possibly squeeze into. I'll have to hitchhike and it might be a long wait. I look at the sun and pull my baseball cap down a little lower. Within five minutes, Victor pulls up in his pickup truck and tells me to get in the back since the front cab's full with his men. Without hesitation, I jump in the back.

We pass the slow transport truck and arrive in Orange Walk Town about fifteen minutes later. I'm thinking about how much I'll be able to get done since I'm getting an early start. This time, I won't go by to see Tim and Matt until I get my shopping done. *No staying to go drinking either, I've got to get my house in order.*

When we get to town, Victor doesn't stop when I signal by tapping the side of his truck. Instead, he drives into one of the neighborhoods and parks in front of a place that looks like all the other houses on the block, except bigger. Then I notice it has a sign over the door that reads "Minerva's."

I still have my bearings and know it's just a short walk to get where I want to go. There are three other men from the village with him that I had met the first time.

"Thank you for the ride."

"You are welcome, Jorge." I turn to walk away.

"Jorge, we would like to invite you for a beer," one of Victor's men offers the invitation.

"A beer?" I'm stalling because I'm not prepared for this, and my first thought is back to my Peace Corps training and being culturally sensitive.

"Yes, mon, a beer." By now, they're beside me, slapping me on the back and encouraging me to join them.

"Okay, I can drink one beer, but then I have to go do my shopping." What the hell, it's eight o'clock in the morning, I never drink that early. My agreeing to drink one beer makes them happy and we go inside, laughing and talking like old friends.

My plan is to honor their invitation by drinking one beer with them and then make a graceful exit. The first beers come, and before they're half done, another round of lukewarm beers are set down in front of us. That's okay. I'll just leave after the second beer. I decide to drink it fast before another round can be set down. The whole time, everyone's speaking in Spanish and I'm trying to be polite and keep up with the conversation. At the same time, I'm looking for an opportunity to escape.

I'm not fast enough and another round is put down. By this time, I notice we're in a brothel. There are lots of women around now, and Victor asks me if I like to see the pretty girls. To be honest, I'm not really attracted to them. Most of them look pretty rough with lots of makeup and cheap perfume. A few have some mean-looking tattoos—skull and crossbones and daggers dripping with blood. Not exactly what I'm used to. But I lie and tell my new buddies that "yes, I like to see them." I want to make sure they know I'm macho and like women in general.

After about six beers and no chance to escape, the girls do start to look better. By this time, I've forgotten about my shopping list. From Minerva's, we make the rounds hitting the most popular bars in town. We go to the Godfathers, the Las Vegas Club, Papa Gayo's, bar after bar. Since they're all brothels, the best bar is judged by the women. They all have loud, cry-in-your-beer Spanish music playing from a jukebox, a rank smell coming from the bathroom, and girls that look hard enough to kick my ass. I watch as each of my new buddies go through the routine of telling them how beautiful they are before they will even smile.

My new friends like flirting with the girls, and there seems to be competition in the bars we visit as to who can have the best and the most girls sitting at their table. The more girls at your table, the more it costs and the more prestige you earn from the men around you. Victor is friendly to the girls, but he also keeps his distance, not letting them get too close. He seems more interested in impressing his friends and having the girls pay attention to us even though he's the one paying for all the drinks. He's always focused on what's going on around him and what he's doing. He knows most of the men in every bar we go to, and he's friendly to the majority of them. Once in a while, he expresses his dislike of someone in the bar. If they leave us alone, he ignores them. If they want to talk to him or sit at our table, we leave the bar.

After a dozen bars, friendlier girls, three times as many beers, and dancing on the tabletops, we head home. It's two o'clock in the afternoon when Victor, Arturo, J.B., and Georgie drop me off at my house. I'm falling down drunk and haven't accomplished anything on my shopping list. But I have some new friends. I also still have money in my wallet. In fact, I haven't spent a dime the whole day. We drank a lot of beer, and at some point, we had lunch somewhere, but Victor paid for everything. I offered several times but each time he made me put my wallet away.

One thing I know for certain, I will never be able to "outdrink" or outlast these guys. They'll drink when they feel like drinking and for as long as they want. I also learned that when I'm with Victor and his buddies, I can go into any bar and be given instant acceptance and respect. It's a good feeling, like I have someone watching my back.

15

Part of the Team

There are fourteen girls and women on the softball team. They range in age from sixteen to midthirties. Right away, I notice the younger girls won't talk to me. Every time I try to tell them something, they turn their heads and ignore me. At first, it bothers me because it seems disrespectful, but I chalk it up to cultural differences and focus on the game. The older women are more cooperative and listen to me. After a few days of this, I ask Junior, "Why won't these girls talk to me when I'm trying to explain something?" He replies, "Because you don't speak Spanish, and they are shy to use their English."

We practice on a daily basis in the evenings, playing until it's too dark to see the ball. I need the exercise and it's fun getting into the game. After practicing for a few weeks, we decide it's time to play another team. The girls have worked hard; now they need some competition.

Junior and Fatima arrange a game with a team from a neighboring village. Our team agrees to host. I'm excited and nervous when they arrive. I introduce myself to the coach of the other team and shake hands. With a big smile on my face, I proudly turn around to look at my team. Every one of them has a big frown on her face. They look like someone just died. I look at the visiting team and they're doing the same thing. I approach my team and ask them, "What's the matter, what's going on?" They all turn away and mumble something in Spanish that I know right away is not good. I pull Junior aside.

"What's wrong? Why are the girls acting like this?"

"That's just the way they are, and besides, this team cheats."

"Cheat? How do you cheat in softball?"

"Oh, you will see!" He takes a step back, shaking his finger at me and shuffles his feet nervously. "You will see."

Meanwhile, a good-sized crowd has gathered from the village, plus the visiting team has their fans along as well. At this point, the players and a few of the team groupies take over, and I feel left out of the whole process. First, they pick umpires for all the bases and home plate. This advantage seems to be the prerogative of the home team. Next, they decide the visiting team will be up to bat first, how many innings they'll play, and a few basic rules regarding backstops and fences. While they're deciding these critical factors, the two teams look like they're ready to fistfight each other. As unfriendly as this whole scenario seems, our team brings out snacks and refreshments for the visitors.

Now it's time to play. Hoping to change the energy a little, I take my place as coach on the sidelines with my team. I may as well not exist because not one of the players acknowledges my presence. I notice that not only are they mad at the other team, but now they're also arguing with each other. I look over at the visiting team, and their players are clearly listening to their coach. Again, I turn to Junior who's arguing and taking directions from his wife.

"Junior, what the hell is going on?" He shrugs his shoulders.

"That's the way they are."

I keep trying to get them to focus on the game. "Watch the other team and study how they hit and field the ball." No response. It's useless, so after a while, I give up and stand by Junior to watch the game.

He had told me the other team would cheat, but he never said anything about our girls cheating. The fans from our village are appointed as umpires, much to our advantage. Christina, my center fielder, hits a short grounder that the first baseman fields for an easy out. But her husband, who happens to be the umpire for first base, calls her safe. A blind man could see that she was out, and it really pisses off the other team. I'm too angry and embarrassed to even watch for fear of another "mistake." The other team doesn't cheat, at least not that I can see. To be fair, they also don't have the opportunity because all the umpires are on our side.

After five innings of bad calls, the game ends with our team as the winners, if you can call it that. Surprisingly, everyone lines up for the traditional handshake and *now* my team is smiling for the first time since the game started.

After they all shake hands, the visiting team piles back into a cane truck and leaves. Everyone else walks off the field with their boyfriends, husbands, and families. I'm left standing there in an empty field by myself. Junior's the only one who says anything to me. He slaps me on the shoulder. "Well, good game, you won. See you tomorrow."

I feel angry and humiliated and I'm considering quitting as the coach. They ignored me the whole game, they cheated, and now they're happy they won. I feel used and unappreciated. I decide to announce my decision to quit at our next practice. I want to do something to let them know their behavior is unacceptable.

The next day, I go to practice determined to keep my convictions and make the speech that I carefully planned all night and day. When I get to the field, the girls are laughing and joking around and behaving like nothing has happened. I ask Junior to translate and call them all in for a serious talk. I give my speech and tell them how I feel about the game and their attitude. For once, all fourteen girls stand in front of me. I'm having trouble staying angry and focused because they're all smiling and seem so happy. I can feel my speech going flat as Junior is translating. He never questions what I say and, as far as I know, translates every word exactly as I say it. I'm not getting the reaction I expect; in fact, they're in a happy mood and it's contagious. "Come on, Jorge, let's play ball." Someone tosses me a mitt and a ball. They're all looking at me and smiling mischievously. No matter how mad I want to be, I can't help but smile back. It all seems so irrelevant right now. They came to play.

I'm still angry and a little offended. I decide I can quit and leave on a bad note or give it another try. I can't imagine not coming out to play ball every day. Junior sees the mood I'm in and gives me a playful shove and mimics the girls. "Come on, Jorge, let's play ball."

We had just won our first game, and even though the outcome was dubious, it deserves some recognition. There were a couple of things that I had noticed while watching the teams play. Our girls weren't running the bases very fast nor were they always touching the bags as they passed them. In a real game, with real umpires, that would count against them. Wanting to be a little creative and have some fun, I come up with an idea to improve their speed and attention to touching the bases. I challenge the fastest girl on the team, Soila, to a race. The rules are we're both going to start on home plate and race around the bases in opposite directions, touching each bag as we pass. The first one back to home plate wins. Junior will be the judge, and I put a player at each base as umpires. I give instruction that if one of us misses touching a bag, that person is out.

Soila is a Creole girl raised in Spanish culture so she's Spanish in every way, except her size and color. She's solid from a life of hard labor cutting sugarcane with the men. She outweighs me by about fifteen to twenty-five pounds of lean muscle. I know she's fast; I've seen her run. Despite her size and speed, I still feel like I can beat her.

Soila rises to my challenge with the whole team cheering her on. We take our positions on home plate. Junior counts to three and we're off. I'm running as fast as I can. *I can't let her win.* I round each of the bases, making sure I have contact with the bag. I'm coming in to home plate, and I can see Soila out of the corner of my eye coming in fast from the other direction and it looks close. I close my eyes and push as hard as I can for the final sprint.

The next thing I know, *bam*! We collide. We run into each other at full speed. I go down hard with the wind knocked out of me, my head hurts, and a couple of my ribs feel like they're broken. I want to stay on the ground and assess my injuries, but I also want to get up before Soila does and save some of my dignity. I struggle to my feet about the same time she does, and with one look, I can tell that I got the worst of it. She looks a little shaken, but she has a smile on her face and is laughing with the rest of the team. The whole team is doubled over with laughter, which is good because that way, they can't see the pain I'm in. By the time they stop laughing, (about thirty minutes later) I've regained some of my composure. I ask Soila if she's okay, and she says she's ready to go again. More laughter. I tell her, "Maybe next time."

Now the rest of the girls want to race. It's the first time I don't have to talk them into something or have them ignore me. Now that we've shown them what not to do, they line up at home plate. They all race and practice touching the bags, which is exactly what I wanted.

Everyone's very gracious and respectful to me for the rest of practice; I'm in pain even though I do as little as possible. Afterward, I slowly, very slowly, walk the fifty yards to my house and collapse on my bed. I go to practice the next day, and they're still laughing about it. Mostly, they're teasing Soila about what she did to the gringo. It takes me a couple of months to recover from my severely bruised ribs and ego. It hurts, but it's worth it because from then on, everyone cooperates and treats me as part of the team.

Summer is almost over, and the schools are scheduled to open in the middle of August. For the last month, I've spent all my time coaching softball and going to games. Now it's time for school to begin, and I have to get my plan together.

Peace Corps has given me a Honda 125 trail bike to use. I decide that I'll visit a school every day, continuing with the three schools I worked with at the end of last school year. I'll expand over the year, visiting more schools and starting more gardens. My Belizean supervisor, Mr. E., works out of the curriculum development unit in Belize City. He expects monthly reports on my progress, but other than that, I don't feel much pressure from anyone.

At first, the hardest part of my job is the lack of structure. My work day doesn't happen unless I make it happen. There's no blueprint or plan. It's a new project and I'm doing it for the first time. Back home when I went to work, I knew what I had to do; there was structure. Here, there is none and it takes me a while to figure it out. Now that I'm getting used to it, I like it. I have control and I wouldn't trade it for anything.

16

Independence

Belize is preparing for independence, and the official date is set for September 21, 1981. The PUP government has somehow managed to receive the reluctant blessing of the opposition party, and Belize will soon be free of the British.

I'm contacted by the wife of the consular general, Mrs. Consular General. She knows I'm a chef by profession and asks me to help her with a banquet she's planning for U.S. and Belizean government officials, who will be attending the official ceremony. Her husband has a good chance of becoming the first ambassador to Belize.

I don't really want to work on Independence Day, but I'm flattered that they've asked me. Plus, I'll have a chance to show off doing something I'm good at. I plan the menu and I give the shopping list to Mrs. General. She makes sure I have everything I need, and I spend the whole day and most of the night in the kitchen. The banquet turns out fine and everyone's happy.

There's a countrywide celebration going on outside her home. Even if you have been against independence, there is nothing to do now but celebrate because it's here. Every town and village is having a party. All the schools plant mahogany trees to commemorate the event. Every home, business, and government agency is flying the Belizean flag.

The government spends lots of money sponsoring big-name soca bands to come from all over the Caribbean. Everywhere you go, you hear reggae or soca music playing. There are big parades, and everyone tags on at the end of the parade and follows it around town. Dignitaries from the United States and other countries in the Caribbean and Central America are invited, toasts are offered, and speeches are made. Belize is now an independent nation.

It makes me think about what our independence must have felt like two hundred years ago. It also brings home the fact of what a young country Belize is; she seems tiny and vulnerable compared to her big and powerful neighbors. The good news is that Great Britain has not completely abandoned her. If Guatemala tries to make good on their claim that Belize belongs to them, they will have to deal with the British army.

17

Where Is Your Mother?

The home is not built on a foundation of cement.
It is built on the woman.
—Mexican proverb

The Americans at the banquet are all high-powered and going a hundred miles an hour in their lives and everything they do. Even being around the other Peace Corps volunteers is a completely different pace than the village. A typical day for me consists of getting up at daybreak, which is the same time year-round at 6:15 a.m. I use the outhouse, pour some clean water in a basin, and wash up a little. Then I do my yoga and meditate while the Cha-cha-lak-cas (a very noisy bird) make their morning racket—"patras, patras." Then I fire up my little stove and boil some water for instant coffee. For breakfast, I usually have peanut butter on bread or a bun. After that, it depends on what day of the week it is and what school I'm working with.

Just daily living necessities seem to take all my energy. I'm always busy making sure I have water, food, and a clean house to keep down the cockroaches, ants, and rodents. I do my laundry in a bucket. A "Peace Corps Maytag" is a pigtail bucket with a small hole cut into the lid for the handle of a toilet plunger to fit into. You put your dirty clothes in with water and laundry soap, put in the plunger, put on the lid, and move the plunger up and down until your clothes are clean. Then you rinse them a couple of times the same way and squeeze out the extra water by hand. The whole process usually takes a couple of hours. The villagers have their own way, which involves an old-fashioned washboard and a laundry basin.

The sun goes down at 6:00 p.m. Once it's dark, I have to use kerosene lamps to get around my house. I cook myself something for dinner and clean up my mess. Then it's time to read and maybe write a few letters. Sometimes, I have work to prepare for the next day. The kerosene lamp is hard on my eyes and makes me tire quickly. Plus, the mosquitoes and humidity distract me, making it difficult to get much work done after the sun goes down.

Before going to bed, I like to go for a walk down the main street of the village. Before 9:00 p.m., there are plenty of men standing around talking in small groups. Women never join in, and they only go out if they're going to church or someone's home. I stop and talk to people I've met and make new friends. I'm lonely so it feels good to get out and get the latest gossip. By nine o'clock, most homes are closed up for the night with very few people left on the streets. I'm in bed by nine thirty and have no trouble sleeping. It's very quiet and peaceful.

I quickly learn there are a few necessities you have to have for survival in a village. Pigtail buckets are used for everything from hauling and storing water to mixing cement and doing laundry. Tying wire is to Belizeans what duct tape is to Americans; it's used for everything, from holding a cane truck together to fixing a softball mitt. The machete is the most versatile of the three and can be used for everything from cutting your lawn to killing snakes. No self-respecting canero would be caught without his machete. Everyone, including women and children, use one for cleaning yards and high grass around their homes. At school, children are sent out daily with machetes to keep the school grounds trim.

That's another thing I've noticed. The jungle is aggressive, and if you're not constantly cutting back, it will take over quickly. In a few short years, everything here would be covered with tropical vegetation.

Once the school year starts, everyone gets busier, and we have to slow down on softball practice. At this time of year, there are weekend softball and soccer marathons scheduled to determine who will be the district champs. Either the game is at home or we travel with the men's soccer team to another village. In a marathon, there can be as many as eight teams, and we play by elimination for first, second, and third place.

Because there are so many games, all the coaches are required to take turns as umpires. This is not my favorite thing to do. There are usually some drunks around that like to give the umpires a hard time. When they don't like my calls, they call me gringo and are generally not very supportive. I learn to ignore them. I know I have enough friends with me from the village to back me up if need be. A couple of times, the girls on my team answer belligerent drunks by saying something in Spanish that sounds like the equivalent of "up yours, village idiot." I pretend I don't know what they're doing or saying, but I know they're standing up for me and it feels good.

During school days, it's back to work. After school, I sometimes stick around to work in the school garden by myself or go into Orange Walk Town to buy supplies or go to the post office. Mail from home has become my lifeline. In fact, distance makes me closer to my family than I ever felt in my life. I love getting mail and reading about what everyone's doing and the changes in their lives. I feel like I can be close to them without being drawn into the drama and having the energy sucked out of me.

My house is directly across the street from the Catholic primary school. Since I live here, I always put in a little more time at their school garden. During the day, we have a full ninety minutes for lunch, and all the students and teachers go home to eat. For me, it's a short walk across the street to make myself a peanut butter sandwich or something easy.

The kids like to eat lunch quickly and go back to school early. The boys play soccer and the girls play softball. I've been working with this school for a few months now, and I'm getting to know the students better. Most of them are children and they act like children. But there is one small group of four or five girls who seem to be much older than their age of fourteen. I notice that they sometimes withdraw from the usual softball to walk around the school yard, observing everyone else and having lengthy discussions. Today, while I'm eating lunch, they focus their attention on me and come over for a visit. They make me feel like a minor celebrity and I love the attention. They're between fourteen and fifteen years old and very pretty. This is most likely their last year of school since very few village girls have the opportunity to attend high school. Their life after this will most likely turn toward helping their family and getting married to start their own families. Their curiosity about me results in some simple but profound questions.

"Mr. Jorge, where is your wife (giggle)?"

"I don't have a wife."

"If you do not have a wife, then where is your mother?"

"My mother lives in the United States, far from here."

"Where is your sister then?" They're starting to look concerned.

"My sister lives in the United States too."

"Who cooks your tortillas and beans for you?" Now they're exchanging glances and looking very serious.

"No one. I don't eat tortillas and beans."

"What do you eat then?" Now they sound skeptical.

"I cook my own food, different things." More concerned looks.

"Who cleans your clothes and your house for you?" Now it's total disbelief.

"I clean my clothes and my house."

"Mr. Jorge, that is not good. You need a woman to cook your beans and tortillas and clean your house." They're scolding me now.

"Well, until I find someone, I'll have to do it." They look at each other with a look of astonishment. They're clearly not satisfied with my answer.

"No, Mr. Jorge. Until you find a wife, you have to bring your mother or sister to take care of you." They all nod in agreement.

The conversation is interrupted when the principal comes out ringing a handheld bell signaling that it's time to return to class. I think the thing that amazes them the most is when they find out I don't eat beans and tortillas every day. They can't understand why I would come live here without my family or some kind of woman in my life to take care of me.

It's hard for me to imagine my mother or my sister being here to "take care of me" or "cook my tortillas." They might cook for me if I'm sick or it's my birthday. Otherwise, they'll tell me that I'm a grown man and can cook my own damn tortillas.

The simple questions from these young girls plant a seed and start me thinking about what family is, what it means to them and what it means to me. To them, the family "is the woman," and I can see it's deeply ingrained in their culture. The woman is the one who holds everything together.

I am thirty-one years old, at a point in my life when I'm thinking about my age. On one hand, getting married and having children are something I want to do when I'll still be around to see my kids grow up. On the other hand, I don't want to get married just because I'm worried about my biological clock. Besides, I'm having way too much fun being single and chasing fast women.

18

Teaching and Learning

I'm impressed with the girl's visit and their thoughts about my situation. Something else that immediately impresses me with all the students is their common sense and knowledge about their environment. They know which trees are good for fence post and what phase of the moon to cut them in. They know what plants to stay away from and which ones produce edible fruit. They know how to build chicken coops and work with machetes and tools.

What fascinates me is when I see kids teaching kids. The older kids are always teaching the younger ones. It's such a perfect relationship and both sides are very patient with each other. There are arguments, but they deal with them in a mature way, and if they can't resolve something, they go to an adult. They're always educating me, especially when I think I'm supposed to be the teacher.

Today, I'm home with nothing to do, so I decide to work on the chicken coop in the school garden. While I'm there, one of the older boys, who is thirteen years old, comes by with a couple of his younger brothers and a cousin.

"Mr. Jorge, what are you working on?"

"Hi, Rafael. I'm working on the post for the chicken coop."

"Mr. Jorge, that kind of wood will not last in the ground."

"It won't? Why not?"

"It is too soft. You need hardwood."

"It'll last for a while, won't it?" I don't like the thought that the work I've been doing all morning might be pointless.

"No, Mr. Jorge. It will only last a year, maybe a little more."

"Where do I get hardwood?" I'm frustrated, but I know Rafael's right.

"You have to go in the bush."

"How will I know which trees to cut down?"

"We will show you, Mr. Jorge. We will help you."

"Okay, let me get my machete." I'm starting to feel better knowing they'll help me.

"Mr. Jorge, this machete is very dull. You cannot cut with this." Rafael and his brothers are smiling as they take turns feeling the dullness of my machete.

"It's sharp enough, isn't it?" Now I'm frustrated again. I know he's right, but I'm getting tired of being wrong.

"No," he says laughing. "Mr. Jorge, this will not cut down even a soft tree."

"All right, do you know how to sharpen it?" I give up. These kids know what they're doing and I don't.

Rafael pulls a small triangular file out of his back pocket. It's wrapped in a dirty piece of newspaper, which he carefully folds and puts back in his pocket to be reused. Then he skillfully begins sharpening my machete. He shows me how to angle the file so that I'm not just sharpening the cutting edge. I know what he's doing because it's the same as sharpening a good knife.

Rafael works with me until I have the right rhythm and we get my machete sharp but not brittle. Then we carefully walk into the bush surrounding the village and cut down a hardwood tree. I say "carefully" because the bush is full of danger including snakes, killer bees, poisonous insects, and even jaguars. I follow the boys since they know what they're doing. They come to a tree that, to me, looks like just another tree. "This tree, Mr. Jorge, this is a good tree for a post."

Of course, not all the kids are good. In some schools, I have some real troublemakers who like to call me gringo behind my back. One of these schools is in Trinidad. For years, they have been using the community center as a school. But they will soon have a new school that the government is building. The principal of the school, Maestro Joe, quickly becomes my friend. He's a very macho guy and he loves to put me to the test to see how, as he says, "you Americans hold up." He's short, stout, and intense. He's in his forties with jet black hair and a "Fu Manchu" goatee. He carries a pistol in his front pocket and you can see it when he's teaching. I ask him why he carries it.

"Let me tell you something, Jorge (he always starts like that). There are many undesirable characters in these parts, so you always have to be prepared for anything. You understand what I am saying, no true?"

"Yes, Maestro, I understand."

"Good, then we have something in common. Let me ask you something. Do you have these undesirables in your parts, where you come from?"

"Yes, Maestro. I think every place has those kinds of people."

"Uh-huh, I see. Well, then everyone should be prepared like me. Don't you agree?"

"Well, I agree we should always be prepared, but I think each of us has our own way of being prepared."

"I think I know what you mean and you make a good point. Okay, let's go to the garden. Boys, grab your machetes. We are going to show Mr. Jorge what we can do."

He is rough but also intelligent and articulate. I like talking to him. It's like having a conversational chess game. He has some very tough boys in his school and he is the perfect one to handle them. Some of them like to challenge me. I get the feeling they don't think I'm a man. They most likely get this idea that Americans are soft from their father or other male role model. I also give them plenty of opportunities to laugh at my lack of knowledge about their environment.

Many of these boys grow up quick and are expected to do a man's work by thirteen or fourteen years old. They're used to doing a day's work in the field with a machete. Some of them are not willing to automatically give me their respect. I'm going to have to earn it. To gain their respect, I show them respect. Whenever there's hard work to do, I jump in and work right beside them, clearing bush with a machete or digging a garden bed.

When I first start working in the gardens, I go to school dressed the way that I would work in my garden at home. I'm wearing overalls with cutoffs underneath, a T-shirt, and sandals. I take the class out and when we reach the garden site, I start explaining how we're going to plan our garden. I notice all the students are giggling at something, and I know it has to do with me. Since I have no idea what it is, I keep talking. The next thing I know, my feet are on fire and in intense pain. I look down and see I'm standing right smack in the middle of a nest of fire ants. Both my feet are covered and they are digging into my flesh. I jump off the pile, stamping my feet and brushing them off as quickly as possible. The students have a great time watching the show I put on. My feet are a mess covered with red welts that itch and burn for days. After that, when working in the garden, I always wear tennis shoes and watch where I step.

I find all the students and teachers to be very direct, which sometimes bothers me. When I first arrived in the village and began working with the school, I noticed that if someone is fat, he or she almost always has the nickname *gordo* or *gorda*, which literally means fat, fatty, or fatso. If someone is not too bright academically, it's not hidden but talked about openly in front of the student. I may be introduced to a student with the comment, "This is Jose and he is very dunce." Jose smiles and acknowledges his introduction. It's not done with any malice; it's done as a matter-of-fact. While I'm hearing that Jose is probably dumb as a post, I'm also hearing that he is respected for the things he is good at. Those things are reinforced everyday by the mere fact that he is recognized and respected for who he is. Jose will get all the support he needs to succeed in school or whatever he decides to do. There is enough family and village support to make these children comfortable being who they are.

This direct and matter-of-fact style works both ways. You may have a teacher that does not challenge his students. He may be lazy or does not have good teaching methods. The students will not hesitate to tell the teacher as well as their parents and the principal that they are not satisfied. The teacher is always confronted with any concerns or complaints, and they are dealt with in a fair way. Like the students, they have an opportunity to defend themselves.

I learn I have to be very careful about what I say. I may think it is said in confidentiality, but by the next day, everyone will know about it. The amazing thing is you're not judged by it. But you are confronted for further explanation or clarification. I may say to a teacher, "I don't like the way so-and-so teaches." The next day, I may need to clarify to so-and-so exactly what I mean. There is no anger, but there is a need and desire to understand.

It takes me a while to realize that you can be honest about a person's shortcomings without offending him or her as long as you accept and respect them for who they are.

19

Death in the Morning

It's my second visit to work with Maestro Joe, and he invites me to the inauguration of the new school, which is taking place tomorrow. I ask him if there's anything I can help with.

"Let me tell you something Jorge, we are going to be starting very early in the morning. The first thing we will do is kill a pig to make a special Mayan dish called Pib. This is something our ancestors used to make. It is tradition."

"How do you make Pib, Maestro?" The chef in me is curious.

"Aha, that is a good question, Jorge. To make Pib, you have to dig a deep hole in the ground and start a fire to heat up rocks. Then you line the hole with the red, hot rocks. The next step is covering the rocks with banana leaves. Then we take the pieces of meat that the women wrap carefully in banana leaves. Then more leaves over that and then dirt to cover the whole thing. After that it has to sit for hours while the meat cooks slowly."

"Pib sounds like a lot of work, Maestro. I can see why you would only make it on special occasions."

"Oh yes, mon, it is a lot of work."

I show up at five in the morning ready to help with whatever is needed. Naturally, Maestro Joe is in charge of killing the pig. I'm surprised at how big this animal is. To control her, they have "hog-tied" her feet together. There are two men on the back feet and two men on the front to hold her as still as possible.

Maestro Joe has a large butcher knife and, of course, he offers me the honors, which I politely decline. He then stabs the pig in the heart and leaves the knife there. She begins twisting and turning violently to break free. Her shrill screams break the peaceful morning calm. I watch, hoping it will soon be over, as the wound in her heart spills her life on the ground. Her breathing gets harder and harder. It's getting raspy now and I can hear the gurgling of blood in her lungs. Finally, she gives one last breath and lays still.

Watching this violent act gives me a primal feeling of life and death. At first, I feel numb and then I feel like a hunter, even though there is no hunting involved. I tell myself it's a pig, a dumb animal, and now it's gone, and we will celebrate by eating its flesh. I also know I'm not going to eat any.

Men and women jump into action, and I sense that it would be wise to stand out of the way and observe. The cleaning starts with scalding hot water that's been boiling over several large fires the women are tending. The steaming water is poured over the skin, and the men start shaving off the hairs with sharp knives. Then they cut down the length of her abdomen and gut her, throwing some parts to the dogs that are always hanging back just out of kicking range. Other parts, many other parts, are saved for cooking including the intestines, which they stuff with blood to make a local delicacy appropriately called blood sausage. The nose, the tail, the ears . . .everything is used. Even the excess blood on the ground is licked up by the dogs. The skin is in high demand and they have a huge urn on the fire where it's put to cook.

The butchering is over quickly. Now the women who are responsible for wrapping the meat in banana leaves take over. Through this whole process, everyone is busy and knows exactly what to do, even the dogs. The whole thing is incredibly efficient and only takes about two hours.

Their attention now turns to the pigskin boiling in its own fat inside the big urn. Someone sends some boys to buy fresh corn tortillas from the village *tortilleria*. My curiosity gets the better of me and I peek into the urn to see how it's done. The skin and fat are being stirred by a couple of hefty women using large wooden paddles. It looks just like a big tub of lard, which it is. When the tortillas arrive, some (super hot) habanero chili peppers are picked out of someone's garden. Everyone lines up at the fire to get their share of the skin and fat. They put the soft, hot, bubbling skins into their tortillas with some fresh slices of habaneros. Then they roll it up and eat it like it's the best thing they ever had.

Someone brings out some rum and starts passing it around for straight shots right out of the bottle. About this time, I'm fading into the background and making myself as invisible as possible. I know I can't handle rum and pigskin at 7:00 a.m. I'm successful at staying out of the way while this little precelebration takes place. The only thing left now is for the meat to cook and that will take hours. I slowly push my motorcycle behind the crowd and get it to the road before starting it. I go home to eat a real breakfast of peanut butter on a bun and instant coffee. Then I go back to bed for a nap.

The inauguration goes off at 2:00 p.m. as scheduled. Maestro Joe, his teaching staff, and the village council host the whole village plus invited guests and officials from the ministry of education. There are speeches and songs, opening prayers and closing prayers. Some of the students are dressed in Mayan garb and perform traditional Mayan dances to celebrate and recognize their heritage. The local priest does a final blessing for the school and the ribbon is cut. The school is now officially open.

It's time to eat and drink. The Pib is very popular, and I manage to avoid eating it without anyone knowing. Instead, I fill my plate with rice and beans and coleslaw. The remaining pigskin has been made into *chicharon* or the same stuff we call "pig rinds" at home. The inauguration is a big success celebrated by everyone. Trinidad Village now has a new school to be proud of, and I now know how to kill a pig and prepare Pib.

20

My Education

Since my arrival, I've been talking with teachers and principals to learn more about the education system of Belize. It's part of my own education. It doesn't take me long to figure out that families and students take their education very seriously. Primary school, which takes a child up to the equivalent of the eighth grade, is free. Some families have children that continue and go on to high school. There's a tuition charge, and the rate varies from school to school, with the best schools charging up to eighty dollars per month.

Getting into high school is also competitive and better schools are more competitive. All students are required to take a national selection exam during their last year of primary school. Their score determines if they can continue their education and which schools they can apply to. The students who score 80 percent or above can apply to schools that are considered prestigious. Students scoring lower get into schools that are not as sought after. To narrow the selection process even further, there are no high schools in the villages. If a student from a village wants to go to high school, he or she will have to pay for boarding in addition to all the other expenses. This makes going to high school an expensive and, many times, unattainable venture for someone from the villages.

Approximately 50 percent of the eligible population actually gets into high school. Of that, approximately 50 percent complete the four years. Do the math and you end up with 25 percent of the eligible population graduating. Once they finish high school, some go to work, some overseas on scholarships, and some join the "brain drain" to the United States.

Working with the primary schools, I'm continually impressed with the way teachers handle discipline. There is an honesty and maturity displayed by both the teacher and the children that I've never seen before. In our culture, if a child misbehaves and another child informs the teacher, that child is branded a "tattletale" or "fink." But here, the children use their own judgment. If they feel a student is doing something wrong, they, usually a group of them, tell the teacher. The teacher then determines if it needs their attention or if the children themselves can handle it by talking to the offender. If a teacher does need to deal with a situation, the children are amazingly honest about what exactly happened. Even the perpetrators are forthcoming and take responsibility for what they did. They accept their punishment without argument. There is a level of responsibility and accountability here that I have never seen before. There is also a sense of justice and the belief that the world is fair and children have rights.

The world I grew up in was not like this. "Children were to be seen, not heard" and adults were always right. I lived my whole childhood learning how to cruise under the radar and I was very good at it. Any time I was unjustly accused of an action or misdeed and tried to defend myself to an adult, I was knocked down. "Even if you didn't do it, you probably did something." As a child, the only adult I ever had a relationship with that would allow me to defend myself was my father. But we were separated most of the time. Now here I am in a third-world country, and I'm experiencing adults listening to children who have the right to speak and, when necessary, contradict or correct an adult. I'm starting to think I was born into the wrong culture.

The first time I'm involved with something that requires teacher intervention is when two students get into an argument over a machete. One boy takes it from another who is already working with it. I stop the argument and scold the boy who aggressively took the machete and make him give it back. Then I take the role of an adult and tell one of the teachers what happened. The teacher and students listen politely as I finish with my version of what I think happened. Then I tell them what I think should be appropriate punishment, which is the boy who took the machete should apologize. The teacher, after listening politely to me, then asks the children what happened. I'm in disbelief. *Wait a minute. I'm the adult here and I just told you what happened.*

The teacher listens carefully to the children as they explain the whole event. The boy who took the machete was taking what was his. The other boy had borrowed it without permission. After listening to everyone involved, I realize I've been rash in my judgment about the whole situation. The children demand and are given the right to defend themselves. The teacher makes a couple of reprimands with the students who accept their admonishments and leave satisfied that both sides were listened to.

After that, the teacher sends them on their way and goes back to his class. I stand there by myself for a while, just taking it all in. I feel humbled. I have never seen children treated as equals, and I'm impressed with their honesty and the level of responsibility I have just witnessed. For a moment, I feel just a twinge of resentment that I never experienced this level of honesty and integrity when I was a child. At the same time, I know that how I was raised as a child made me who I am today, and I have no regrets about that.

As a child, school was a painful place for me that always felt like prison. I was there because adults told me to be there. Like everyone else, I had to follow all the rules. That meant being on time, doing my homework, participating in class, avoiding the bullies, sometimes being a bully, and most important, try to gain respect. If you got caught doing something, you lied. Everyone knew that worked better than telling the truth. Then you had to pick your friends for protection. You were either followed or a follower, and if you didn't belong, then you got harassed and bullied.

Here in the village schools, there are no threats or none that I can see. Conflicts are dealt with openly and there are no secrets. It is a learning environment and a safe place for kids to be and they want to be here.

Students and teachers have very few resources to work with but they make it work. The blackboard is the only visual aid they have and it's used for everything. Even paper is a valuable resource, pencils are used right down to the nub, nothing is wasted. I'm always impressed with how resourceful the teachers and students can be with what they have to work with. I'm also amazed at how artistic and creative the culture is. Almost everyone can draw very well like it's completely natural to be an artist.

The teachers I work with are required to teach in English. But all teachers have a first language that is either Creole, Spanish, Garifuna, or one of three dialects of Mayan. Many times, they fall back on their first language; in this case, Spanish or Creole to get a point or lesson across. These kids not only have to learn to speak and understand a second language—English—they have to learn to read it and write it as well. Considering what they have to work with, I'm amazed at how much they accomplish together.

21

Food

I like living in an agricultural community where people's work revolves around the seasons. The cash crop is sugarcane, but every farmer also has a *milpa*, which is a small vegetable garden located someplace close to his cane fields. In the milpa, farmers grow whatever they like to eat. Mostly they plant beans, corn, cabbage, peppers, and okra. Everyone has a garden and takes pleasure in working with the earth.

During the off-season for sugarcane, July through November, I see farmers going to their fields every day with their water bottle, machete, and a light lunch of tortillas and beans. Many times, the wife goes, and I see them walking back together carrying their harvest. Most farmers also have fruit trees with lush tropical fruits like mangoes, papayas, bananas, custard apples, plantains, guavas, plums, and bread fruit. These are things that supplement their diets of rice and beans, and what I'm missing from my diet.

By now, I'm ready to give up and admit that I can't cook for myself. Without a refrigerator, I never know what to buy or how to store it. I try to do my own cooking, but it's too much work and I'm wasting food. Plus, I quickly discovered that even the tiniest crumb attracts cockroaches, ants, and mice. I'm still spending too much money eating at restaurants. Many times, I end up eating bread and peanut butter for breakfast, lunch at a Chinese restaurant in town, and rice for dinner. I need to do something about my food and diet situation.

I decide to swallow my pride and see if I can pay Chabby to cook for me. I figure out how much of my budget is for food and what I can afford to pay.

By this time, I know enough about the culture to know that I need to approach Samuel about the idea before I talk to Chabby. If I get his blessing, it's almost a sure thing. I approach him one day as he's coming home from the sugarcane factory.

"Samuel, do you have a minute?"

"Yes, Jorge. What is it?"

"I want to ask you if I can hire Chabby to cook my lunches and dinners for me."

"What's the matter, Jorge, you do not like to cook anymore?" Samuel had observed my cooking experiments several times but was unwilling to try my creations.

"No, I still like to cook, but I don't have time, and I never know what to buy or how to keep it from going bad."

"So you want to hire my wife to cook for you, no true?"

"Yes, but only lunch and dinner. I can make my own breakfast."

"Okay, I will talk to her, but it is up to her if she wants to do it, that is fine with me."

"Great. Thanks, Samuel. Tell her I can pay eighty dollars a month."

"Okay, I will tell her, Jorge."

The next day, Chabby stops me in the yard before I leave for work.

"Mr. Jorge, Mr. Samuel said you want me to cook your lunch and dinners, no true?"

"Chabby, that will really help me if you can do my cooking."

"But I am worried you will not like my food, no true." She starts blushing and hides her face.

"I'll love your food. Don't worry about that." That made her happy.

"Okay, then you can start today if you want."

"Great. Thank you, Chabby. I won't be here for lunch, but count on me for dinner."

After work, I go home knowing that my dinner is taken care of. I don't have to stop at a restaurant or resort to bread and peanut butter. When I reach home, the first thing I do is go in the bathhouse to clean up. By the time I'm finished, it's almost dark.

"Mr. Jorge, you can come and eat now." It's Chabby calling me from her doorway. Samuel is at the sugarcane factory, so she leaves the front door open to keep the rumors down. I sit at the table with Olga and Pedro, who are both so shy they hide their faces from me. Chabby puts a plate of refried beans with a generous piece of chicken and some fresh, stewed tomatoes in front of me. "Mr. Jorge, the tortillas are here in the leck." She taps the side of a dried out gourd shaped like a small pumpkin that's hollowed out for keeping tortillas warm. Inside are fresh flour tortillas, thick and hot. I watch how Pedro and

Olga eat their beans using their tortillas like a spoon and I try to mimic them. They both giggle at everything I do. I eat everything on my plate plus about six of the thick tortillas. I can eat more, but I know I've had enough and I don't want to eat more than my share. I might eat my eighty dollars worth in one week if I don't control myself. Chabby offers me more but I decline. "Thank you, Chabby. That was very good."

"You are welcome Mr. Jorge." The kids giggle. I offer to help with dishes but she laughs and refuses. I play with the kids for a while and then leave to go on my nightly walk.

Hiring Chabby to cook for me turns out to be one of the best moves I ever made. If I make it home by six o'clock, I eat dinner with the family. If I get home late, Chabby has covered my meal with clean linen and put it inside my house for me. Dinners are always handmade flour tortillas and beans with chicken and stewed tomatoes. Lunch is the bigger meal of the day with rice and beans, chicken, coleslaw, and fried plantains. The only days I have lunch with her is the one day I work with the San Lazaro School and on weekends. On Sundays, we usually have a special Belizean dish like tamales or *escabeche* (spicy onion soup with chicken).

The change is a big improvement in all ways. I save money, have someone to talk to, eat a healthy diet, and avoid having a big mess to clean up afterward. I manage to salvage some self-respect as a chef by making my own breakfast. I never have to worry again about what to buy or how I'm going to store it. I feel like I'm being taken care of, and I love it.

22

Hazards to My Health

I've been in the village for about six months now, and I feel good about being here. Instead of hanging out full-time with my Peace Corps buddies, I'm finally experiencing another culture and spending time with Belizeans. I'm still out of shape and still smoking cigarettes but less and less. It helps that the usual "cues" are not here. There's not a night club or parties to go to with friends when you get off work.

Bottom line is I have to give up smoking. It is the most addicting and unhealthy habit I have. Every day that I keep smoking is more time off my life. It nags me like a bad dream.

I'm walking with Arturo on my way home from my evening walk, and we're talking about soccer. He's a "striker" for the village team. A striker is a player on offense positioned to make goals. To be in that position, you have to be a very fast sprinter. I've seen him play before and I know he's fast. Just for the fun of it, I challenge him to a race.

"I want to see how fast you are. How about a race?"

"You want to race, Jorge?" He laughs at my challenge.

"Yes, come on. Let's see how fast you really are."

"Okay, let's go from here to my house." Which is about fifty yards away. I start us off by counting to three and we're off. I cheat and take off on the count of two, sprinting as fast as I can. He quickly catches and passes me so easily that he turns around and runs the remainder of the race backward laughing and taunting me. I can't even finish the fifty yards. I'm blowing so hard I feel like I'm going to have a heart attack. Arturo continues on to his house still laughing. I manage to say good night, glad that I don't have to face him after my humiliating defeat.

At that moment, winded from my short run, I make a decision. I know if I quit smoking, I'll be accomplishing something every day that is good for my health. Even if I accomplish nothing else, I know I'll be giving myself a longer, better quality life. I make a silent prayer to choose life over death and never pick up a cigarette again.

Right after I convince myself to live a little longer, I stop by JB's. He has a park bench sitting under a coconut tree in his front yard. It's a good place to sit down, rest, and reflect on the decision I've just made. There's a crooked stick lying on the bench and just as I'm about to pick it up, it moves, by itself. It's a snake, a big one and I almost grabbed him.

I remember my conversation with Samuel. Since then, I've been told by others in the village to watch out for snakes because they're all bad. At the same time, I've been told by a Peace Corps friend (who happens to be a zoologist) that the locals are probably killing 1 percent bad and the other 99 percent are most likely harmless. I immediately look around for something to kill him with. I don't like the fact that I came so close to finding out first hand if he was good or bad.

While looking for a weapon, I lose track of where he goes. It's a dark night and, as usual, I don't have a flashlight with me. About that time, JB comes out his front door. "Be careful, JB, I just saw a snake."

"Where is he?" JB only speaks Spanish but I understand him.

"I don't know. I lost him." I'm standing in one place doing a 360, looking for a snake in the dark. I'm afraid to take a step in any direction until we find him. JB runs back in his house and returns with his machete and a flashlight. Now we have an advantage. After carefully searching, we find him crawling slowly up the coconut tree behind the bench. JB slams him hard with the flat side of his machete. When he falls to the ground, he slams him again. We wait a few minutes to be sure he's dead before getting close. I ask JB what kind of snake it is. "It is a very dangerous snake, Barba Amarilla (yellow beard), tommygoff, the worst kind." They all look the same to me. Until I know better, I'll take his word for it.

According to my zoologist friend, a tommygoff is a fer-de-lance and a very bad snake. I decide to save this one so my friend can identify it for me. I carry it home draped over a long stick and then put him in a jar covered with alcohol. I want to find out if the locals really know what they're talking about. For all I know, it's a perfectly harmless snake.

For the next few days, I show it to everyone I see and ask, "What kind of snake is this?" Everyone without hesitation says, "It is a tommygoff, Jorge."

When the weekend comes, I go to Belize City and take my little prize to the zoologist. He takes one look and says, "It's a tommygoff." Scientific name—Bothrops asper, also known as Central American lancehead, two-steps (referring to the toxicity of his venom), fer-de-lance, barba amarilla, and a very dangerous snake.

My friend, who is excited over the specimen I brought him, shows me how to identify them by the "pits" they have on either side of their nose used for heat detection. He also points out the yellow jaw and the triangular shape of its head. I take a good look and study his features. His reputation is so bad that even when he's dead, he looks dangerous and I keep a respectful distance. Obviously, the locals know what they're talking about. The bad news is there are a lot of these guys around. The good news is I quit smoking.

23

Crop

My work with the girls on the softball team has been dwindling for the last month and ends with the beginning of sugarcane season (crop). This is what makes the village tick and what they've been doing for generations. Everybody has a job to do when crop is on.

Like an alarm goes off, everyone is preparing to cut their sugarcane and deliver it to the factory. The men are getting their trucks and tractors ready and checking their fields. The women, girls, and young boys now have more responsibilities for different aspects of the home life. They pick up jobs the men usually do like cleaning the yard with a machete and cutting firewood for the *fogon*.

I watch as cane cutters line the streets each morning to be picked up and taken to the fields. Every village has a team of cutters and truck drivers, and every farmer has his turn. When it's your turn, the team goes to your cane field, cuts it, loads it, and delivers it to the factory. Victor coordinates this activity with the farmers. The factory keeps track of how many tons each farmer delivers and pays them at the end of the season in June. Meanwhile, the plantation owners borrow money from the banks to pay the cutters and drivers who get paid by the ton on a weekly basis.

This is about the time I notice the other population in our village. Some families are poorer than others. For the most part, Belizeans are fairly well-off with their modern cement homes and cane fields. But every village had a population of "aliens." That is the official name and the polite term given to refugees who settle in Belize from neighboring countries. Most Belizeans refer to them as *paisa*, short for *pizano*, meaning "my fellow countryman or patriot."

Most of the aliens in San Lazaro are cane cutters and do some farming on the side, selling vegetables door to door. They live on land assigned to them by the village lands committee. This land is leased to them at no charge, but they're responsible for taxes of about ten dollars a year. They're also given an option of owning the land. To make it their property, they have to build a structure that is valued at eight hundred dollars (BZ) or more.

Their homes are made out of bush sticks and thatched with bay leaves. The floors are made out of white marl, a type of limestone that gets hard when it's packed down. They seem more like camps with an open fire going throughout the day and night. They always have three or four worm-infested, mangy hunting dogs around. Their livestock (chickens and pigs) live in their yards with them in crude pens made from bush sticks. The pigs are the local variety—small, black, and hairy.

I can usually distinguish an alien from a Belizean within a few minutes of meeting them. They're darker in complexion and speak Spanish with a faster rhythm. The adults look healthy enough. The children appear malnourished with bloated stomachs, skinny legs and arms, and their hair often looks oily and stringy.

Many of them come from the remotest parts of Guatemala, El Salvador, or Honduras. They're sometimes called "Indians," but I'm not sure of their actual descent. At first, I thought they might be Mayan. But their language is Spanish so I'm assuming that's what they are. Many are escaping a very violent war aimed at wiping them out. I hear stories of horror from Belizeans who have talked to them. They describe the things that soldiers do. Sometimes they go into a village and kill everyone—men, women, and children. Only those hiding escape death. Terrible things are done to the bodies as a message to rebels. Heads, arms, and legs are cut off and placed across the bodies. Pregnant women are ripped open by bayonets and their unborn fetuses torn out of their bodies. Their government justifies these attacks by saying "even if the villagers aren't rebels, they're still helping the rebels."

Some of the men escaping the war are rebels and have been fighting ever since they were old enough to carry a rifle. They've been around violence most of their lives and are used to it. Many Belizeans believe they may be too used to it and are too quick to go for a machete when angered. An increase in crime nationwide is quickly blamed on the aliens, and they earn a reputation for being violent. I'm advised by Victor not to trust them "because they will smile to your face in church but take off your head when you turn your back."

I have little contact with this population. At times, I sense mistrust and hostility from them. Understanding the role the United States plays in their civil wars, I can't blame them. My status in the village and my friendship with Belizeans keeps me in a safe position.

From my observations, most aliens realize that Belize is their new home, and they have to behave. They live rough by anyone's standards but work hard to adjust to their life in a new country. With crop on, they are now the main work force in this part of Belize.

24

The Bad Eye

Christina's baby is dying and Chabby asks me to watch Pedro and Olga so she can go over to see her for the last time. Kind of like a wake but before the person is even dead. Christina, married to Walter, is JB's daughter, and they live next to Samuel's and Chabby's.

"What is the baby dying from, Chabby?"

"Fever!" That one dreaded word used to describe every condition experienced by children in the village.

"Did she go to the doctor?"

"Yes, she has been many times, and the doctor gave her injection but says he can do no more." I know that when villagers go to the doctor, they don't feel they're getting their money's worth unless they're given an injection. The doctors also know this and almost always give some kind of injection.

"How long has she been sick?"

"She has had fever for five days now."

I agree to stay with her kids while she goes to visit. About an hour later, she comes back and explains very matter-of-fact that "the baby is still alive but will soon die."

Since I consider Christina and Walter friends, I decide to honor tradition and pay my respects. I walk over through the dark on the narrow dirt path that winds through the coconut and palm trees between their house and Chabby's. When I get inside, the first thing I notice is how stifling hot it is. All the windows are closed and people are standing all around the perimeter of the room adding their body heat like a furnace blowing hot air.

The baby is fully clothed, including shoes and a baby bonnet. She's lying on a table in the middle of the room gasping for air. I have to control my disbelief and anger at the scene in front of me. I'm not a doctor, but I know a baby with a fever or anyone with fever needs fresh air and to be cooled down, not heated up. At the same time, I also know that while I have status as a teacher, I'm nowhere near the status of a doctor who is up there close to God.

The long and short of it is they've been to the doctor and he's given up. I know they won't listen to me. I pay my respect to Christina, who's sobbing in the corner, and to Walter, who's greeting people and behaving like a good host. I leave and stop to talk with Chabby. I'm hoping maybe I can convince her to convince Christina to give the baby some breathing room. If she would just take off some of the clothes confining her little body, she might have more of a chance.

"Chabby, that baby needs some fresh air and to be cooled down. It is way too hot in that house." I'm trying to control my anger.

"But Mr. Jorge, the night air is not good for children, everyone knows that."

"Look, Chabby, I'm no doctor, but I know that when anyone has a fever they need to reduce it by cooling the body down. Do you think you can go over there and ask Christina to let the baby cool down?" I can see that this is going nowhere.

"Mr. Jorge, I have to tell you something."

"Okay, what is it?" She looks very serious.

"Mr. Jorge, someone has given the baby the bad eye, and when that happens, no one can do anything." She's shaking her head as she tells me this.

"The bad eye? What is the bad eye?" Things are getting worse.

"*Obea!* Someone who does obea looked at the baby with bad intentions." I know that *obea* is Belize's version of voodoo.

"So the baby will die no matter what? Not even the doctor can help?" I can see I'm fighting a losing battle.

"Yes, Mr. Jorge. No one can do anything." She shakes her head sadly.

I give up and go home feeling sad for the baby. I thought for a minute about running into the house and snatching the baby, but I know that won't work. This is a cultural thing that I need to accept.

About 5:00 a.m., I wake to Christina's sobbing and wailing from her home one hundred yards away. I know the poor baby has finally passed on. Normally, there would be a wake, but they have already done that. Later, they have a funeral and a burial. I don't go to the funeral. I've already been around all the mourning I can handle. I stay home and read.

Ironically, a cold front is coming through, and it's a nice break from the heat. If it had only come a day earlier, it might have helped the baby. Then again they would have probably just wrapped her up in blankets. The temperature drops to a cool sixty degrees. That night, a thick fog comes in the evening and lays down close to the ground. Lanterns light people's homes and dot the landscape. It gives the whole village a mystical look.

Christmas is coming and I decide to spend it in the village. Since the Catholic religion is so strong here, it promises to be a religious event. I don't care much for the religious aspect. For me, it will be the first time I don't have to work on Christmas Day in fifteen years.

There are preparations. Don Salus gets the generator ready for Christmas Eve. Some people make a special black fruitcake with strong rum in it. It is delicious and I eat it whenever I have the chance. All the religious services are planned out, and the women are busy cleaning the churches and putting flowers on the altars. Yards are cleaned and homes are painted. Some families get Christmas trees, which they cut about ten miles down the road at a place they call Pine Ridge.

All the schools get a full month of holiday time for Christmas and New Year's. The kids are excited as much for the vacation as they are for Christmas. I also appreciate the vacation. I've been working hard and it feels good to have some time off.

On Christmas Eve, the generator comes on just as promised. I actually have a light in my house. It's just one big bulb in the middle of the room with no decorative light fixture. It seems so bright and out of place like the full moon is pulsating right in the middle of my living room. The generator also brings water to the faucet in my yard. The power stays on the whole night and all of Christmas Day. I find out that the reason they don't use the generator throughout the year is because it breaks down so often.

On Christmas Eve, there's a procession through the village that's entertaining to watch. All the families are involved, and they pick a young couple with a child to step in for Mary, Joseph, and Baby Jesus. Everyone walks very slowly, carrying lit candles through the village going past each house. People not in the procession are outside watching as it passes. I watch with Samuel and Chabby who patiently explain everything to me. I can't help but think about the baby girl that just died and how it fits into their religion. According to their belief, she is with God now.

On Christmas Day, everyone cooks their favorite meal, and it is tradition to have cake and something to drink for all visitors. This is the first time I've seen cake in the village since Belizeans don't normally have dessert-type foods.

I have a delicious Christmas meal of rice and beans with chicken, fried plantain, and coleslaw with Samuel and Chabby. Afterward, Samuel and I take a walk around the village to visit his family and others. Everyone is so welcoming and kind. It seems like every house wants to feed you. People are in the spirit, and we're feeling pretty high by the end of our visits. No one is into exchanging gifts, except maybe once in a while for the children. It's Christmas without all the commercialism, and it's the best Christmas I've ever had.

25

Death in a Cane Field

School starts up again and it's time to get back to work. My regular schedule includes a visit to the school in the village of San Jose once a week. To get there, I travel ten miles of rough dirt road and another ten miles on the two-lane paved road called the Northern Highway. I'm using a loaner bike while my regular motorcycle is getting worked on. My temporary transportation is a Peace Corps-issued Honda 90. It's slow going but it gets me down the road, barely.

After school, I get on the highway, and just outside the village, a Creole boy runs out in front of me and makes me stop. He looks like he's between eighteen or twenty years old, and he's scared, very scared. I can feel it, and I can see the panic in his eyes. He's soaked with sweat, crying and trembling. He keeps looking over his shoulder and I know someone's after him.

"Pleeze, Mister. Pleeze give me ride, pleeeeze?"

"Whoa! I can't give you a ride. This bike is too small."

"Pleeze, sir? Pleeze?"

While begging for a ride, he goes behind me and tries to force himself on the back seat. I can't give him a ride because, first of all, the little Honda barely carries me and this guy is bigger than me. Second, the quickest way to win a one-way trip home from Peace Corps is to ride your bike without a helmet, or worse, give someone a ride that's not wearing one. I'm trying to explain this to him while pushing him off the back of my bike. But he's running from someone, crying with fear, and he can't hear anything I say.

He runs in front of an oncoming cane truck waving his arms. The big truck swerves across the road to avoid hitting him and keeps going. I want to help him but I'm not sure what to do.

Another cane truck pulls over just ahead of us and stops. He starts toward the truck, thinking he has a ride. Then the driver and two other guys, who are Mestizo, very calmly get out with their machetes. Already panicked, he starts screaming in Spanish, "Yo no fui" (I didn't do it), over and over. He turns and runs into a tall cane field that's right beside us. The men coming out of the truck spread out and go in after him with slow determination. I stay there not knowing what to do. These guys don't look like they're in the mood to listen to anything I have to say. My first thought is that he must have done something very bad for them to be after him with machetes. My mind automatically runs down a list of things he might have done—*stealing, no machete for that; rape, maybe; child molestation, that might call for a machete.* But I have no way of knowing what he did or is being accused of doing.

I'm praying that he'll be silent, and maybe they won't find him in the high sugarcane. He's not, and they do. I know when they catch him because I can hear and feel the intensity of his screams change to pure terror. Then, complete silence. The natural sounds start coming back to me. The birds start singing again, and I can hear the sound of someone chopping wood.

I don't know how long time stops before I realize I'm standing by myself in front of a sugarcane field on a highway in Central America. There's no one else around and I'm not sure what I should do. In a minute, those men will return and they might not like it if I'm still here. *What should I do? What did that boy do to deserve this? What can I do for him now?* My intuition tells me to get out of there and figure it out on my way to Orange Walk Town. *If I was home in Lake Tahoe, I would call 911, but here I don't even know where a telephone is, and even if there was a telephone, what number do I call?* I feel sad and angry. I'm sad that something so brutal can happen to another human being. I'm angry that I can't do anything about it. I know if I go to the police station in Orange Walk, nothing will happen. I'll spend time filling out a report, and they won't even have a car to go back and check the scene of the crime. I tell myself what's done is done and go home.

When I get to San Lazaro, the first person I see is Georgie walking down the road. I want to tell someone what just happened, so I stop and share what I had just witnessed.

"I feel like I should have done something."

"No, Jorge, you cannot do anything. You do not know what that boy did to those men, and they will not let you interfere with their business."

"Do you think I should have gone to the police and reported it?"

"No, mon, you did the right thing. The police cannot do anything now and they will not find the men who did it. Did you know them?"

"No, I never saw them before."

He told me a story about a time during the 1970s when the cane farmers in Orange Walk were receiving very big bonuses because the price of sugar was high.

"When those bad boys from Belize City found out that we were getting our bonus, they got on the bus and came here to rob us."

"How did they rob you?"

"They just waited until we left the bank, and then they came with a gun and took our money."

"What did you do?"

"We had to arm ourselves, Jorge, and the next time they came—*pow*! We shoot them. They did not come back after that. We had to do that because they hurt some of the farmers who try to resist."

It's around this time I begin to notice some subtle racial differences between the Creole and the Spanish. In the district towns, they live together, work together, and play together. Interracial marriages (rice and beans in Creole) are very common. But in the villages, each culture stays to themselves. You won't find many Creole in a Mestizo or Maya village. In some Mestizo villages, Creole may be assigned there as teachers or policemen. These people are highly respected for their profession and the villagers work well with them. But I have seen some resentment on both sides. The Creole don't particularly like living in a village that is not their own culture. Sometimes, they will say village people are "bushy" and think "bushy." The Mestizo, in turn, say the Creole don't really care about them. Overall, it eventually works because they all see themselves as Belizeans first. For the most part, they're willing to tolerate the differences.

The experience with the boy in the cane field haunts me for a few days. I find myself still curious about what he might have done to justify such a cruel punishment. But there is no way to find out.

I notice a difference when things happen here involving death or crime. When something unexpected or tragic happens, people tend to forget about it quickly and go on with their daily lives. I think partly because in the United States we have the media that keeps the news in front of us for days. Because of that, I'm used to processing things a different way.

The natural rhythm of life in the tropics makes life seem harsh at times. It's also typical of the environment and climate. The intense Caribbean sun and all the moisture are merciless on anything fragile or careless. For the same reasons, it creates an aggressive, fertile environment. If I'm going to survive here, I need to adapt to my environment, including the culture. Speaking of which, my daily life was about to change and I had no idea it was coming.

26

My Diet, My Lifeline

I'm not exactly sure what happened. This morning Chabby tells me that she can't cook for me anymore. I can tell she feels bad about it so I don't question it too much. I'm a little bummed out, but there isn't much I can do about it, except look for someone else to do my cooking. I ask Chabby if she knows anyone that might be interested, and she sends me to see one of Samuel's sisters.

Gorda is a widow with two little boys and her father, Don Pablo (my landlord), to take care of. She is obese and everyone affectionately calls her Gorda, which literally translates into big and fat. She readily agrees to cook for me and life is good again. I don't even have to miss a meal.

My good fortune is short-lived. After eating with her for a couple of days, I realize why she and her father are obese. She uses lard and salt, lots of it, with everything she cooks. Now I'm eating my beans in a pool of lard and I'm not too happy about it. But I'm not sure how to get out of our agreement. She was so happy when I asked her if she would cook for me. Every opportunity I have, I let her know that I don't like so much lard and salt in my food. But I don't think she knows how to cook any other way.

Gorda's husband was killed in an accident three years earlier. He was delivering a load of sugarcane to the factory when it happened. Her brother, Luty, was in the truck with him as his "sideman." There was so much dust on the road they didn't see the other cane truck until it was too late. It was a head-on collision. At impact, ten tons of sugarcane shifted forward onto the cab of his truck crushing him to death. Luty escaped by falling to the floorboard, where he was trapped until they cut him out.

Now Gorda is left with two little boys and no job. Her brothers and her father all help her, plus she has her own home to live in. But she owes the bank and needs all the money she can get. I know my payment for food is helping her, and she was so confident that I would like her cooking. Now I don't have the heart to hurt her feelings or take away the payment. I figure I'll stick it out for a while and keep looking for an excuse to get out of our agreement. In the meantime, I pick around the lard as much as possible.

To top it off, whenever I go visit the school in the village of San Jose, the students are taking turns inviting me home for lunch. It's a very nice gesture and one I can't turn down, but it's a little like Russian roulette. I never know what I'm going to get. Many times, I eat food that I normally would never eat. I eat it because I don't want to offend anyone. When I was eating with Chabby, at least I could look forward to going home and eating a good meal at the end of the day. But now I know I'll be going home to eat salty beans in a pool of lard. My eating situation has gone from great to bad.

After a month, I figure out a new eating routine, which includes picking around the lard and eating more peanut butter at home. Gorda sees I'm not crazy about her cooking and says she needs to talk to me. It's late evening and Don Pablo is snoring in his hammock and her boys are getting ready for bed.

"Jorge, I will not be able to cook for you anymore." She appears nervous but firm.

"You won't?" I'm trying to hide my relief.

"No, you see I need more time to take care of my father. He is not well."

"I see. Well, I understand. I guess I'll have to find someone else." I'm trying to act disappointed. I think it's easier for her to let me go than learn to cook without lard.

Now I'm back where I started and I have to find someone else. Since I've been here, I've made friends with the family of the village chairman, Don Salus. His sons, Arturo, Rodel, and Thomas, are my friends and three of his daughters are on the softball team. On my way home from Gorda's, I stop and speak to Don Salus about the possibility of eating with his family.

"Good evening, Don Salus."

"Good evening, Jorge."

"Don Salus, I have a favor to ask but I don't expect you to answer me right away."

"What is that, Jorge?"

"I need a place to eat. I've been eating with Gorda but now she can't cook for me anymore. I'll pay for my meals and I promise to eat whatever you eat." I hold my breath.

"I will talk with my wife and let you know tomorrow."

"Thank you, Don Salus. I promise I won't be any trouble."

"Okay, Jorge, I will talk with her. It is her decision."

"Thank you, Don Salus."

Tonight, I pray they'll cook for me. I have a peanut butter sandwich for breakfast and pray again. For lunch, I decide to spend some money before I overdose on peanut butter and eat at a Chinese restaurant in town. For dinner, I'm trying to figure out how creative I can be with rice and peanut butter when Arturo and Thomas come and save me. Their mother, Mrs. Eck, has agreed to cook for me.

I'm happy. This seems like the right family for me to eat with. They have older children who help their mother and make it less of a burden, and I enjoy the company of Arturo and Thomas. They're also brother-in-laws to Victor, who is married to one of their sisters and lives next door. Things are looking better, and once again, I feel like I'm being taken care of. I give my thanks to the food gods tonight.

27

Women

This is going to be very bloody. I just finished breakfast when Chabby calls me over and hands me a machete. She's cornered a rat behind her stove "Mr. Jorge, I will chase the rat out and you will kill him with the machete."

"Okay." While I'm standing there looking at the machete and thinking there must be a better way to do this, the rat comes running out. He's looking for a way to get around me. I swing the machete down hard, taking off his tail and just missing his body. I also make a big dent in Chabby's cement floor from the force of my swing. Now there's a trail of blood where the rat turned around and ran back under the stove. She gives me a strange look and takes the machete away from me. "That's okay. You go home now. I will finish," she said and almost pushes me out the door. I leave feeling like I've done something wrong.

I'm a little bummed out because it's the first time Chabby, a female, has asked me to help with something, and I feel like I haven't been much help. Much later, after I learn how to use a machete, I realize what I did wrong. I should have used the flat side to kill the rat. It's less bloody and you have a better chance of hitting your target. The flat side is also used to kill a snake because if you use the blade, the head can fly off and still bite you.

I'm not having any trouble meeting the men of the community. If I'm involved in a school project that requires help like building a plant nursery or I need fence post, the men come out with their machetes and work with me.

When I'm with the girls on the softball team, we're friends, but off the field, it's a different relationship. When I walk past women or girls in the streets, they never acknowledge my hellos. Some of the older married women respond on occasion. Sometimes, I walk past a group of young women gathered around the water pump getting their pigtail buckets filled. I always say hello in my best Spanish, hoping to get their attention. They look at me with interest for a second or two, but they never say hello back. It's like there's a secret password or knowledge I need to have before they'll talk to me and I don't have it yet.

There is something about the women here that attracts me. It's not that they look so healthy and beautiful or that they always seem so relaxed, clean, and attractive (like they just finished getting a message at a health spa). Even when they're working in their yards or getting water (always cause for me to sweat profusely), their long black hair is always shiny and neatly done up in braids or a ponytail. Their brown skin glows against the gold jewelry they like to wear. They almost always have on a dress or skirt, simple clothes but with rich earth colors. Even their clothes look relaxed and clean. I have never seen white look as white as it does when it's on them. They're strong in a womanly way, and their light cotton clothing shows off every curve. They look natural with no makeup or high heel accessories to distract from their beauty. I love to hear their laughter, which is always happy and genuine, and they laugh a lot. All of this is very appealing to me to say the least. But there is something else, something unique from the youngest to the oldest that speaks to my very soul. It's their certainty of who they are; they are family and tradition.

In every relationship I've ever had, the woman was the aggressor. At least initially, and then once they have my attention, I become the aggressive one. I've always liked confident women who know what they want, especially if they want me. But these women are different. They know who they are. They are women, feminine and maternal with every breath they take, and they glow with the certainty of knowing that and they are grounded in it.

But they will not even look at me and appear to have no interest at all. My substantial experience and knowledge of women seems to get me nowhere. My failed attempts at communication only add to the mystique that surrounds them. It is important to me to learn more about this culture and be accepted. That includes the women, but I am not being let in.

One of my favorite things about the village is observing family life. Everyone's extended relatives live in close proximity, and the village revolves around family, work, and church. The closeness and togetherness of families is something I'm learning to appreciate.

Sometimes, I wait at a home for the man of the house to arrive. I always wait outside, talking to the children that are usually around. When they see their father walk into the yard, their eyes light up. And they run to him—"Papa, Papa!"—giving him hugs and kisses, like they haven't seen him in weeks. The whole time "Papa" has a big smile on his face and you can see the love in his eyes. When he sees me, he meets my gaze, says hello, and offers me some water. He tells the younger ones to put away his machete and water bottle. The older one, he tells to go and ask her mother to bring some cool coconut water. All the children hang onto his every word and jump to do whatever he says without question. We then find a comfortable place in the shade to sit and talk.

I find myself envying the fathers and the treatment they get. I can't help but think about my relationship with my father. I feel like I lost him at an early age when we were separated by divorce and my mother's marriage to his brother. Whenever we were together, the hurt and anger he felt was like a wedge between us. I always wanted a different relationship with him but didn't know how to do it.

I'm attracted to the simple but honest life the families have here. They live in a harsh environment where tropical diseases and snake bites are common events treated by a bush doctor. They seem in tune to the fact that life could end at any moment for any one of them, and they cherish their time together. This is something that's inherent in their beliefs and customs.

As I learn more about village life, I realize the majority of villagers have lived here for generations, ever since their ancestors escaped from the caste wars in Mexico. All men born in the village are entitled to a house lot, which is granted to them by a village "lands committee." Family land and homes are passed onto each generation. The tradition is for the youngest son to stay home and care for his aging parents, eventually inheriting the family home. The sugarcane fields or other valuable possessions are usually divided among all the sons. If several sons are involved, the family helps them get house lots and build homes of their own, one at a time. It may take years, often building a little at a time if extra money is available. Many times, the building process does not start until a son gets married. It may be a thatched house made from materials found in the bush, or it may be a more modern home made from cement. Until the house is complete, the newlyweds stay with the man's family, and most of the time, the man is in no hurry to leave. When a family has no sons then the tradition is passed onto the daughters.

A woman born in the village is only entitled to a free house lot under special circumstances. For example, if she were to marry a man from outside the village then she can approach the lands committee for a house lot.

This family bond I'm observing is new and curious to me. I'm seeing family as an asset, something I never realized was possible. I grew up doing my best to be an outsider in my own family. To see the unconditional love and communication that these families have is a new experience for me. They discuss things openly that I would have never felt safe sharing with my parents. There are literally no secrets. Once again, I'm seeing children being accepted for who they are. They get all the love and support of a family to help them reach their full potential as good, decent human beings. The only expectation in return is for them to do their best at whatever they do.

I think about my visit from the young girls and their advice. "Mr. Jorge, you need a woman to take care of you."

28

Fire

It's a lazy Sunday and I don't have anything to do, so I reluctantly decide to catch up on some letter writing I've been putting off. Just in time, Victor, Arturo, and Thomas drive up in Victor's pickup to save me from certain death by boredom.

"Vamos (let's go), Jorge."

"Where are we going?"

"We are going to burn cane. Grab your machete."

"All right, hold on a minute." I grab my machete, thankful for the opportunity to get out of the house and jump into the back of Victor's truck with Arturo.

Burning sugarcane is done throughout the harvest season, and cane cutters do not like to go into a field unless it has been burned. The fire gets rid of all the snakes, poisonous insects, and killer bees. The only things left of a burned field are burnt cane stalks and ashes, leaving a bleak landscape until the green cane grows out again.

I feel like it's a privilege to be invited to help with something so important. I know how dangerous it can be and how careful we have to prepare. A cane fire out of control can burn down more plantations than you intend to.

It's April, toward the end of cane harvest, and it is the dry season. Already, the feeder roads are turning into thick layers of dust. Anytime trucks drive through it, they create a huge mushroom cloud so thick it blots out the light from the sun. I can see how Gorda's husband had a head-on collision, and I'm surprised there aren't more.

We drive several miles down a maze of feeder roads to reach the job for today. Once there, we slowly walk around the plantation we're going to burn. The sun, always intense, is even more so at this time of year. Other cane fields surround this particular one for as far as you can see on three sides. The fourth side has the feeder road we came in on to provide a natural firebreak. The wind is blowing in hard gusts in every direction.

"I'm worried about this wind. It wants to start a fire," Victor says as he looks at the fields around us.

"Does it have to be done today?" I can see the potential danger.

"Yes, I want to bring my cutters here tomorrow."

"Let's make our fire path and each one of us can take a side to mind." Thomas is anxious to get it done.

We listen carefully as Victor gives us directions. "Okay, Jorge, this will be your side. If the fire jumps, you have to put it out fast. Arturo, you take the left, and Thomas, you take the right. I will go wherever the fire is." Each of us goes to our sides and starts to prepare our firebreaks by clearing a four-foot path with our machetes. Victor has given me the safest side with a natural bare spot in the middle. End to end, I have approximately 150 feet to worry about. It looks like a lot of ground to cover. After finishing our preparations, we carefully walk around inspecting and looking for anything we might have missed. Satisfied that we've prepared as much as possible, we get into our positions surrounding the plantation. Once we spread out, we can't see each other through the tall cane, but we can hear each other if we yell.

Picking up a handful of dry cane leaves, Victor uses a Bic lighter to light his homemade torch and begins lighting the field running around the perimeter of our firebreak. Everything is so dry the field practically explodes into flames. Right away, huge gusts of wind start blowing, and we have fires jumping on all three sides almost immediately. I see fire jump on my side, and I run to cut the stalks that are burning and pound them out with the flat side of my machete. This requires a certain amount of skill with a machete that I have not quite mastered. I turn around to check behind me and see at least three other places that are burning. I run down the path as fast as I can and I yell for Victor. "I got fire!" Then I hear Arturo and Thomas. Everyone is yelling, "I got fire! I got fire!" I know he can't help everyone so I move as fast as I can, cutting, slashing, and pounding out fires. When the wind blows in my direction, the heat from the main fire is unbearable. I have to duck down low and use my arms to protect my face. When the wind direction changes, I get back up and move to the next fire. There are a few places where the fire has jumped and is out of control.

When I'm not putting out a fire, I'm cutting firebreaks in front of hot spots that are too big to put out. We're working as hard and as fast as we can to keep the fire under control, and I have this sinking feeling that we're losing.

There's a sense of panic because all there is for miles in every direction are dry cane fields, and we have just started an inferno. I feel the pressure and keep moving as fast as I can on my side of the field, trying to keep it under control. I get lucky because my one big fire heads toward the natural break, and I'm finally able to stop it there. Everyone gets control about the same time. Then the main fire runs out of fuel and burns out. The wind stops, and just as suddenly as it started, it's over.

I'm exhausted and about to collapse. The adrenaline, the heat, and the exertion have taken a toll on me. I'm covered in black soot, the hair on my arms is singed off, and I think I may have lost my eyebrows. Mucus is streaming out my nose, my lips are dry and puffed up, my tongue feels thick, and I can barely move. I can't hold up the machete without my arm shaking, and my legs feel like Jell-O, but I can't stop yet.

Now we're going around looking for burning embers that remain. We have to make sure there are no more live spots in the perimeter around the firebreak. After careful inspection and putting out a few small fires, we're finally done. We sit down to drink some water and laugh about what had almost happened. We had burned down a considerable amount of sugarcane. But somehow, we managed to keep from burning down half the countryside.

"Did we burn down anyone's cane?" My voice is hoarse from yelling.

"Yes, we burned part of two other plantations." Victor's surveying the damage.

"Whose?"

"Mr. Tillett and Mr. Moh. I will have to go and talk to them."

We pile into the truck, and it's all I can do to lift my heavy, tired legs over the tailgate. The first thing we do is go talk to the owners of the fields we just burned. Both men understand and are thankful that Victor bothered to come and tell them. I also appreciate the fact that he took responsibility for what we did. I know that this kind of thing happens all the time and that sometimes the ones at fault don't report it. That results in a loss for the farmer. But Victor assures them he'll make arrangements to get their cane in for them and they're happy. From there, we head to a bar in the village of Trinidad for a cold beer.

I'm proud of myself for holding up my end of the job during the fire. That's something I don't think I could have physically done a year earlier.

29

Family Secrets

Sometimes, families in a village are too close, and there are no secrets. If something happens, it's only a matter of time before everyone knows about it. I've learned some of the signs that tell me when something out of the ordinary has occurred. Like today, as I'm returning home from a long day at work. Even though it's still daylight, there are already groups of men and, a more ominous sign, groups of women in the streets talking. I know something unusual has happened.

Slowing down and navigating my motorcycle through the small groups, I notice that Don Luis's shop is closed. All the doors and windows are locked up tight. This is strange because normally, it's a busy time of day for him. I park my bike and find a group of men that I know. They're talking about what had apparently just happened five minutes earlier between Don Fido and Don Luis. First of all, I discover they're brothers, which is not surprising in this small village where everyone is related by blood or marriage. Apparently, Don Luis's son, Luis Jr., has been screwing around with his cousin, Emilla, Don Fido's daughter. Now she is pregnant, and Luis Jr. wants nothing to do with her.

Don Fido, who is well-known for his ability to overdrink, gets drunk and goes to have a brother-to-brother-to-nephew talk with Don Luis. The only problem is he takes a very big knife with him (I suspect his wife hid his machete). When Don Luis sees him and the knife coming, he closes his door and locks it. Don Fido proceeds to beat on the locked door with his knife, yelling, threatening, and kicking the whole time. The whole village hears the commotion and comes out to watch the drama. After a while, he gives up and staggers home, yelling threats that he will kill both his brother and his nephew.

The men in my huddle aren't very sympathetic. Victor summarizes their feelings very gracefully by saying, "Everyone knew they were doing it. (*Everybody except me*). They should have been stopped long ago." The others chime in, "No true." I thought about all the times I had seen the two together, not realizing they were cousins. Had I known then they were "first cousins," I would have seen it differently, as I do now. I agree with Victor. It should have been stopped long ago.

Once they're sure the action is over for the day, the groups slowly start breaking up and everyone goes their own way. Don Luis stays closed for the rest of the evening and takes a loss in business. Don Fido is most likely passed out at home dreaming about defending his daughter's honor. I know that tomorrow things will be back to normal, and the incident will be forgotten. Later, when I go for my evening walk, there is very little talk about what happened.

In the morning, I see that Don Luis's shop is open and everyone survived the night. The word is already out on the street that Luis Jr. left the village during the night to go stay with relatives in another district. Emilia, his pregnant cousin, now has to face the shame of her deed. The reality is that the only support she'll be receiving is from family and friends.

I feel sorry for her. She's one of my players on the softball team, and although she isn't one of my favorite players, I've learned to respect her. Being in a small village, her choices are limited. The most likely option is to have the baby, and if she's lucky, she might find another man willing to care for her and raise her child.

When I go to the school, one of the teachers, Alicia, and I talk about the incident. She nudges me with a flirtatious look and says, "You see, village life is not as boring as you think. We can have excitement too."

I think about Alicia's reference to a more "exciting" village life. I know any excitement with a white man would be hard to conceal. There's also the fact that any excitement is bound to be connected to a logical consequence, which I'm not willing to pay. For the time being, I'll have to limit my excitement to partying in town with other Peace Corps volunteers and wild women.

30

Rain

I wake up to a sound I'm not used to, but I know what it is. It's heavy rain beating against the ground and foliage on its way to my house. I feel apprehensive as the heavy rain closes in and hits my thin tin roof. I half expect it to give way under this mighty volume of water. It doesn't, and somehow, it feels strangely exhilarating to be inside safe and dry. It's hitting my roof so loud that it sounds like I'm underneath a freight train.

Just like clockwork, on the first day of June, it starts raining and it rains nonstop for sixteen days. All the roads are flooded and there is mud everywhere. In some places, there's as much as three feet of water across the road, where creeks and rivers have overflowed.

Some of the villages I visit are close to the Rio Bravo (angry river). Normally, I ride my motorcycle across a bridge to reach them. Now after two weeks of steady rain, I have to park my bike three miles away and take a boat the rest of the way in. Homes close to the river are flooded out, and those families move into the school or stay with relatives. I have never seen so much rain.

If I'm outside during an occasional break, I can hear the rain coming, beating against the trees and the earth. Visually, I can see a solid wall of water stretched across the horizon for miles, coming toward me from half a mile away. This gives everyone plenty of time to take cover. For Belizeans, this is the rainy season, and it's business as usual. For me, it's exciting to experience such a force of nature.

Ever since the rain started, the volume of noise at night has been incredibly loud. There must be billions of frogs surrounding my house. They orchestrate their song into one tremendous croak that plays over and over. The mosquitoes and crawling insects have increased, and now I'm fighting mosquitoes during the days as well as nights. When there are little breaks between outbursts of rain, the humidity becomes unbearable. Just the slightest movement results in sweating. At nights, things cool off, and there's enough of a breeze that I can sleep comfortably.

Every so often, we get thunder and lighting. It's so close you can hear it slicing and hissing through the air a second before the thunder comes. It's scary. My house shakes from the thunderbolts, and they keep coming one after the other. I feel like I'm in the middle of a war zone. I've been in what I thought were strong thunderstorms in Lake Tahoe, but nothing there even comes close to this. I stay away from doors and windows and get into the middle of the room, hoping that's the safest place. Sometimes, it continues for hours.

The weird thing about the weather is I never know what to expect. In Tahoe, I listened to forecasts and knew when a snowstorm was coming days before it actually arrived. After days of rain, all the homes are still closed up. Everyone stays inside. When I go over to eat with the Eck family, I ask about the weather, and their answer is always vague. "This is the rainy season, Jorge." I listen to the news on radio Belize, and it says the same thing every day: "Seas light chop to choppy, expect rain."

Meanwhile, I sit in my house, waiting for lightning to strike me at any second. I start reflecting on the past year and make a mental checklist of what I've accomplished. Most importantly, I've made friends. Even some of the single girls are talking to me now. Coaching the softball team along with living and working in the village for the last year has helped to boost my status in the community.

Whenever I feel like I need a dose of Americanism, I head for town and stay with Matt or Tim and Susan. When I'm with them, we get together at someone's house to listen to music, cook dinner, or go out to eat. I also date a few of the new female volunteers, which improves my love life and helps keep me sane.

I'm still attracted to some of the prettier Mestizo women in the villages, especially those with the oriental look that makes them seem so exotic. But I know any kind of relationship isn't likely to happen. I'm not part of the culture. For any Mestizo girl to consider me, she would also have to consider the risk that I could leave at any time and go home to the United States without her.

My health is much better, and I haven't smoked a cigarette in four months. I still start my mornings with yoga and meditation, and I'm gaining weight and getting stronger every day. In general, I feel healthy and focused.

My assignment has turned out well. Peace Corps gave me a faster motorcycle. I now have a second-hand Yamaha 125 trail bike, and when it's working, it's very fast. I love getting on a cane road, opening up the throttle, and going through the gears. I expanded to work with several more schools this year, which made my Belizean supervisor happy. Plus, I now have a much better idea of what my job is and how to do it.

Some of the Belizean friends I've made and Belizeans in general have a false impression of the United States and Americans. Many believe that the streets in the United States are made of gold and that everyone from the United States is rich. They say to me, "You're an American. You have money, like sand." This pushes my buttons since most of the Belizeans living in San Lazaro are better off financially than my family or I ever was. During the sixties and seventies, when they were getting big bucks for sugarcane, most farmers invested wisely. They built nice homes, planted more cane fields, and invested in trucks and tractors to work their cane.

In comparison, my mother is fifty-nine years old and lives in the suburbs in a house that will take her thirty years to pay for. Like many Americans her age, she's worked hard her whole life for a fraction of what the families here have.

But in their eyes, they will never be as wealthy and well-off as Americans are. Once I realize this, once I understand the perception that America presents and that we as Americans present, my mission changes. My priority is now more of a cultural sharing and understanding rather than a "technological transfer." That's the Peace Corps buzzword for training someone how to do a particular skill.

I'm determined to show them what the majority of Americans are made of. We aren't born rich. We work hard and have problems just like anyone else. For the first time in my life, I feel like I can do something that is patriotic. I know their perception of the United States and Americans is wrong, and I can help change that perception.

I hear some of my fellow Peace Corps volunteers talk down to Belizeans. It happens when Belizeans open the door by giving up their seniority and empowering Americans to feel their way is the best way. It's a vicious circle like a self-fulfilling prophecy. And both sides are angry about it.

The Belizeans invite us here to teach them something that will help Belize become a more developed country. We come here and try to get them to do it our way. But it doesn't work. They don't have the same values, beliefs, resources, or work ethics that we have. They don't need to do it the same way we do it.

Peace Corps does a good job training us to be culturally sensitive, but sometimes we become the opposite in trying to accomplish something. Many of us never get out of our own culture. Even though we are physically in their country, in our minds we still carry the values and beliefs that were raised with. We believe that our way is the "best" way and especially that our work ethic is the best. Until volunteers can see our culture as "different," not better or worse, we will always be frustrated by our perception of how things "should" be.

Some Belizeans assume we know more than they do and give up their seniority, only to become resentful later. They assume we know more because we are from a rich, powerful nation. But wealth and power do not make you a better person or translate into more knowledge.

The best thing I can do is be myself, relating and sharing my values and beliefs while working to understand theirs. After that, I can be a Peace Corps volunteer, a chef, a softball coach, a teacher, or anything else I want to be.

Once I realize what I want to do with my time here, life becomes easier. I learn to adapt to a different pace, and my priorities change. Daily necessities like getting water for drinking and bathing are more important to me than reading the news or what I wear to work. I'm talking and listening to people more and learning about their culture. People here have an honesty that's reflected through acceptance of others. In some ways, their beliefs are simple. If you do well, you are rewarded. If you misbehave, you are punished.

I came into the village as an outsider, just another American passing through. I've made friends, and I'm generally accepted and respected as a "maestro." Somehow through the blur of alcohol and drug abuse, I managed to salvage some of the better characteristics from my family and the American culture. I'm honest, hardworking, and consistent in all aspects of my life including having a good time.

The support and acceptance from the people here has made all the difference in my having a positive "Peace Corps experience." In particular, eating with Arturo's family has been good for me. The whole family treats me like they would anyone else, and I have gotten close to them. One of the sons, Rodel, is a young teenager. He's intelligent and speaks English very well compared to other members of the family. He is also the first one to attend high school.

For reasons of puberty, Rodel has become fascinated with the word "masturbation." He makes me laugh because he uses the word at the most inappropriate times. Fortunately, no one else knows what he's talking about. Sometimes when I go for my dinner, he's in the bathhouse, which is situated close to where we eat. When he hears me talking to his parents at the dinner table he hollers out loudly to say hello. I return his hello and continue talking to his family. Other times, he hollers out loudly knowing that I'm the only one who will understand what he's saying.

"Hey, Mr. Jorge, guess what I am doing?"

"I don't know. What are you doing, Rodel?"

"I am masturbating!" Then he laughs like a crazy man while I try to keep a straight face and talk to his father.

31

Down South

School will be out soon for summer vacation, and I've been told that the ministry of education (MOE) will be doing workshops out in the districts. Their plan is to involve teachers from the districts in developing resource guides for use in the classroom. My job is to help with logistics and, once in a while, do a presentation on school gardens.

They pick one village in each district and then invite all the principals and one teacher from each of the primary schools in that district. The workshops last for three days each and there are six districts.

The best part about it is that I get to see other parts of Belize and meet all the teachers in each district. We go from one end of the country to the other and see remote villages that the average Belizean or tourist doesn't normally see. In each district we visit, I make new friends.

The last district we go to is the southernmost tip of Belize. The deep south receives almost three times as much rain as the north. It is also the most remote part of the country. It is approximately 160 miles from Belize City to the district town, Punta Gorda. That's not too far by home standards, but here, it is a good eight- to twelve-hour trip by bus down a half-paved road called the Hummingbird Highway, then a dirt road called the Southern Highway.

Since it's the rainy season, the roads are bad and the rivers are overflowing higher than some of the bridges. At one point, we come to a river and we can't see a bridge at all. There's just a huge, wide torrent of water rushing by. Not being able to see where the bridge starts, the bus driver eases down an embankment until his front tires are touching the water's edge. Some teenage boys are standing where the bridge begins, and they're directing the driver. Their bare feet feel what we can't see. They line up with the front tires to guide us. Then they walk slowly across the underwater bridge, feeling their way with their feet. They have to hold onto the bus to keep from being swept away by the powerful current. The river is about as wide as the length of a football field, and it takes forever to get to the other side. At the highest point, water begins to pour in under the door of the bus.

The whole thing is a little scary especially when I see trees go floating past in front of us. I'm thinking if one of those trees broadsides us, we might be pushed off the bridge. I notice that a few of the Belizeans on the bus are concerned about it as well. Everyone gets quiet when we see a tree coming from upstream. In my mind, I'm checking out escape routes in case we get pushed off. All the windows are open because we're in the tropics and it's hot, but they only open halfway. If I can squeeze through, it looks like the safest and fastest way out. I know how to swim in the currents of a strong river. I'm more worried about being able to get out through the window. After a tree passes safely by, everyone relaxes again. As refreshing as a swim might feel right now, I'm glad I don't have to take it.

Finally, we arrive in Punta Gorda, which is on the coast directly across from the Bay of Honduras. The population is mostly Garifuna and their livelihood is fishing. Garifuna is a culture that originated from slave ships that sunk in the Caribbean. The surviving slaves made it to the island of St. Vincent and mixed with the population of black Caribs. In 1832, they set out from the island in dugouts and made their way to the coastal towns of Belize, Honduras, Venezuela, and other countries. All Garifuna have Spanish last names but their language is uniquely Garifuna. They practice and believe in obea, a form of voodoo. They have reputations for being good educators and fishermen.

I make friends with Elvis Garcia, a Garifuna who is the district education officer from Stann Creek. He's a very jolly man and he's always in a friendly mood. "Good morning, how is Jorge?"

"Morning, Mr. Garcia, I'm doing all right, but I'd be doing better if I slept in a bed last night."

"So you don't like the floor, no true?" He laughs as he says this.

"No, not too much, but I did get some sleep." I don't want to come across as a complainer.

"I am staying with my cousin and I would invite you but he is already full."

"Oh, no problem. I'm fine where I am," I lie.

"It is too bad they do not make better accommodations for us, no true?"

"Yeah, well the food's good."

"So you like Belizean food, no true?"

"I love Belizean food, Maestro."

"The next time you come down, I will invite you for some real Garifuna food."

"That sounds great. What is Garifuna food?"

"Garifuna food is mostly seafood cooked many different ways. We like boil-up and fish sere'. That's fish soup made with coconut milk. We eat a lot of ground foods too, like sweet potato and cassava. You will like it, Jorge."

"It sounds good and I love seafood." He's making me hungry.

"You will like it then, no true?"

"Yes, Maestro, I'll like it. Now I'm hungry."

"Vamos, Jorge, let us go eat some breakfast."

From talking to Elvis, I learn that most Garifuna speak several languages. In addition to Garifuna, they usually speak Creole, English, and Spanish. Some of them can even speak some of the Mayan dialects.

I want to check out a few of the villages while I'm here, so I talk to David, my Belizean supervisor, about the possibility. He introduces me to the local district education officer for the Toledo District, Mr. Tun. He politely offers to take me with him on some of his rounds.

32

Into the Green

I make arrangements to extend my stay, and we leave at 7:00 a.m. for some of the more remote villages. Mr. Tun explains to me that the villages we'll be visiting are K'ekchi Mayan and Mopan Mayan.

"They are two different cultures, similar in many ways, but their language is different."

"They live next to each other and speak different languages?" I ask.

"Yes, sometimes their villages are very close, just a few miles apart."

"Do they ever live together in one village?"

"No, they normally prefer to stay with their own people."

"How do they communicate? Do they speak Spanish?"

"No, they do not speak Spanish. But they can speak Creole and some English."

Their villages are spread throughout the countryside and they live in the "real" rainforest. It's an incredible sight to go down winding dirt roads deep into the jungle. I'm amazed with the variety of plant life, trees, bamboo, and all the different shades of green lining the road. I can only see about four yards into the plant life before it becomes all green. I know it has to be loaded with wildlife, but I can't see any through the density of the jungle. There could easily be a jaguar, perfectly camouflaged, watching us from the bush.

We go deep into the countryside. My eyes are glued to the window, watching the jungle terrain. After a few hours, we cross a wide shallow river and go around a corner to find a village. Mr. Tun informs me that the population of this village, Falling Creek, is Mopan Mayan. Their homes are bush houses built low to the ground and covered with bay leaves. Because it's the rainy season, there are low patches of fog, and every so often, we get a brief outburst of heavy rain.

First, we make contact with the school principal. The school house is small, about twenty feet by thirty feet, and built out of concrete with a zinc roof. It looks out of place with the bush houses and surrounding jungle. The principal is a Garifuna man, Mr. Zuniga, in his early twenties. He's a small but energetic man, and he comes forward eagerly to greet us and shake hands. Mr. Tun introduces me, and I notice Mr. Zuniga seems happy to see people from the outside world. There are two other teachers, one woman who is Creole and one man who is K'ekchi Mayan. As we enter the school, all the students, around thirty of them, stand and say in unison, "Good morning, sir." They stay standing until the principal tells them they can sit down. The students and their teachers then return to what they were doing before we arrived. From what I can see, the children are divided into three classes with portable blackboards as the only division between them. This is similar to what the schools in the North do as well.

The principal takes us to the teacher's house, which is built out of milled lumber and a zinc roof. It's small, about ten feet by fifteen feet with a covered porch. We sit on the porch and Mr. Zuniga offers us lime juice and fresh mangoes. He and Mr. Tun have some school business to take care of, so after our little snack, I leave to take a walk through the village.

It's very different from the villages I'm used to in the North. For one thing, in the North, we have a main road that goes through the village and then smaller feeder roads throughout the village. All the homes are built around these roads. The only road here is the one dirt road we came in on. No one has cars so it makes sense. Instead, the homes are connected by worn foot paths and are scattered with no clear pattern that I can see across the rolling terrain.

The villagers are small, especially the women. I don't think there's anyone here over five feet tall. People stop and stare at me and I feel like a giant. I can hear water close by so I follow the path down to the banks of the river. There's a group of women standing in the water doing their laundry topless. They see me and stare but make no attempt to cover themselves. It doesn't bother me, so I wave, and a couple of them wave back before returning to their laundry. I watch them beat their clothes against the rocks for a while and then head back to the village.

By the time I get back to the school, it's lunch time. The principal takes me and Mr. Tun to the village chairman's house. After introductions, the chairman, Mr. Puk, invites us for lunch. His wife, who is also topless, serves us chicken soup with corn tortillas she is making right before us over an open fire. Mr. Tun tells me that lactating women make the best tortillas. I notice that this woman is not lactating, but the tortillas and the soup are delicious. I take seconds when it's offered but decline thirds. I can eat the whole thing, but I know they probably have children that still need to eat. Afterward, we go back to the school, and I spend the afternoon watching the kids and teachers work. Some of the children stand, not moving, to stare at me. A couple of them see me and run away terrified. I think it must be the first time they've seen a white man.

I find out from Mr. Tun that they aren't used to strangers, especially the children. He also told me that many times the government purposely stations teachers in a village that don't speak the local language. That way, they're forced to use English as their common language.

After school, Mr. Puk directs us to different host houses where we'll spend the night. We're given space inside the home and a hammock to sleep in. I put my backpack on the ground and rest for a while in the hammock. My host family is Mr. and Mrs. Pol, but only Mr. Pol speaks to me.

Later, Mr. Tun and I return to the village chairman's house for dinner. In the twilight, we see glimmering fires scattered around hillsides where meals are being cooked under thatched outdoor kitchens. It looks like something you might see in a *National Geographic* magazine.

Our dinner is stew beans with corn tortillas. After eating, we thank our host and go back to our hammocks. I feel tired and peaceful. It's around 7:30 p.m. when I fall asleep.

Very early in the morning, around 3:00 a.m., I wake-up to see the woman of my host house building a fire. I see other fires starting in nearby homes through the open door. Once the fire's going, she starts grinding her corn on a flat rock with another cylinder-shaped rock. Then she mixes it with water and kneads it into small round balls, about the size of cotton balls. Using a flat rock and her hand, she quickly flattens the masa and shapes it into perfectly round corn tortillas. As she makes the tortillas, she puts them on a flat piece of iron that's balanced over the open fire. She moves quickly and quietly, turning the tortillas over when one side is cooked. In the dim light made by the fire, she seems to know exactly where everything is. By the time she has the tortillas and beans cooking, her husband is up and they talk in low whispers. They aren't really having a conversation, just short statements every now and then. I sense a familiar intimacy and bond between them that I admire.

Around 4:00 a.m., after eating some of the beans and tortillas, the man leaves for his milpa (farm). He takes some of the food along in a sling bag he carries over one shoulder. Over his other shoulder, he slings the strap of his rifle, and he carries his machete in his hand. I hear low whistles in the distance as the men acknowledge each other while walking to their farms in total darkness.

By early afternoon, the men return from their milpas. Their sling bags are now fully loaded with fresh-picked corn and fruit. They carry it by putting the shoulder strap of the bag across their forehead, leaning forward close to the ground, and balancing the load on their backs. There are easily fifty to eighty pounds of fruits and vegetables in the sling bag.

Mr. Tun explains to me that the people in these Mayan villages are subsistence farmers. The land they have is passed down from generation to generation and has probably been in their families for hundreds of years. They use very little money. Everything they have is bartered for with food from their milpas. They grow rice, corn, and beans. Other crops are grown as the seasons allow like cabbage, peppers, tomatoes, and okra. There are plenty of fish from the river and enough fresh indigenous fruit around to supplement their diets. They also hunt for wild game like deer and turkey. My host has a jaguar skin hanging on his wall. I ask him where he got it.

"I mi hunt fo deer ina di bush. I mi hear someting back a bush and weh me stop fi look, ih stop." He spoke slowly in Creole.

"What did you do?"

"Mi wait till ih come closer and mi si ih deh." (I saw him there.)

"How did you see him?" I knew they did their hunting at night.

"Mi lamp shine pan ih eyes." A lamp is a small battery light they strap to their foreheads.

"Do you think he was hunting you?" I was imagining what it would be like to be stalked by a jaguar in the bush.

"Oh yes, mon. Weh ih di com close, mi turn and shoot ih." (When he was close enough, I turned and shot him.)

"Where did you hit him?"

"Here, ina da head." He points to the side of the jaguar's head with a black spot on it.

Being in this village and watching people's lives is like going back to more primitive times. We eat out of dried gourds and use our tortillas like forks. The villagers have recently been blessed with latrines (outhouses) built with help from the ministry of health. Not everyone is using them yet, preferring their traditional squats in the bush. In all my walking around and exploring, I never come across anything that resembles bad sanitation habits.

The women think nothing of walking around bare breasted, even in front of strangers. They live incredibly simple but peaceful lives, and once again, I'm amazed at the family life I'm witnessing. The same commitment, unconditional love, and devotion I see in the families of my village are here as well. Their knowledge of their environment impresses me the most. They live and work with it knowing how to use all the resources the jungle offers in a way that's sustainable. They are completely in tune to their surroundings.

Mr. Tun wants to go visit another village that does not have a road, so we have to leave the truck and walk through the rain forest. To go anyplace on foot, you need a guide, and the men of the village are happy to take us. The jungle is immense and they call it going "into the green." Once I step into it, I feel like I'm being swallowed up in a green world filled with darkness and danger. I start out being very careful, watching wherever I step or put my hands. There are so many things to watch out for—roots and vines on the ground that pop up to trip me, mud that's slippery. There are branches with nasty thorns that puncture my skin to the bone when I grab them to keep from falling. There are lots of high creeks to cross, and we just wade right through with water sometimes coming up to my chest. I'm also watching out for poisonous snakes and spiders.

We're traveling on a trail that intersects with many other trails constantly going up and down small hills. The guide moves very fast, and it's hard to watch where I'm going and him at the same time. A couple of times, we lose him and have to whistle and holler until he comes back for us. We keep up with him for a while, and then he's off again without saying a word. It's hard work, and after miles of trying to be careful, I give up and concentrate on keeping up with him. Even at our best pace, he's always just barely in sight.

After four hours of brutal hiking, we reach our destination, Sunday Tree, another Mopan Mayan village. How anyone can even know it exists is a testament to their knowledge of the bush. We've just walked about sixteen miles through the rain forest. We went up and down hills, crossed through high creeks, and experienced at least six tropical rain showers. I fell down in the mud 150 times, got cuts and bruises on my body, hands, and feet. We saw scores of beautiful toucans, macaws, and other tropical birds. When we finally stop, we're dead tired, soaking wet, and sore.

Twenty minutes after our arrival, our guide, who seems just as fresh as when we started, turns around and heads back home alone. Mr. Tun and I spend the night with similar arrangements to those we had in Falling Creek. After some school business, the next day another guide takes us back. The return trip is just as amazing, beautiful, and brutal as the first time. Even though we've traveled the trail once, I would have never been able to find our way back without a guide. I'm not even sure we went the same way. On our own, we would have been lost in the first ten minutes.

After Mr. Tun completes his business in the villages, we go back to the district town of Punta Gorda. The town is still small, but now that I have been to the villages, it seems much bigger. It has a few Chinese restaurants, a gas station, and a hotel. There's a British camp close by, so they have a few bars and whores that cater to the soldiers. I also get to meet the Peace Corps volunteers that are stationed in town.

By the end of the workshops, which last until the middle of August, I'm ready to go back to my village. Soon, softball season will be starting, and I look forward to going home and coaching the girls again.

On my way home through Belize City, I stop to say hello to my host mother. She's home by herself and invites me in.

"Well, look who come. Come in and let me fix you a cool drink."

"Thanks, Ms. J. How have you been?"

"Bwai, I feel good. Everyone all right. But look at you. You done get big. You look like if you hit dehn boys it will knock dehn down and dehn no wan get back up."

"Yeah, I quit smoking and gained some weight."

"It look good on you. Dehn bwai no wa mess wit yu, no true?" (Those boys will not mess with you.)

"I hope not."

I stay for awhile and drink a nice refreshing glass of cool watermelon juice. I ask her to say hello to everyone for me and go catch my bus.

33

Invasion

There's a change in the village and I call it an "invasion." Television! Belize City and the district towns have been watching it for almost a year. Now it's here in the village. During the short time I was gone, everyone went out and bought these little twelve-inch, black-and-white Korean TV sets. All the Hindu shops in town are selling them as fast as they can get them for seventy-five U.S. dollars.

The majority of villages only have electricity when their generators are running, but these TVs can also run off a car battery. In the evening, everyone hooks up to the battery from their cane truck to watch TV. During the day, they run their trucks to charge the batteries again.

The only reception we get is a popular TV station from Mexico. Univision plays *novelas* (Spanish soap operas) all the time. Now when I walk down the street, instead of hearing reggae music coming from radios, I hear the *novelas*.

A political cartoonist summed it up best. He did a drawing labeled *Belize City 1981* as a city in need of repair with leaning, tumbling down houses, and shacks with patched-up roofs. Next to this cartoon is another drawing, *Belize City 1982*, and it's the same picture only now everyone has a TV antenna. A Belizean politician is quoted in the newspapers as saying, "American television has done more to damage our cultures than a thousand invading armies could ever do."

On my first day back from the districts, I take my evening walk and notice a difference. The usual groups talking on the streets are now inside one of the shops watching soap operas. Don Luis, being the entrepreneur that he is, goes to Mexico to buy a color TV with a nineteen-inch screen. It is the biggest TV anyone has ever seen. Then he lines up benches in his shop and charges people a shilling (quarter) to watch the *novelas*. When the benches are full, people stand in the back or hang out around the doors and windows. They also spend money on Cokes and sweets, making Don Luis a happy man.

There are some people that aren't too interested, who don't get sucked into it right away. Victor has no interest and neither does Arturo. I still find small groups to talk with, but the presence of television definitely makes a difference in conversation.

I think one of the things that make it so interesting is that it brings the rest of the world to our little village. I'm still amazed at how many villagers have never been to Belize City or even out of their district. Incredibly, I find out that eight of the fourteen girls on my softball team have never even been outside of the village. Now they're seeing things on this little box in their homes that they've never seen before.

I stop by to visit a friend, Don Francisco, who is fifty-five years old and a fairly successful cane farmer. He has to work hard but he makes a decent living. I also know him to be an intelligent man. For one thing, he speaks four languages. He speaks Mayan to his wife, Spanish to his children, Creole on the streets, and English to me. When I visit him, he's sitting right in front of the TV with his face just three feet from the screen. He's watching a Spanish soap opera for the first time. I can tell he's fascinated by it because he's concentrating so hard that he barely notices me. The novela he's watching has been filmed in Venezuela, and they're showing scenes of busy streets with fancy cars, skyscrapers, and everyone dressed in the latest elegant fashions. I respect his concentration and watch with him for a few minutes. Then he turns to me with a puzzled expression on his face. He points at the TV and says, "Jorge, do you know what they use those big buildings for?"

He catches me by surprise and I have to think for a minute. Finally I say, "In a big city, thousands of people come together. They need the big buildings for apartments and offices so everyone will have a place to live and work."

"How do they live in those? Do they need such a big building?" He seems perplexed.

"No, those big buildings have offices and some have apartments where everyone's living space is divided. Hundreds of people can live or work in one of those buildings because the offices and apartments are stacked up on top of each other."

He looks confused and asks, "Where are their fields (sugarcane)? Where do they work?"

"They don't have fields. They're not cane farmers, they work in offices."

Surprised, he asks, "Where are their milpas (gardens)?"

"People in the city don't have milpas."

"Where are their families?"

Again, he catches me by surprise. His questions are making me think about my own culture.

"Most people live far from their families. In the United States, people's lives revolve around work and people go wherever their work is. They may live hundreds or even a thousand miles away from their closest relative."

Shaking his head with a look of concern, he says, "But how can they live apart from their family? I cannot do that."

"Well that's the way people live in the United States and other developed countries."

He shakes his head and says, "No, mon. I would not like that at all."

34

Che Chem

Chan Pine Ridge Village is the site of an annual agriculture trade show. My idea is to have a demonstration garden as an example of what a school garden can accomplish. If everything works out right, it'll be a model for other schools to follow. With the support of the school principal, Mr. V., I apply for and receive a small grant from Peace Corps.

Mr. V. and I gather the students and begin planning our master garden on two acres of land close to the school. First, we'll plant a fruit orchard with orange, lime, custard apple, and cashew trees along with other local varieties. Then we'll plant field crops like corn and beans. We'll build a chicken coop and a compost pile. We also reserve a section for each of the students to have their own vegetable plot. Chan Pine Ridge is well-known for its watermelons, so we have to have a watermelon patch. With careful planning, we'll stagger our planting dates so everything is at optimal growth for the fair.

It's a big project and we only have four months to prepare. I start spending all my spare time at the site, working with kids during school and some of the parents after school. In addition to the principal, two of the parents are especially helpful. Arnufo and Terrance come out and work every time I show up. If they know what I want done, they work on it while I'm away.

The first thing we have to do is put a fence around the two acres to keep roaming livestock out. I ask Terrence and Arnufo to organize some of the men to cut fence post. Bright and early on a Saturday morning, we all pile into a cane truck and go out to the bush. Once there, we split up to cut our post. I'm looking for a tree that's fairly straight so I can put one end in a hole and nail barbed wire to the other end.

I've been in the bush before and I know I have to be careful. The jungle is thick with no trails and it's easy to lose your bearings. I'm also paranoid about snakes and jaguars. I've heard stories about jaguars stalking people in the bush, and I know what snakes can do.

I don't have to go far before I find a couple of good solid trees about the right diameter and straight as an arrow. I carefully check around the base and branches for snakes, and everything looks safe enough. Using my machete, I cut down two trees. I then cut off the narrow ends so they're about eight-feet long and trim off the branches. Wasting no time, I pick them up by the heavy end and tuck one under each arm to drag through the bush back to our truck.

It's hot and humid, and I'm sweating more than usual from all the exertion. I don't go far before my eyes start feeling funny and I stop to wipe the sweat out of them. They feel itchy and a little swelled up. I ignore it and keep going. When I get back to the truck, some of the men are already there. They point at my post like I've done something wrong.

Something is wrong. I can make out some of what they're saying. "Che Chem muy peligroso." I know peligroso is Spanish for "dangerous," but I don't know what Che Chem means. I drop my logs with the others as the men are backing away from me. "What? What's going on?" Just then, Terrance comes back with his posts, and the men start talking to him and pointing at me. He looks at me and says, "Jorge, dem trees yu cut down da Che Chem."

"What is Che Chem?" I can see he's concerned.

"Dehn kinda wood da poisonous."

"What does it do to you?" I notice that everyone is keeping their distance from me and my fence post.

"It can make yu very sick, suh."

"Can we at least use these as post?" I want to get something for my efforts.

"No Jorge, dehn post no good. Uno betta left dehn righ deh." He translates to the other men, and they smile, shaking their heads in agreement to leave the post there.

"What should I do to keep from getting sick?"

"Unu betta go di bush docta or di hospital, up to unu, suh."

Now I know why my eyes are itching. By this time, they feel hot and tender and are already swollen halfway shut.

We have enough posts, so we load them in the truck with everyone working carefully to avoid the Che Chem. We leave that behind and head back to Chan Pine Ridge. By this time, my eyes and forehead are badly swollen. Under my arms, where I had put the trees, is swollen, red, and itches like poison oak.

When we get back to the garden, I hop on my bike and go to the hospital in Orange Walk.

The health care system is free, but free is not always better. It means getting a number and standing in line with about twenty other sick people and waiting until your number is called. When they finally call me, I'm all swelled up and feel sick to my stomach. The doctor gives me some pills and tells me how to take them. I take one right away and go home. I go right to bed and wake up in the morning with a fever and blood on the bed where open sores are forming. It's Sunday and I'm sick the whole day. It doesn't feel like the pills are helping me much. Mrs. Eck sends food to me but I can't eat anything.

By Monday morning, I'm worse, so I decide I need to see a private doctor. I still have a fever and I'm getting weaker. I make it to town on my motorcycle and find the doctor's office. He tells me the medicine the hospital gave me is the right medicine but it's been expired for over a year and is not doing me much good. He charges me for some good drugs. He also gives me an injection to get things going.

Within one day, I feel better. Within one week, I'm completely over it. The twenty dollars it cost me was well worth it. Che Chem (botanical name—Metopium Brownei) is dangerous stuff to be avoided at all cost.

35

Canero

Life in the village has become easier for me. I have more friends now, and even people I don't know are talking to me. But my relationships with some of the men in the village still seem superficial. They're polite and treat me according to my status as a teacher. But I spend most of my time with the girls' softball team and school children. Very little of my time is with the men. It reminds me of what it must have been like to wear a six-gun in the Wild West and be comfortable with it. I feel surrounded by gunslingers without my gun. Only here, the six-shooter is a machete, which is used for everything including defending yourself. All the men carry one, and they even have holsters for them or "machete scabbards."

Sugarcane season (crop) is about to start, and the whole village will revolve around harvesting sugarcane for the next six months. I have two weeks of my Christmas vacation left with nothing in particular to do. I decide to spend some time working with the men in the cane fields. I'll meet them on their terms and become a canero (cane cutter). I might make some friends and a little extra money in return. I find out they're starting with Mr. Eck's plantation and ask for a job. The foreman hires me without hesitation, and by the smirk on his face, I know he doesn't believe I'll make it through the day. He and the caneros are getting a good laugh at my expense.

The sugar factory is closed for six months of the year. When it opens for the season, they will only accept green cane for the first two weeks. They do that to make sure all the machinery is running properly. Green cane will last up to two weeks. Sugarcane that's been burned in the field will only last three days before spoiling. It's common for the factory to have problems with machinery in the beginning. If the problem takes long to fix and you have trucks in line with cane that's been burned, it will spoil and the farmer loses money.

Caneros prefer to work with burnt cane. When you burn a field, you get rid of all the snakes, killer bees, poisonous insects, and extra foliage. Cutting green cane means you have to be extra careful to avoid all of the above. It also has tiny prickles on the stalk that manage to work their way into your hands like annoying little thorns. There are some caneros that refuse to work the first two weeks of the season. They prefer to wait until the fields can be burned.

The first day of crop, everyone gets dropped off at the plantation, and Don Juan assigns us our rows to cut. Since this is the first week of the season, we're cutting green cane. Each cutter has four rows to work on. Don Juan shows me mine and gives me a quick demonstration of how to cut and stack.

Sugarcane grows in clumps of three to six stalks with each stalk about two inches in diameter. On your first cut, you gather a clump together by grabbing the tops with your left hand. With your right hand, you swing the machete at the bottom hard enough to cut through all the stalks. Once you cut, you let it fall into your left arm, and in one movement, you turn and stack it behind you.

While you're working, you try to keep up with the caneros on both sides of you. At the end of each day, the cane is loaded into a truck. Some farmers have a mechanical cane loader called a "crab" that picks up large bunches of cane and puts it into the truck. At other plantations, the cane is loaded by hand. It's the "checkers"" job to estimate how many tons each cutter cuts. The team I'm working with uses a mechanical cane loader.

In the beginning, I watch the other caneros work with their machetes. I'm amazed at how easily and gracefully they handle this tool. I feel clumsy after watching them. Within an hour, I'm getting blisters on both my hands since I'm switching hands whenever one hand gets tired. I have a bandana with me, which I use to wrap around the handle of the machete. That keeps my blisters from getting worse.

Within two hours, the Caribbean sun is coming on strong, and there's nowhere to get out of it and still cut cane. I keep my head down and let the sweat drip off me. The humidity is heavy, and by 10:00 a.m., the slightest movement causes perspiration. Once in a while, a little breeze kicks up and cools me down momentarily.

The first few days, I have to stop often to drink water from a gallon jug I keep by my side. The other cane cutters show me how to cut off a section of cane and peel it with my machete. Then I stick the peeled end in my mouth and slowly chew on it. It feels refreshingly cool and sweet. I chew on it until all the sweetness is gone and then cut off another piece. One stalk of cane easily lasts for the whole day and helps distract me from the heat and humidity. I'm not sure how good it is for my teeth though.

I've been told to watch out for snakes. Whenever I make a move, I look first. The cutters on both sides of me have killed a couple of bad ones, which tells me they're around. I'm just not seeing them.

The cutter on my right stops for a break and lets his hand fall to his side naturally, with the machete hanging down beside his right leg. At that very instant, a snake strikes at his machete. He expertly swings his machete to the side, first stunning the snake and then killing it. Damn snakes. Another time, a shout goes down the line from one person to the next, and everyone ducks down. I imitate them without knowing why. Within seconds, the air above me is filled with a dark cloud of killer bees swarming in one direction. As soon as they pass, everyone stands up and continues cutting.

Compared to the other cutters, I'm slow. To try and keep up, I start going to the fields an hour earlier and staying an hour later each day. This means I'm at the field cutting on my rows by 7:00 a.m. I only take fifteen minutes for lunch, eating in the field. The other cutters take an hour to go home, or they find a place to eat and rest in the shade. I also decide to stay an hour longer than everyone else, until 5:00 or 5:30. By doing this, I'm almost able to keep up—almost. Every morning, I come close to catching up with the caneros on both sides of me. Then they arrive, take five minutes to sharpen their machetes, and within fifteen minutes, they're ahead of me.

I stay with it for two weeks, working ten hours a day and six days a week. In the end, I make a grand total of forty-eight dollars. At four dollars per ton, I've cut twelve tons of sugarcane. I figure I've worked approximately one hundred and twenty hours, which comes out to about forty cents per hour. Fortunately, school will be starting soon to save me from getting rich as a professional canero.

I make some new friends. I also gained respect from the men in the village. It shows whenever I pass them in the street and they slap me on the back and say, "buen trabajo," (good job).

36

Stealing Watermelons

I'm anxious to get the demo garden planted so we'll have a good-looking crop when the fair comes. I know I can always count on Mr. V., Terrence, and Arnufo to finish the chicken coop and ramada for me. I'm having trouble getting my corn planted. Every time it germinates and sprouts, the birds get it. I try kid patrol and arm the students with rocks, but they're easily distracted. The birds end up having dinner in our field of corn while the students throw rocks at each other. After planting for about the third time, I remember something I read once in one of my gardening books. It's an old homestead method to keep birds out of your garden. I decide to give it a try. First, I put wooden stakes around the garden. Then I go around the perimeter with white yarn and crisscross it over several times in the middle. The birds think it's a trap and are afraid to land within the outline of the white yarn. My corn sprouts come up and the birds leave them alone.

Everything's ready and the fair is only three weeks away. We've all worked hard and everything in the garden looks great. I'm worried about the watermelons though. We have some potential entries for the largest watermelon contest, but everyone tells me that they'll be stolen before the fair. They know their own culture better than I do, and if they say our watermelons will be stolen, I believe them.

I'm trying to figure out a way to keep our prize watermelons from being stolen. I think about picking them ahead of time, but they're not quite ready yet. Then I have an idea that I think is sure to work. I decide to psych out the thieves by putting up a sign that reads, "One of these watermelons has been poisoned!" That should make anyone think twice before stealing them.

While I'm there in the garden, feeling very proud of myself for coming up with this solution, two farmers coming from their fields stop by to visit. I proudly share my idea and wait for their approval. I can see right away they're not impressed. They exchange glances and smiles and then very patiently explain.

"That is a good idea, Jorge, but it has already been tried."

"It has? What happened?" I'm already starting to feel a little bummed out that the idea has already been thought of, tried, and failed.

"Well, Mr. Torres, who grows ten acres of watermelons, was tired of thieves getting half of them every year. He put up a sign that read, 'One of these watermelons has been poisoned.'"

"And what happened?"

"Well, the next day when he returned to his field, the thief had crossed out the 'one' and the sign now read 'two' of these watermelons have been poisoned!"

That was the end of that idea. The fair came and, yes, my prize watermelons were stolen the week before, but it didn't matter anymore. I accepted the fact that it would happen.

The prime minister of Belize, the Right Honorable George Price, attend along with the minister of agriculture, the minister of education, and other government officials. It's a very special day as I meet each one of them, shake their hands, and introduce them to the principal, Mr. V., Terrence, and Arnufo. They're very humble men, and they give me the time I need to explain the concept of our demonstration garden as a model for all schools. I compare it to meeting the president of the United States and cabinet secretaries. We receive a lot of praise for our garden.

After the fair, I get together with some Belizean teachers, and we go out to celebrate. We celebrate all night long, and I watch the sun come up on my way home. All our hard work paid off. Teachers visiting the fair were commenting that they want their school gardens "to be like this one."

37

Ever-Present Danger

"Terrence is dead." It's early afternoon, and I'm at home when Samuel comes to tell me. At first, I feel shock and the finality of his words. Then I feel like I need to do something to help his family, but I don't know what. I decide to do the only thing I can. I get on my motorcycle and go to his wake to pay my respects.

Bad news like this travels fast through the sugarcane wireless. They say he had gone hunting with two friends, walking into the bush for hours. They were hunting Gibnut, which is the world's largest rodent, weighing in around thirty pounds. It is also a favorite Belizean game meat.

Terrence had shot at one and followed it as it ran into a hole. At the entrance to the hole, he shoved his machete in. A tommygoff was lying in the darkness and bit him twice before he could pull his hand out.

The men with him tried to get him to a bush doctor as fast as they could, but they had gone too far. In the bush, there are no roads and no telephones, and it took hours to get him home. When they finally got back to the village, the bush doctor took one look and told them it was too late, and she could not do anything. They rushed him to the hospital in Orange Walk Town, but they also said it was too late.

They say dying from a snake bite is very painful. Victims describe the pain as a fire burning inside. They thrash and throw themselves around until they finally die. On the inside, they're bleeding to death.

Terrance died a horrible death. I'm going to miss working with him in the garden. He was someone I could always rely on to help me. Mostly, I'll miss his friendship.

38

Reality Check, 1983

There are a million different ways to die, and I guess which way you finally go doesn't matter much. How I'm going to die is not something I normally think about, but I know I don't want to die from a snake bite. It can be so easy to forget where I am and drop my guard. Just a week ago, I caught myself reaching into a dark hole in the trunk of an avocado tree to feel how deep it went. Halfway in, someone said, "Careful, Jorge, there could be a snake." I jerked my hand out at the speed of light. I can't let my defenses down like that, not here. I don't want to be paranoid about it either, so I make an agreement with myself to *be careful*. I only have a few months to go before finishing my two-year tour.

I make my weekly run to the post office in town and receive a letter from Peace Corps. They're reminding me that my time here is almost over. They want me to go to Belize City for my Close of Service (COS) conference. This is something they do to help volunteers tie up our loose ends before going home. It's also a good time to get together with the original group I came in with for a reunion party.

For the conference, they keep us in Belize City for one day of paperwork and medical stuff. On the second day, they take us all to San Pedro by water taxi and put us up in a nice hotel right on the beach.

It's great to see everyone again. A few have returned to the United States early, but most of our original group is still around. Everyone's talking about how good it's going to be to get back home and the first thing they're going to eat or do. John and Linda are planning their wedding. Sabrina's going back to Los Angeles; Ryan and Olivia are extending with Peace Corps for another year. It starts me thinking about what I'm going to do. I'm glad I've completed my two years, but now I'm not sure I'm finished and ready to go home.

I start asking myself questions: *Am I ready to go back? What will I do?*

I feel good about what I'm doing now and what I've accomplished. Here, I'm somebody people recognize and respect as a teacher. I feel like I'm doing good things that make a difference in people's lives, not to mention the good I'm doing for my own well-being. I can't help but ask, *"What's waiting for me in the United States?"*

The conference is designed to start the process for going home. The truth is that the thought of going home scares me. I don't feel like I can handle it yet. I'm just not ready. *What do I do now?*

After snorkeling on the reef and some serious partying, the water taxi takes us back to Belize City. We arrive late and the last bus for Orange Walk has already left. Olivia and Ryan invite me to stay at their place. They have a small two-bedroom, downstairs apartment directly across the street from the Caribbean Sea.

After eating a nice dinner, Ryan's lying in the hammock taking a siesta and Olivia's in the kitchen. I'm sitting by the window reading the local newspaper when I hear a woman scream, "help, help!" I know right away it's a real scream from someone in trouble. I look out the window and see a car parked across the street in front of the sea. I can see a man beating a woman in the passenger seat. His arm is swinging over and over again as he punches her. I see her go down and her screaming stops, but he keeps swinging hard, too hard. I can hear the sound of flesh hitting flesh. All of this happens in just a few seconds. "olivia, call the police!" She also heard the screaming and knows it's for real.

"Ryan, wake up. Someone's in trouble." I give Ryan's hammock a shove as I go out the door.

My adrenaline's pumping as I hit the gate. I yell, "hey asshole!" He turns to look at me and then he goes back for a couple more hard hits to the girl. Now the sound of flesh hitting flesh is accompanied by a muffled sound, like grunting. I go out the gate and start walking diagonally across the street toward the front of the car. I can no longer see or hear the woman.

The guy gets out of his car and says, "Mind your own business."

"This is my business. She's screaming for help." My plan is to stall this guy long enough for the police to get here. In the meantime, I'll try to avoid him and go around the car to get the girl out of the passenger side. I don't want to fight him if I don't have to.

By this time, Ryan's up and coming out the gate. The abuser is fairly big, short but stouter than both of us. But there are two of us, so I'm not too worried about him. He starts walking toward Ryan, telling him to mind his own business. I'm still going with my plan heading toward the passenger side and the girl. Keeping my eye on him, I see he wants to fight Ryan, and instinctively, I know Ryan will be in trouble. He's moving in fast and Ryan starts backing up. Then the guy pushes him and slaps him in the face. Now Ryan needs help.

I direct my voice toward the car and the girl. "get out of the car!" I know she's there but I can't see her. I make a quick decision to help Ryan first and start for the bad guy. I yell at him to get his attention away from Ryan. He turns to face me, and I go in fast with a couple of left jabs that go high. He starts backing up, sensing I'm not going to be as easy a target as Ryan or the girl had been. He keeps backing away, and I know I have to move in and get it over with.

I went in too high the first time. This time I'll go for a body shot. He's against his car now and can't back up anymore. Just as I start to move in, Ryan grabs me from behind by my shoulders and says, "He just took a knife out of his pocket." I don't see it but I believe him. He has one of his hands down by his side. I quickly look around for anything I can use as a weapon against a knife, but there's nothing in the empty street.

He's backing into his car now, cursing and threatening to come back and get us. I remember the girl and begin yelling for her to get out of the car. *Is she hurt, or hiding?* Turning, I tell Olivia to call the police again. He's still cursing and telling us that he's going to come back and take care of us. I tell him to get out of the car. "Let's finish it right now." He starts driving away slowly with his head out the window, cursing us. Then I see the passenger door open a couple of inches, and even though I can't see her, I know she's hurt and trying to get out. He must have heard her because he stops the, car reaches over, and pulls her back in. Then he slams the door shut and hits her again. God, I'm mad and this guy is getting away. It seems like we've been here for twenty minutes. *Where are the police?* "Olivia, write down the license plate number." I want him to know we have something to track him down. "Get out of the car and fight, you punk."

"I'll come back for you." He points his finger at me. Then he drives away.

I'm really bummed that this guy is getting away, and there's nothing we can do about it. We've been here for what seems like a long time. and the police haven't responded. I call the police again and give them the license plate number, telling them what happened. I can tell by their attitude over the phone that they really don't give a damn. No police ever shows up to take a report or ask questions.

I spend a sleepless night alternately worrying about the girl and what happened to her and the fact that I'll be going home soon. Did I do everything I could to get the girl out of the car to safety? I don't feel like I did. Am I ready to go home back to everything that drove me away in the first place? I don't feel like I am.

39

Rites of Passage

The next day, I get on the bus and second guess myself the whole way. *I should have concentrated on getting her out. But I thought the police were on their way. The guy might have used his knife on Ryan if I got the girl out.* After a while, I convince myself that maybe he didn't hurt her anymore because we had his license plate number. I doubt it, but hopefully, she got out of his car alive.

When I get back to the village, I find out there's a *quince anos* I'm invited to. The literal translation is "fifteen years." This is probably just what I need to take my mind off the night before. Basically, it's a birthday party that marks a very important time in a young girl's life. It's a rite of passage where she passes over from being a little girl to a woman and everything that that means. I've heard of them and I know they're important, but this will be my first one. I decide to go and observe this cultural event from beginning to end.

The ritual starts with a special mass at church. Abby (at this point she is still considered a little girl) is escorted down the middle aisle by about twelve *padrinos* (godparents). There can be as many *padrinos* as the girl's parents wish, and each one is financially responsible for at least one contribution to the party. It could be the band, food, drinks, or her dress. For obvious reasons, the more godparents she has, the better.

She's escorted slowly down the aisle and kneels at the front of the church. The priest begins his usual mass. He also has special instructions and advice for the new woman to be. He tells her and the whole congregation that she has to be careful in life and remember to go to church and pray. She is reminded that being a woman brings more responsibility, and she needs to stay away from temptations. "Being a woman does not give you a license to experiment with men." When the priest finishes his lecture, he smiles and introduces Abby to everyone, addressing her with the proper introduction for a young woman. "Ladies and gentlemen, permit me to introduce Senorita Abigail Sosa." His introduction is followed by loud applause.

After mass, we walk over to Abby's family home for a reception. With everyone in attendance, another ceremony begins with Abby escorted by twelve *chambelans* (cham-be-lans—young boys she has picked to be her escorts). These boys have been practicing for weeks for this occasion. The *chambelans* are all dressed in white. They march in cadence, looking very serious like they are there to protect her against fire-breathing dragons if necessary. She is now escorted in front of all the guests, and the *chambelans* flank out to the sides, surrounding her like stone-faced guards.

She stands facing the crowd in a dress that resembles a wedding gown and makes her look like a beautiful fairy-tale princess. With procession music playing, her parents march up to her arm-in-arm and present her with her last toy—a doll. This brings lots of applause. Then her father, dressed in his best Sunday clothes, humbly steps forward and expresses his love for his daughter and what she means to him. It's very moving to see this strong man stand in front of family and friends and share with the world his love for his child. Before he's done, tears are rolling down his cheeks. Then Abby's mother does the same, only she is openly crying. By this time, I'm ready to cry myself.

Now it's Abby's turn to express her love for her parents. Sobbing, she addresses each one separately and thanks them for all they have done for her as a mother and father. All the times they protected her and taken care of her when she's sick, the guidance and advice they've given her. She remembers everything and thanks them for always being there for her. When she's done, everyone applauds and cheers.

This whole time, the *chambelans* have not moved one inch. They are still on guard, forming a solid perimeter around the girl and her parents.

After the speeches, a waltz is played, and the birthday girl dances with her father, and the lead chambelan dances with her mother. Then, one by one, all the godfathers and godmothers are called up. The first godfather cuts in on her father, and the father waltzes with the godmother. As each set of *padrinos* get their turn dancing with the father and daughter, they continue until the floor is full. The whole time, the *chambelans* are still there symbolically guarding the birthday girl.

After the waltz, another ceremony begins, and Abby is presented a satin pillow, which she puts on the ground in front of her as she sits on a chair. Next, her father kneels on the pillow and presents his daughter with her first pair of high heels. This produces much cheering and applause. Now she is a woman, and I can't help but notice the transformation that's happening right before my eyes. She looks beautiful.

After receiving her high heels, Abby disappears, and everyone gets busy eating and drinking. I take a seat with some friends I spotted earlier. The women are serving our food and, one of them brings me a big bowl of escabeche with corn tortillas and a Coke.

When Abby returns thirty minutes later, she's wearing a dress that has nothing subtle about it. The music changes from a waltz to an upbeat, charging tango. If I came into the party at this moment, I would never believe that this is a fifteen-year-old girl. She and the lead chambelan break into a dance they've practiced to perfection.

After a lengthy display of their talent and discipline, the dance ends. They face each other and hold hands for a moment. Then they turn and give a low bow to all the guests. Everyone applauds, whistling and yelling their approval for the performance.

After that, the party continues with traditional dances. They also do some role playing (mock) with potential suitors for the birthday girl amid more whistling, cheering and applause. Being here and watching this ceremony is emotional for me. All of the birthday girl's relatives are present, from great grandparents to little brothers and sisters, cousins, aunts, and uncles. Everyone who cares about Abby is here to share this very special time in her life. At this moment, she is the most important person here, and everyone's energy is devoted to her. She has just gone through the rites of becoming a woman. She said good-bye to the little girl protected by her parents, and she's celebrating her new status as a woman now available for men to court.

All the women are dressed in their finest. The men are also dressed in their best clothes that look in bold contrast to their sun-weathered skin and rough nature. Children are running around, little girls covering their mouths and giggling, little boys hanging out together blowing off firecrackers and playing with a soccer ball. Just to see everyone here and the expense and effort made to recognize this very special event makes me realize that this is the kind of closeness and reality I want my family to have. Not the family I was born into, the family that I'll create one day, my own family.

Everyone knows there is a good chance she'll be a mother before she's twenty. She will no longer be the little girl that rushes out to greet her father when he comes home from working in the fields. Her responsibilities at home will increase, and she'll be depended on to help her mother even more than she has been.

But tonight, Abby is special; she'll still be special tomorrow, and she'll still be a little girl, fifteen years old. But it's the beginning of womanhood and all the responsibilities that come with being a woman. This whole event has been a reflection of tradition, family, and unconditional love. It's a powerful demonstration of reality that shares the joys and hardships of life that come with growing from a child to an adult.

After the party, I walk home in the darkness of a moonless night. The stars are so bright I feel like I'm part of the sky. The whole way, I'm giving thanks for being where I am with this incredible culture that is teaching me so much.

I wake early feeling grateful in general and happy about my new life. Then I remember that I'm going home soon, back to my old life, and all my fears come back. I'm worried that I'm not strong enough. *I'll fall back into the same rut I was in when I left.*

I don't want to leave. I'm not finished with the healing process I've started here. I'm in the place that I need to grow in for right now physically, mentally, spiritually, and emotionally. Since the COS conference in San Pedro, I've been thinking about extending my time as a volunteer. It was an option offered at the conference.

Since I've been in Belize, I've felt closer to my family than I ever did when I was home. I write regularly to my mother, who shares my letters with my brothers and sisters. There are also a couple of close friends that I stay in contact with, including my ex-girlfriend, Lisa. I love getting their mail and getting updates on their lives. All these thoughts are coming to me as I decide to extend for one more year. Now that I've made my decision, I feel confident that it's the right thing to do. I get busy writing everyone letters to tell them about my new plans.

40

The Beginning of Change

I decide not to coach softball for my third year. I talk to the girls and they also feel it's time for a break. Several of the "girls" are now married and pregnant. We're not a complete team anymore, and we don't have the spirit or energy to form a new one. By not coaching softball, I'll have more time to focus on my third year and my job.

Walking around the village, I'm beginning to notice some of the changes that television has made. There are now two guys that own satellite dishes in Orange Walk Town. They're political rivals, and they each point their dish in the direction of the villages. This gives them the opportunity to broadcast their political messages to the masses. At the same time, it gives the villagers a little more variety to choose from on TV and we're getting more American stations. My only complaint is that I can be watching a good movie or a soccer game and at anytime, without warning, it's switched to another channel by the owners of the dishes.

The popular novela right now is *Christina*. Everyone watches it in the evening and then talks about it the next day. I hear people talking about the latest "*Christina* episode," and it sounds like a real life crisis is happening. Before TV, when women from the village met at the water pump, they talked about life in the village, things like education, politics, or religion. That still happens, but the bigger news seems to be what happened on *Christina* the night before.

There are other changes happening in the village. Men are gathering in their small groups on the street and complaining about the price they're getting for sugarcane. They're used to getting decent money and having protected markets, but now something new is happening. The global market is coming and they're losing money. The price of sugar has gone down and threatens to go down even more. There's some angry discussion going on. I stop by to listen in on a group that Victor is with.

"They cannot pay us such a low price. We will lose money like that." The man talking is shaking his head. "We have to organize a demonstration against the sugar board."

"It will not do any good. If they don't have the market to sell it, they cannot sell it." It's Victor telling them not to waste their time organizing a demonstration.

One of the men responds, "This is the fault of the government. They have a responsibility to protect us from things like this."

"Yes, the government should protect us, but they did not and now it is too late."

"I cannot make a living selling my sugarcane at that price. I will have to sell some of my land to pay the bank this year."

"Yes, it is going to be a hard year, but 'ni modos?'" (What can we do?). Victor shrugs his shoulders as he says this.

"This is your fault, Jorge." It's Pedro, a friend, and he's smiling, but I can tell he's part serious.

"How is it my fault?" I know he's referring to the United States and not directly to me.

"Your government does not want to buy our sugarcane anymore." Other men in the group nod their heads in agreement.

"How come?" I'm totally ignorant to the politics involved with selling sugarcane.

"They will buy it, Jorge, but they don't want to pay us for it."

"Why? What's going on?"

"They say that now we have to compete with their farmers, and we cannot do that. They are much more advanced than we are."

"I will talk to the president and see what I can do." That relieves some of the tension and makes them laugh.

"Yes, Jorge, tell him to come over and live with us for a while."

"Okay, can he stay with you, Pedro?"

"Oh yes, mon. That is no problem. You know we are just playing, Jorge, but this is a serious problem, and we are not sure what to do."

"But it doesn't sound like it's all the fault of the U.S. It sounds like a lot of things are involved on both sides."

"Yes, that is true, Jorge. We only say those things to you because we are friends, no true?"

"Yes, mon."

"They should make Jorge president and then we will have no problems, no true?" It's Victor and everyone laughs in agreement.

Slowly, the group starts breaking up, and men walk away shaking their heads with worry. It's an attitude I've seen before. They are already convinced that they can't compete against anything the United States does.

41

Mota

The U.S. Agency for International Development (USAID) comes to our village within days of our conversation. They have a plan to train sugarcane farmers to diversify and become vegetable farmers. They know hard times are coming for sugar prices, and they want to prepare the farmers by introducing other cash crops. They meet with the farmers and offer funding to encourage them to try new things. Several U.S. companies and consultants will come in to assist with the export process and provide a market if enough farmers agree. It sounds like good logic, and I'm impressed that AID is being proactive with the farmers.

Not everyone is receptive. Victor and others say, "It will not work. You cannot make vegetable farmers out of cane farmers. The difference is too great." Sugarcane, part of the grass family, takes very little effort to maintain and harvest. It has no serious threat from pests or disease. You put it in the ground, fertilize it once a year, spray herbicide once or twice, harvest once a year, and collect your money.

Vegetables, on the other hand, require constant daily care. They need irrigation in the dry season and protection from flooding during the rainy season. The amount of diseases, insects, and other pests present in the tropics requires qualified technicians, chemical pesticides, and fungicides for crops to survive.

Lately, I've been hearing rumors of farmers diversifying but not exactly the way the United States wants them to. They're growing another cash crop—*mota* (Spanish slang for marijuana). I'm not seeing it, I'm only hearing about it.

Victor starts changing around this time. I see less of him, and when I do, the only thing he wants to talk about is money and guns. He seems to have more of both lately, and he always wants to show me his newest gun. One day, he takes me to a cane field, where he's set up a scarecrow for target practice. He shoots a few rounds and then hands the gun to me. I take a couple of shots, but I don't like shooting at a mock-up of a man. I hand it back and tell him I don't like guns. That's the last time he invites me to target practice.

I hear rumors constantly, and like the Creole say, "If it no true, it nearly true." The latest rumor is that a runway has been built by the ministry of works. They're the ministry responsible for the repair and building of roads. The rumors must be true because I begin seeing small planes landing behind the village and flying out on a daily basis.

All the signs are there for the establishment of drug trafficking. There's discontent and anger over the loss of their protected market. Men talking about how easy it is to grow marijuana and how good the money is. There are planes coming and going and new faces in town. I hear gangs are being formed to control the trade. I see Victor slowly building an army of men. Many of them are aliens, and they're not carrying machetes, they're carrying automatic weapons.

One day, he introduces me to an American in the village. He seems friendly enough. I say hello, shake hands, and move on. I meet the same American in town a few days later and have a few beers with him. He invites me to smoke a joint, and when I decline, he asks if I want a snort of coke. I take a deep breath and say, "No, thanks."

He doesn't say it, but I've been around drugs and drug dealers enough to know he's here to set up business. He spends money freely and has plenty of it. He's also dangerous. I can see and feel it in his mannerisms and the subtle innuendos he occasionally drops. He's a hard-core businessman and not someone to cross. I feel like the grim reaper has come to take care of business in our small peaceful village.

42

How to Get Married

I know what Victor and some of the other farmer's are doing, but I decide to ignore it and mind my own business. They're not asking me for advice and I can't tell them what to do. My plan is to focus on my job and stay out of the way. If I'm not involved, it shouldn't affect me.

A few days after meeting the "reaper," I'm outside my house getting ready to leave for the day when Chabby comes over. She has a big smile, and I know she wants to tell me the latest village gossip. "Sergio and Goya got married last night," she says in a conspiratorial whisper and waits for my response. My first thought is, *how the hell did I miss a wedding in a village this small?* I'm also beginning to feel a little bummed out. *Why wasn't I invited?* Sergio and Goya are both friends. Goya is Maria's (pitcher) sister, and she used to come and practice with the team.

"Where did they get married? In the village? In a church? Did they go to town?"

"No, no," she says, "Sergio went and stole Goya last night."

"Oh! So they really didn't get married, they just eloped last night."

"Yes, Sergio took Goya home to his father's house."

"Well, what happens now?"

"Now Sergio's father will have to go and speak to Goya's father."

"Will that make everything all right?" I notice she has to consider the personalities involved for a minute.

"Yes, I think so."

It takes me a while to figure out that not everyone in the village is actually married in a church or legal ceremony. In fact, the only ones that are, are the ones that can afford to top the last wedding with invited guests. The majority wisely prefers to elope and live together rather than go to the big expense of a wedding. From a cultural standpoint, if you have daughters, there are two things that are going to happen for sure. They're going to get pregnant and they're going to get "married." You just pray that it's to a man who treats her well. If you have sons, you don't worry as much. They're expected to behave like men and take a woman when they have the opportunity and not always with marriage in mind. Girls and boys tend to marry young in the village. Many are married by the time they're twenty years old.

I still see Maria around the village. She has become a woman since I met her that first day on the softball field. She's a real beauty—tall and slender with jet black hair and dark eyes that sparkle. I notice that she's paying more attention to me, and I feel a sexual energy between us.

I've learned a little about her family since I've been here. Two of her five brothers are my favorite students. In addition to them, she has five sisters. Her three older sisters are very attractive, with one married, one recently eloped, and one about to get married. Her mother and father are always courteous to me when I see them around the village or in town.

Sometimes I daydream about the possibility of a relationship with her and what it would mean. I'm not sure but I think I would have to speak to her father before I did anything or maybe become friends with him? I'm not clear on the protocol. How far can I go before I have to speak to her father? It seems like such a serious thing to do, and I'm not ready to make that kind of commitment over a brief flirtation. I need to be logical about the whole thing and not let my emotions get in the way. The problem is when I'm not around her, my logic works, but when I see her, I want her. She knows this and seems to like it. I have to be careful because something like this can have consequences that I'm not ready to deal with right now.

43

Globalization

A new threat to Belize and Belizeans in general is globalization. It is affecting the whole Caribbean in a dramatic way. Island nations that historically rely on agriculture, citrus, bananas, and sugarcane have always enjoyed a protected market. Without that protection, they have to compete with larger countries that have the resources to control the market.

The result is a drop in the value of their exports. Less income means island nations can't pay back money they've borrowed from the World Bank. The Bank, who wants their money back, uses their persuasion to convince Caribbean countries into promoting ecotourism, which has proven effective in bringing in foreign dollars.

The problem, as they discovered in Jamaica, are the social issues tourism creates. In small countries where agriculture has been a tradition, the change to tourism creates unanticipated consequences. Valuable farm land and seaside property that has been passed down for generations is now sold for commercial development. Tourism creates job opportunities away from home, and extended families begin to break up. People leave their rural homes to work as taxi drivers, security guards, maids, cooks, and become part of the tourist economy.

I also discovered, from reading about the issues in Jamaica, something termed the "demonstration effect." This is what happens when tourists vacation on an island in the Caribbean for two weeks. The locals see someone who seems to have unlimited amounts of money to do whatever they wish. Some vacationers are low-key, demonstrating responsible behavior. But many go to party and have fun. What else do you do on an island? These are the tourists that party every day, drinking, doing drugs, and exhibiting promiscuous behavior.

The locals see this and interpret that this must be the way to live, that this is what life is about. They see people living a good life with no visible consequences, and they begin to think that they can live that way too. Life is just one big party. They start by supplying tourists with drugs and women. Before long, they begin using the drugs and the woman they're selling. Then the social problems begin. Families break up, people begin robbing tourists, dealing drugs, and prostituting.

The traditional social fabric for dealing with family problems is the extended family. Built into this structure are strong role models. If a man is not treating his family right, he has brothers, uncles, cousins, and his father who counsel and steer him back to his family. The woman and children are also taken care of with support from their families.

If you break up the extended family, the social infrastructure falls apart. Cultural norms are exchanged for making easy money and satisfying the bases of human desires. As the level of desire increases, so does the need for more money. The levels of poverty and crime go up, and the government finds itself in a tough situation. They need the money that tourism brings in, but they're not able to deal with all the baggage it brings.

In our area, the price of sugarcane has gone down even more than predicted. Historically, cane farms are passed on to the younger generation, but that's not looking too profitable. The problem is they don't know how to do anything else.

The students we work with in the villages have few options if they don't continue their education. They work with their fathers in sugarcane or they leave the community to look for work elsewhere. When sugarcane is only paying enough to pay back what you've borrowed to produce it then there is no incentive to work with it.

The other threat we're beginning to see among our students is defeatism. If they can't continue their education either because they've failed the national selection exam or they can't afford it, their opportunities become minimal. They don't feel like they can do anything else. Sugarcane is not profitable, and they have no marketable skills. A few resourceful individuals go out and find apprenticeships in the mechanic or construction trades but these are limited. More and more are getting into bad habits like drinking and drugs.

Recently, the Belize government has begun promoting ecotourism as its number one priority to bring back the economy.

44

Vision

"We need a school for students that don't pass the national selection exam."

"But how can a school like that compete with other high schools, Jorge?"

"Maybe we don't need another high school."

"What do you mean?"

"Everyone is focused on higher education and academics. Families sacrifice so their kids can go to high school and get a good education. After high school, some move on to sixth form (junior college) and from there to a university. The best students go to the U.S. or the UK. The students that stay in their communities have very few opportunities for a successful career. Look at what happens when a good job is advertised—thirty people with degrees apply for the same job."

"Yes, that is true, but what kind of school are you talking about, Jorge?"

"What is it that Belize has an abundance of and that all of these students have access to?"

"Rice and beans?" They all laugh.

"No, mon, I'm talking about land. These kids we're working with have access to all this real estate around us, and they don't know what to do with it. Look, normally these kids would take over their family's sugarcane plantations, no true?"

"Yes, that is true."

"But everyone knows that sugarcane is not paying well, and we don't know if that will ever come back, but there are other things you can do with land.

163

Look at Jose's father. He's a successful cattle rancher, but how many of our students know how to do that? There are lots of things they can do. What about pigs, chickens, or even specialty crops like papaya and passion fruit? There's a market for those things. The Agency for International Development has identified other crops besides vegetables that will sell and can be grown here. It doesn't have to be sugarcane or vegetables."

"What kind of school would that be, Jorge?"

"Listen, the students that get good grades continue their education so we're not too worried about them. In one way or another, they're taken care of and have some options. This will be a school for the others, the ones who don't get good grades." We can call it anything we want. Call it a school of agriculture, appropriate technology, or resource planning. It can be a two-year school instead of four years. Students can identify things they're interested in and focus on that as long as they use their land. We could send students to learn from people who are doing it, like Jose's father. The main thing is we keep them in the community by teaching them how to plan and think outside the box, how to be entrepreneurs."

"That sounds like a good idea, Jorge, but where will we get a school like that? That will take a lot of money and resources, no true?"

"I know, but it's something to think about."

"Yes, no true?"

The whole idea is very intriguing to me, and I can't help but think about my own situation. When I went to school, it was toil and drudgery. I know now that my bad experience in school was partly because I didn't know how to learn the way the majority of kids learn. It took me until I was thirty-one years old and living in a different culture before I "learned how to learn." Perhaps I'm slow, and maybe I'm the consequence of an education system that doesn't have the resources to accommodate everyone's learning style.

The other part of that equation was the fact that I gave up on the system before I had finished the sixth grade. Defeated, I became defiant and aligned myself with others who reinforced my rebellion. We cut classes, drank at school, got into fights, and challenged all authority. It's a miracle I got through high school at all.

During my sophomore year, I was called to the principal's office on a weekly basis. One time in particular, two men in suits were waiting for me. I did a quick mental check list of anything I might have done to bring down the FBI on me. The vice principal, who is also the school disciplinarian and my sworn enemy, introduced us with a smirk on his face. They explained to me that they were there because of my score on recent state testing. Apparently, myself and a girl from Las Vegas received the highest scores in the state. They asked me a few questions. I knew the vice principal had already filled them in on my reputation as a bad student. Maybe if I had been in a room with just the two of them I would have reacted differently. As it was, I became defiant and acted like I didn't know what they were talking about. The vice principal assured them that my score was a fluke and I returned to class. That was the last I ever heard about it.

Maybe if I had more support or someone who believed in my ability, I could have received a better education. Or maybe if I had other options after my bad performance in the world of academics, I wouldn't have gotten into my bad habits with drugs and drinking. As one of the "others" myself, I could have used some support and other options for education.

The only good memory I had of school was a class I took called "Family Living." The teacher talked about real-life situations. He shared stories about what it was like to be married, have children, and a career. To me this was practical, real life knowledge that I wanted to know more about. I couldn't see how algebra or world history were going to make a difference in my life. When I think of a school for the others, this is what I think about. A school that teaches students knowledge they can translate into their daily life. I know a school like this can benefit the children of the villages. The problem is I have no idea where we would get the money to start a school like that.

Meanwhile, it's becoming more and more obvious that some of the better entrepreneurs are making effective use of their land with marijuana. I make a point of never talking or asking questions about what's going on, especially around Victor. But I listen, and I can see what's right in front of me.

45

Street Fight

It's Saturday night and the bar in Orange Walk Town has a big crowd. I'm hanging out with Matt, Tim, and Kathy, but I'm also trying to make time with a cute cocktail waitress. She gets off work at midnight, and I go outside to keep her company until her sisters come to walk her home. They come and she goes without giving me much hope for a future relationship. I decide to stay outside for a while and enjoy the fresh air. I sit down and make myself comfortable on a cement curb at the entrance to the bar.

The bar is located at one end of the central park, and the street is full of people. Some are out taking a walk, and others are out looking for some kind of action. It's one of the cultural things I like about the tropics—people get out of their homes. Where I'm situated, I have a view of the whole park. I'm enjoying the peacefulness of just being able to sit here drinking a beer watching the night life.

Then without warning, a fight starts brewing right in front of me. An old man is getting into an argument with three tough-looking Creole boys. The biggest one keeps shoving him. The old man's trying to stand up to him, but he's too drunk and the thug's too big. He hits the old man square in the jaw, knocking him out. Then he spins around and plants his foot in the middle of his chest. The old man goes down hard on his back about three feet in front of me. All of this happens in just seconds before I can react or do anything.

Something inside me snaps and the adrenalin starts pumping. It doesn't matter that he's bigger or that he has two of his buddies with him. I feel like I have enough adrenalin going to take on all three of them. I jump up and point at the big guy. "You want to try someone your own size?" I start for him but he and his two buddies turn around and run. They disappear behind a van that's parked across the street. I start to follow, and they come back around the van with their hands behind their backs. The big guy's being brave now and says, "I'll fight someone my size. You want some, you come over here, white buoy."

They say God takes care of drunks and fools, and it was never truer than this moment. I'm foolish enough that I start to go over. Someone from San Lazaro is playing the role of God tonight and grabs me by the shoulders. "Don't go, Jorge. They just got something out of that van." By this time, my head's clearing up enough to know I'm outnumbered and outsized. I figure I don't need anything else going against me. The punks are really mouthing off now and attracting a crowd. I decide it's time to leave. Before going, I tell them, "I'll be around anytime you want to fight someone besides old men." Then I slowly start back for the bar.

I know they're relieved I'm leaving because they don't want to fight anyone who might have a chance. I look around for the old man, who was out cold just a few minutes earlier, and he's gone. Back in the bar, I find Matt and another friend doing shots of tequila. They offer me a shot, and I make the mistake of telling Matt what just happened. He's already mad because someone broke into his house a couple of days ago and stole his camera. He's still angry about it and ready for a fight.

"Who beat up an old man?" He's drunk and talking loud above the bar music.

"Some punks outside."

"Where are they? Show me where they are." He starts for the door.

"It's over, Matt, besides there are three of them."

"Come on, Rick, we need your help." Rick's our Frenchman drinking buddy, who's been listening to the conversation.

"Matt, man, let it go."

"Show us who they are, Jorge. I want these guys." He goes out the door with Rick and me following him.

To be honest, I'm feeling kind of good because when I faced them before, I was alone. Matt's athletic but on the slender side, and he doesn't look threatening. I have no idea how he handles himself in a fight. Rick's all skin and bones, and I can tell he's not happy to be with us right now.

The bad guys are still outside and this time we do get into it. Matt goes straight for the big guy and takes a hit on the chin with a Coke bottle. His chin splits open with blood everywhere, but he's so drunk and mad he doesn't even feel it.

I want to make quick work with these guys, but now there are more of them and they seem to be coming from everywhere. Tim and Kathy leave the bar and follow us to see what's going on. Tim ends up in the middle of it, trying to keep them from ganging up on Rick while I'm busy keeping them off myself and Matt. It's hard to go one on one because as soon as I square off with one, somebody else gets me from behind.

Matt and I are doing okay, but Tim and Rick are not. It's time to get out of here because it seems like more are coming, and things are getting mean. They're using beer bottles now, and luckily, they're very bad shots. Then a bottle grazes my head, and I know they're getting closer or their aim is getting better. Somehow, we've gotten ourselves on the opposite end of the park, far from the bar and safe refuge. I grab Matt and holler at him to get through his drunkenness. "we need to get out of here now!" He hears me and sees the danger we're in. We start backing out of there, covering each other's backs as we grab Rick and Tim along the way. When they see we're retreating, they regroup and come after us with beer bottles. By this time, we're close enough to the bar that we make a run for it. As the swinging doors close behind us, we hear about a dozen beer bottles hit—*bam, bam, bam* . . .

We feel safe in the bar because we know the owner, and we're friends with his son and daughter. The son, Godsman, is managing the bar tonight. We come in breathing hard, Kathy's crying, Matt's still bleeding, and I'm giving thanks for making it back in one piece. Godsman asks, "What's going on, Jorge?"

"We just got into a fight with some Creole guys for beating up an old man."

"That old man?" He points behind me.

I turn around to see the old man dancing around the bar room with a bottle of beer, completely oblivious to the fight for justice on his behalf.

"Yeah, that's the one." I'm glad to see he's okay.

"But I paid a Creole five dollars to throw him out about a half hour ago."

"You what?"

"Yeah, I paid the guy to get him out of here and keep him out because he's too drunk and keeps bothering the customers."

"You're kidding me."

"No, now I have to throw him out again."

"Oh, hell no. We just got into a big fight over this guy, you're not kicking him out now."

"I did not know they would hurt him."

"The bigger one knocked him out cold."

"You mean Hercules?"

"I don't know his name, but I guess if that's who you told to throw him out, that must be the one."

"You got into a fight with Hercules, Jorge?"

"Well, we all did at one time or another. Matt got the worse of it."

"You have to be careful, Jorge. He is a very dangerous person."

"The fight's over. I don't want any more to do with him."

"Listen to me, Jorge. He is the kind of man that people hire to kill other people."

"No way, you mean he's like a hit man?"

"Yes, for fifty dollars, he will murder you or anyone."

"I guess I better be careful for a while. If you happen to talk to him tell him I said no hard feelings. Tell him I'll give him fifty dollars not to kill me."

"Keep one eye over your shoulder, Jorge."

"I will."

Hercules knows me better than anyone because I'm the one who originally challenged him and started the whole thing. Plus, at one point, we had squared off in the park, and I managed to land a good, solid punch to his rib cage before one of his friends kicked me in the back. I know he'll remember that because I heard him grunt in pain when I connected.

The following Monday, I have to go into town. I'm walking down the street and see Hercules about a block away coming toward me. Being a small town, I knew this was going to happen sooner or later. I figure the best thing to do is play it out and see what happens. He sees me at the same time and ditches into a store. That's fine by me. It's not in my nature to look for trouble.

Two years ago, I could not have stood up against those guys or, if I had, they would have stomped on me. They're too big and I wasn't strong enough. Size makes a difference on the streets.

That was the last time I saw Hercules. Two weeks later, I read in the paper that he was found shot to death in front of People's Stadium. The word on the street says he cheated the wrong guy out of some drug money. There's always someone bigger and meaner.

46

The New Crop

It's early in the morning and I wake up to the unmistakable sound of cane trucks moving down the road. It's a sound I hear constantly throughout cane season. Only this isn't cane season. It's October, at least two months before crop starts. I look out my window and, sure enough, cane trucks are picking up cutters that are lined up on the road. But these are not the usual cane cutters. They're young boys and girls, women old and young, as well as some older men. *What the hell's going on?* I get dressed and go outside.

Samuel's in front of his house watching the procession of trucks.

"Samuel, que paso (what's going on)?"

"Mota, Jorge. They are going to the fields."

"What mota? Are they planting it?" I can't figure out why they need such a large workforce.

"No, mon," He laughs. "They are going to harvest, Jorge."

"This many people are going to harvest mota? That must be one big plantation."

"Oh yes, mon, no true? The Belize Defense Force found it on a search and destroy." They had started doing these patrols under pressure from the U.S. embassy.

"I guess they didn't destroy it."

"No, mon. They gave them two weeks to get rid of it. That's why these people are going. They will pay them good money to harvest and pack it."

"Where did they find the plantation?"

"Behind San Felipe."

"Somebody got paid off?"

"It looks so, Jorge. It looks so."

San Felipe has a reputation for being lawless even though there's a police substation there. It's also the last village up the road, which means they must also be picking up people in Trinidad and August Pine Ridge, the two villages that lie between us and San Felipe. *Must be one hell of a plantation! I wonder how much the commander got paid to leave it alone.*

47

A School in the Jungle

There's a section on the road where the Mennonites are working and I have to stop. They've cleared an area of bush off to one side to dig up limestone for repairing big holes made from recent rains and cane trucks. While I'm waiting, I notice something barely visible through the thick foliage of the jungle. It's the corner of a large cement building.

Instantly, in a rare moment of clarity, I know I've found our school. I park my motorcycle, grab my machete, and cut my way carefully through the bush to a large rectangular building. It's about thirty feet wide by one hundred feet long with solid concrete walls and a steel-framed roof. All the doors, windows, and partitions have been stripped from it. Now it's just the shell of a building.

Using my machete, I explore more and find a smaller house that had probably been used for teachers. Both buildings are completely covered by the jungle. I've been driving by this same exact spot for almost three years and didn't even know it existed. If it had not been for the Mennonites clearing the jungle, I still wouldn't know it was here. It had been a school at one time, and somehow, I know that it will be again.

After a little investigating, I find out that it had once been a primary school strategically placed and shared between the villages of San Lazaro and Trinidad. When San Lazaro built their own school, they moved out. Then the Trinidad students moved out and began using their community center for a school. The land and buildings have been abandoned for thirty years. They sit on six and a half acres of land that belongs to the Roman Catholic Mission. With no one to keep the jungle cut back, it took over and everyone forgot about it. It looks just like one of the hundreds of Maya ruins that dot the countryside. If it wasn't for the Mennonites working on the road, I would have never known it existed.

I'm excited with this discovery because I know it can make the vision we have for an alternative school a reality. After talking with local leaders of the communities and teachers that I work with, I decide to go for it. My plan is simple. I'll apply for a grant to get the project started. Then I'll ask Peace Corps to request another volunteer to take over where I leave off. I'll still go home at the end of my three-year term just as planned.

There is no doubt in my mind that this will be the school I've envisioned for the last year. I have eight months before my third year is up so I have to get moving. I'm not even sure where to start. I know we need permission from the church to use the buildings and land. Father Wright is the local priest and manager of the district's Catholic schools. I make an appointment to see him and explain my idea to make the abandoned land and building into a school again. He likes the concept and agrees to talk to the bishop for me. I also have a good friend, John Masson, who's a manager at Belize Sugar Industry (BSI) and friends with the bishop, so he also puts in a good word. With their support, I quickly get the blessing of the Catholic Mission. They offer me a proposal to lease the land for one dollar per year with a ninety-nine-year lease.

Now that I have the approval to use the land and buildings, I go to the Peace Corps director and explain my plan. The director, Bill, is very supportive and says he'll back me up all the way. He agrees to the condition that Peace Corps will provide a volunteer leader to take over when I leave and two Peace Corps volunteers to help staff the school. He suggests we go to the United States Agency for International Development (USAID) for the money since he feels it will take much more than Peace Corps can provide.

One of the main differences between USAID and Peace Corps is that AID has money. Both agencies are there to build capacity. AID does it through strengthening infrastructure like building roads and bridges and then leaving the equipment there for the host country to use. Peace Corps builds people capacity through training programs and providing volunteer support.

Bill is friends with the director of AID, Neb, so we set up a meeting. Once again, I explain my idea. Neb is also very supportive and sends me home with an outline of what he wants to see in a proposal. He tells me he needs to see the communities around the school involved. He also says he can't give any money to me as an individual. It can only be given to an agency or organization that is a legal entity.

I meet with the village councils of San Lazaro and Trinidad, who agree to host the school and perform community work to clear out the bush. I do a presentation at the local Rotary Club from Orange Walk Town, and they agree to act as the legal entity receiving the grant.

I know I have to go to a ministry and get support from the government. I can't do it without their involvement. I make a decision to go with the ministry of agriculture instead of the ministry of education because I want the students to focus on using their land. I talk to the chief agricultural officer for the Orange Walk District and he agrees to support the project. He also agrees to talk to the minister about providing teachers and agricultural resources.

Everything is quickly coming together, and I'm a little surprised that everyone is being so receptive and supportive. There has not been one objection to the idea.

Neb has offered financial support, but I still have to write a grant proposal to get the money. I don't have a typewriter or a computer so everything I do is written in longhand under the light of a kerosene lamp. What I at first thought was going to be drudgery and work turns out to be exciting and challenging. I finish the first draft within three weeks and take it to Neb. He reads it and sends me back to gather more information. For the next few weeks, I keep up my regular schedule with the schools and work every spare minute during the evenings and weekends writing out my vision for the school.

48

Premonition

It's late afternoon, and I'm still about three miles from home when my bike breaks down. After several tries to restart it, I give up and start walking to find help. There's no traffic on the road and it's unusually quiet. I start feeling paranoid like something bad is going to happen. It's the time of year for "crop," and the feeder road I'm on should be busy with trucks going and coming from the sugarcane factory. I look around to get my bearings. On one side of me is a bare field that has recently been harvested, and all that remains are charred stumps of cane stalks. On the other side of the road is tall, green cane for as far as I can see, with their straight, fuzzy "cane arrows" blowing in the wind. Nothing out of the ordinary, but I still have a bad feeling.

I hear the car before I see it. A quick backward glance tells me it's an old Chevy Caprice, one of those big tanks that use a ton of gas. The white paint is dirty and it has rust spots all along the side. The tires are bald, no hubcaps, and a squeaking sound is coming from one of the wheels. I hear it slow down as it comes up behind me. I turn to look again. There are several men in the car and they're strangers—not good. If they're aliens who don't know me, I might be in trouble.

They drive up slowly until they're right beside me. It's a little dark inside the car, but I can see there are two in the front and three or four in the back. I can also tell by their look and skin color that they're aliens from either Guatemala or El Salvador. The two in the passenger windows on my side look mean. They're glaring at me and muttering obscenities at me under their breath.

I weigh my options. The harvested, charred cane field is on my right, and their squeaking car is on my left. Behind and in front of me is nothing but an empty, dusty road. There's no way I can outrun a car or five guys. The best thing to do is try to bluff it out. I can't show them any fear. I glance at them again and the shotgun passenger points an automatic weapon out the window at me. I hear him say in a thick Spanish accent, "You are going to die, gringo." I have to make a split-second decision, and a dozen thoughts are racing through my mind: *Is this the end of my life? Am I going to die here on a sugarcane road in Central America, far from my family and my home? Will anyone know what happened to me?*

My best option is to turn around and try to make it behind their car. If I can do that then maybe I can make it across the road to the tall cane field. I might be able to lose them and hide in the cane. I've got to be fast and make no mistakes, no time for panic. Just as I turn to run, a flock of noisy parakeets passes overhead and distracts me. I stop to watch them pass as if they're more important than the gun pointing at me.

I wake up in a panic—another nightmare, one in several I've been having recently. The last few months I've been feeling the tension build as I watch our village and the region change from a peaceful, family home environment to a place of danger and violence with gun-toting strangers. Belizeans know me and I feel safe with them. They know I'm not CIA or DEA. I was here in their village, in their homes, way before drugs were. It's the hired guns that worry me. I have to be careful if I want to finish my time as a volunteer and go home in one piece.

For the last few months, it seems like every time I go around a corner, there's another roadblock set up. Sometimes it's the police and sometimes it's one of the drug gangs. Both hold their weapons on me until I'm cleared to pass.

The newspapers have been full of bad stories lately, and they're all happening in our district. They now refer to Orange Walk as "Rambo Town." Every day, there are murdered bodies being found. Sometimes, I meet someone from another district and when I tell them where I live, they express fear about even visiting our district. But it's different if you live here because you know what's going on and who it involves. All the people found murdered were involved with drugs. It might be rival gangs or someone who tried to cheat someone they should not have. I know that if I stay away from the drug business, I'm fairly safe.

But there are times I worry. Some of these drug dealers are very mean and very violent. I've been saved several times because everyone knows me and watches out for me. Otherwise, some of these guys will not hesitate to have me taken out. I have to be careful all the time.

49

Big Decision

I turn in at least six draft proposals in a six-week period before I finally have something that I'm satisfied with and that Neb will accept. I ask for $100,000 U.S. to get the school up and running. My budget includes windows, doors, furniture, paint, classroom extensions, bathrooms, agriculture supplies, and tools and materials to build pig pens and chicken coops.

After turning in my last draft, Neb decides he wants to see the site before he makes his final decision. The idea of using an existing resource to meet a need is what makes him so interested in the project. The empty school building, the land, and the teacher's house are my best selling point, and they are still covered with overgrown bush. I cut a fresh trail so I won't have to worry too much about all the snakes I'd seen around the place earlier. I don't want to scare off Neb and Bill when they come to visit. Carrying my machete, I take Neb and the Peace Corps director down the trail and inside the main structure. I get them comfortable, making sure there are no snakes around, and I describe to them how I'm going to transform this empty, deserted structure into a functioning school that will benefit hundreds of students for years to come. By now, I've got my speech down perfect, and I know out of all the times I've given it, this is the one that will count the most.

Everywhere you look are termite trails, spiderwebs, jungle debris, and dried-out snake skins. I describe to them how it will look when it's done, with classroom divisions, doors, windows, skylights, outdoor classrooms, and an office. It's my opportunity to show them my vision while they're standing right there in the school. I finish by talking about the six and half acres we have to grow crops and raise livestock on. I pause and look at them for questions.

"Do you think you can get students to come here?"

"With the help of the villages and teachers, I know we can."

"Do you think the ministry of agriculture will come through with the teachers?"

"Well, I'm working on it. Right now, I have the support of the area representative who is the minister of trade and industry, the district agriculture officer, and the REAP district council."

"Is the Catholic Mission still supportive of the idea?"

"Yes, they agreed to lease the land for ninety-nine years at one dollar per year."

"And the villages will help?"

"Both San Lazaro and Trinidad are willing to support the school with free labor and other services."

"You'll need a legal entity to receive the money. I can't give it to you."

"The Orange Walk Rotary Club has agreed to do that part of it." Neb and Bill look at each other and seem to be considering their answer. They're both smiling and I feel like there's more to come.

"Okay, I am willing to give you the money on two conditions."

"Anything, just let me know what you need." I'm excited and ready to agree to whatever Neb wants.

"One, you have to stay for another two years as a volunteer to manage the project, and two, you have to add a pickup truck to the budget. You can't have a school of agriculture without a truck."

I'm excited and perplexed at the same time. *This isn't what I planned. I'm going home in June after being gone for three years. If I say yes, that means I'll be a volunteer for a total of five years. If I say no then everything I've worked toward—my dream, my vision of a school for our students—will not happen.*

"The truck's fine. I was just trying to keep the budget down, but I wasn't planning on staying another two years. I've already been here three years."

"That's the only way I'll agree to it. I don't believe anyone else can do it, George. It's your vision. If you want it, you'll have to stay and do it."

"That means I'll be a Peace Corps volunteer for a total of five years. My plan was to get the school off the ground, go home, and let another volunteer take over where I leave off."

"Those are my conditions." I can tell he's sticking to it, and I look to the Peace Corps director for some help.

"Bill, can I actually do that? Can I be a volunteer that many years?"

"It can be arranged." I can tell he and Neb have already agreed.

"I need some time to think about this. How about if I let you know in one week what my decision is?"

"That's fine, but I need to know in one week if you're going to do it or not."

"All right, you'll have an answer by then."

It's a very hard week for me. I go back and forth between staying and going. Originally, I decided to stay for my third year because I didn't feel strong enough to go back into my own culture. I was afraid I'd fall right back into my old habits. Starting my third year, I made a goal to get myself ready, convince myself really, that I can go back and be okay. Recently, I've started looking forward to going home and being around my family and friends.

I feel stronger and much more confident about surviving in my own culture. I'm also very aware that I will soon be thirty-four years old, and I need to decide what I'm going to do with the rest of my life. I like what I'm doing here, but without a degree, I'll never be able to get a job designing schools for others in the United States. I know how to cook, and maybe if I start in a kitchen in a lower position, I can work my way back up to where I'm making decent money. Another option is for me to go back to school, assuming my ability to learn extends to a real university. The thought of being back in my own culture has become appealing to me. If I stay, that means I'll be a volunteer for five years. That's a long time to be away from home and out of the system without making any money.

At the same time, how many opportunities like this will I ever get in my life? Here's a chance to build and design a school the way that I want to. I want this to be a school that will last a lifetime and provide opportunities for hundreds of young kids. It's a chance to fulfill a dream I have of teaching young kids to be self-sufficient using agriculture and getting back to the land. I think part of me sees some of myself in those kids that are academically challenged.

My desire to build and develop the school is not as altruistic as it may sound. As much as I want to do it for the students, I want to do it for myself. It's a challenge, the biggest challenge I've ever been presented, and I want to know if I can do it. Not only is everyone here sure I can do it and 100 percent supportive, but they also "don't believe anyone else can do it." Once again, there's that instant empowerment that I seem to thrive on.

I started this journey thirty-two months ago with the awareness that freed my ability and desire to learn. I said then that, "I'll count my time and learning here as the college education I never had." Maybe now I've achieved my bachelor's degree, and this is my opportunity to go for my master's. The other factor, and maybe the most important one, is the fact that I've fallen in love with the people here. It has been so healing and rewarding for me to observe, learn, and become a part of this culture.

All these thoughts keep running through my head as I lay awake at night trying to decide what to do. I talk to friends, hoping to get some guidance, but it all comes down to me. I have to make the final decision.

After a torturous week of indecision, I decide to do it. I get word to Bill and Neb and tell them I'll stay for another two years and get the school started. Now I have to tell my family and friends back home.

50

The Chief

Once I agree to stay and manage the project, Neb promises to make sure I get the funding. The final figure is one hundred thousand U.S. dollars plus a brand new pickup truck. Now that I know for sure the money is coming, I have to start finalizing agreements.

I stop by to see the chief agriculture officer and give him the good news. He's been supportive of the school, and I'm depending on him to get the support I need from the ministry of agriculture. He's seated at his desk when I walk into his office.

"Good news, Chief. AID has agreed to give the money for the school."

"That's good news, but I think we should put the school at the agriculture station in Yo Creek." Not only is he not matching my excitement, but he also doesn't even seem interested.

"What? Why would we do that? That's not what we agreed to, and that's not what I told AID."

"It will be better there, I've decided."

"But all the planning and work is for the other location."

"Yo Creek will be better. You will see."

"But there's no school building there."

"We can build one with the money from AID."

"I'm not sure AID will agree to that, Chief."

"Yes, they will agree if they want the school."

"So that's it? You want the school in Yo Creek?"

"Yes, that's my decision."

I'm angry and disappointed, mostly angry. It's all I can do to keep from losing my temper with him. He hasn't done one thing to help me get to this point, and now he wants to make the decisions. The fact that it's his country and his people is the only thing that keeps me from telling him what I think of his decision. I still need his support if I'm going to build the school. I'm not sure what or why, but something has happened. The whole time I've worked on the school being in San Lazaro he's been in agreement. Now he changes his mind just when the money is approved. Somebody must have talked to him. I'm not sure what the problem is, but it goes against the vision I had when I first saw the abandoned school.

My proposal is based on bringing the existing buildings and land back to life, making use of the resources we already have on the land. It will be a living demonstration of exactly what we want to teach the students. That's the only way they'll learn how to be resourceful with what they have. The Yo Creek Agriculture Station doesn't have an abandoned school building on it. All it has are a few cabins for workers and a pig-breeding facility. I make an appointment to see Bill and Neb and then hop on a bus to Belize City.

"I won't fund it there, George," Neb says.

"I don't want it there either," Bill agrees.

"Somebody's convinced him to change the location."

"That could be, Bill, it does seem like someone has talked to him."

"You have to go back and tell him that we will fund the school at the original site or not at all."

"Do you mean that? The original site or no funding?" I look at Neb.

"I won't fund the school at Yo Creek, and that's final, George."

"Okay, I'll tell him."

Things are getting tight for me time wise. My home leave is coming up in a few months. If they're not going to let us do the school, I won't be taking "home leave." Instead, I'll have to start making plans for returning home permanently. I'll do my best to argue my case with the chief. I know that I need to be willing to let go of my vision, if it comes to that.

I start preparing myself for the possibility that I might be going home after all. Until now, all my energy has been directed toward getting the school up and running. Now I need to consider that it may not happen. I'm feeling the pressure, and I need to know, one way or the other.

The money from AID is the only leverage I have, but it's good leverage. Bright and early, I go in to see the chief ready to lay everything on the line.

"Chief, I went to see AID about doing the school in Yo Creek."

"Yes, and what did they say?"

"They said they will not give the money to build the school in Yo Creek. It has to be in San Lazaro at the original location."

"They will change their mind." He acted dismissive like we have all the time in the world.

"I don't think so. They don't like the idea."

"Well, let's bring them out and show them the site and convince them. They will change their minds."

I stand up, and putting both my hands on his desks, I lean down to eye level. I'm tired and angry about his attitude. I speak evenly but firm. "Look, Chief, I've been working too hard on this. I have everything lined up for the original location. I've made arrangements with both San Lazaro and Trinidad to host the school. The bishop and the Church have agreed to a ninety-nine-year lease at $1 a year. The Orange Walk Rotary Club has agreed to be the fiscal recipient. Peace Corps has agreed to provide volunteers to help staff the school, and USAID has agreed to fund it. I have the money and resources to make it happen. Now you change your mind, and I don't even know why. I'm telling you, the school goes where we planned it or it does not happen. There will be no money and I'll be on a plane to go home next week. Your decision, but I need to know right now what it's going to be—school or no school."

He looks at me like he doesn't know whether to kick me out or agree with me.

"We need this school, Chief. The students in the villages need it. We've worked too hard to get this far. Don't let it disappear."

"Okay, all right, do it in San Lazaro then." Leaning back in his chair, he looks frustrated or angry. I can't tell which and I don't really care.

"Will you still support it with the minister?"

"Yes, yes I will tell him." He seems reluctant, but he's nodding in agreement.

"Thank you, Chief, thank you. You won't regret it."

I leave his office with mixed feelings. I want the chief's support and now I don't feel like I have it. I have a feeling that someone put pressure on him and I'm not sure who. I head straight for a phone to call Bill.

"Bill, he changed his mind. He'll support the school in San Lazaro."

"What did he say?"

"Well, at first he didn't want to agree to it, but I told him it was San Lazaro or nothing."

"You think he wanted some money?" Bill asked.

"No, I think someone who wanted the school at Yo Creek talked to him and was putting pressure on him."

"Well, good job, George. I'm glad we got it."

"Yeah, now it's time to get to work."

"I'll call Neb and let him know."

"Thanks." I hang up the phone. I feel emotionally exhausted from being on the roller coaster of uncertainty. Now we're moving ahead, and that gives me a new surge of excitement and energy.

51

Finding Teachers

I know for the school to have credibility and be successful, we'll need well-known and respected teachers. I make a list of all the teachers and principals I've worked with over the last three years. I've gotten to know most of them in the classroom. There are several that I think can do the job, and I choose two that I feel have the qualities needed for a school like this.

Jose is my friend and the principal of the school in San Lazaro. He's a very patient and fair man who deals well with students and parents and is highly respected by both. He's also familiar with farming and cattle ranching.

Francisco is the principal of another school I work with. He's an excellent educator and disciplinarian. When he's teaching, you can be sure the students are learning and learning well because he will tolerate no less. But his problem is that he's not good at working with parents. He doesn't have the patience, and he could care less if they're happy as long as the students are learning.

Both men are well-known and respected in the community and the district. I talk to them, one at a time. I ask Jose to be the principal because he can work with the parents. I ask Francisco to be the vice principal so he can be the disciplinarian. They both understand the purpose of the school. It's something we've discussed many times. I explain to them that they'll have to be transferred to the ministry of agriculture since the school will be under them. They both like the idea and tentatively agree as long as it doesn't affect their status and tenure as teachers. I assure them that I'll do everything to make sure that doesn't change.

Earlier, with AID's help, we worked out a verbal agreement with the permanent secretary (the equivalent of an assistant cabinet secretary in the U.S. government) of the ministry of agriculture to sponsor the school. That means they will provide support and payment for teachers, agricultural resources, and school supplies.

To work out the arrangements for Jose and Francisco to be transferred to the ministry of agriculture, I'm working with the local area representative who is the minister of trade and industry. The school will benefit his constituency so it's to his advantage to promote it. I convince him to secure the release of the teachers by promising that the ministry of agriculture will pay their salaries, which has been agreed to by the permanent secretary (PS).

The last step is to go back to the ministry of agriculture and work out the final details. The capital of Belize is Belmopan, and I have to travel half a day by bus to get there. When I arrive, I discover that the permanent secretary we had worked out all of the arrangements with, Mr. G., is gone on long leave and will not be back for a year. The acting PS agrees to meet with me.

"Now what can I do for you?" He's talking down to me, and right away, I don't have a good feeling.

"Well, I met with Mr. G about one month ago regarding an agriculture school we're starting in the Orange Walk District, and I'm here to follow up on our agreement."

"Mr. G did not mention anything to me." My heart sank.

"Well, is there any way he can be contacted?"

"No, I'm afraid not. He has gone on long leave and will be out of the country for the next ten months. Is there something I can do?"

"I hope so. The agreement I made with Mr. G is for the ministry to provide the funding to pay for two teachers to staff the school."

"I'm sorry, but I'm afraid that's out of the question. We cannot afford to pay the salary of two teachers for a school we know nothing about." I feel like I've been kicked in the stomach.

"But you don't understand. I have been working on this for months, and everything is lined up, even the money that AID has agreed to provide to renovate the school. All I need now are the teachers and your support, which is what Mr. G had promised." I was pleading with him.

"Well, why don't you use the money for something else?" He has no idea what he's asking.

"I can't use the money for anything but a school."

"But there are plenty of things that much money can be used for. Why don't you start an agriculture project with some farmers?" He says this like it's the greatest idea in the world and will solve all my problems.

"No, I can't do that. We have plans and agreements in place." I can tell this guy has already made up his mind not to support my project. Maybe the same person who pressured the chief to change the location of the school got to this guy as well.

"Well, I cannot give you the teachers and that's final." He says this with a smile and a wave of his hand as if to dismiss me.

"All right well, thanks for your time." I don't want this guy to get the satisfaction of seeing me give up.

I leave his office feeling weak and discouraged. I've based my whole plan on the ministry of agriculture sponsoring the school and teachers, and now one person has just dismissed the whole idea. My vision is turning into a lot more work and worries than I ever thought possible. I can't let it get to me; this is one roadblock and there will be more. I'll just have to be a little more creative about how I do it.

The only thing left for me to do is turn to the ministry of education (MOE). They're the ministry I'm assigned to as a volunteer, and over the years, I've become friends with the chief education officer. I talk to him first and convince him to introduce the idea to his boss, the minister, for me. Then I go to see the area representative. I explain what happened at the ministry of agriculture. I tell him we need Education to give us the teachers. I specifically ask him to promote the idea "minister to minister" with the minister of education.

He seems supportive and promises to discuss it with him at their weekly meeting. I wait a week and go to see him at his home in Yo Creek.

"I'm checking to see if you had a chance to meet with the minister."

"Yes, I spoke to him about the school, Jorge, and he will agree to provide the teachers on the condition that the ministry of agriculture is paying the teacher's salary. He also wants the school to be turned over to the ministry after two years."

The condition about the teacher's salary being paid by the MOA was not something we had discussed, and I wasn't sure how to deal with it. They want nothing to do with the school, so I know they won't pay teachers. I quickly decide to go along with it and hope that by the time it's discovered, it's too late to withdraw support. I know that agreements made at the ministerial level don't always make it to the actual implementation.

"That's not a problem. In fact, that's exactly what we want to do once the school is up and running with an enrollment."

"Okay, you can go ahead with your plans, Jorge."

"Thank you very much, Minister P. I really appreciate your help and support." We shake hands.

"That's okay, Jorge."

Putting the school under the MOE means that we'll have to change our curriculum. We can still teach everything we want to teach, but we also have to meet the basic requirements established by the ministry for all schools if we want their credentials. I make an appointment to talk with the chief about our teachers and the curriculum.

"I came to check on the status of the teachers. Minister P told me he has worked things out with your boss."

"I have not heard anything, but let me check with the PS." He picks up his phone, and I hold my breath. *Oh no, please, not again.*

"Hello, PS. I have Mr. LeBard here to check on the status of the school in San Lazaro. Did the minister mention anything about that? He did, okay, thank you. Good news, George. The minister has approved two teachers for your school." I start breathing again.

"That's great news. Now I need to ask you a huge favor. Can I tell you the teachers I want?" I had mentioned to him earlier about the importance of having well-known, respected teachers to add credibility to the school.

"Yes, tell me who you want and I will tell you if I can do it."

"I would like to have Mr. Jose P. and Mr. Francisco B."

"I see. They are both currently principals and they won't be easy to replace.

"Whatever you can do is appreciated, Chief." I know I'm lucky to get anything so I don't want to push it. I especially don't want the issue of salary to come up.

"I'll see what I can do."

"Thank you, Chief. I appreciate your support."

"Not a problem. I wish you luck with your school."

"Thank you. And that reminds me, we need to develop our curriculum, and I could use your help." Before he was chief education officer, he had been head of the curriculum development unit. As a volunteer, I had participated in workshops he facilitated for developing curriculum materials.

"When you're ready, contact David at curriculum development, and he will set you up." David is technically still my Belizean supervisor and we're good friends.

"Sounds good, Chief. I'll take care of it."

"Not a problem. Let me know if you need anything." We shake hands and I leave with a big sigh of relief.

Things are starting to feel right again. Instead of trying to get me to do something else, the chief's supporting the school. It feels good to have support from the ministry, and I can sense that all the pieces are starting to fall in place.

52

Building a Road

On my way back to the village, I stop by to tell Jose and Francisco the good news. They still seem a little tentative about starting a new school. I can understand their hesitation since I'm asking them to give up their positions and do something that no one is even sure will work. Plus, right now there is no school and no students to be transferred to. It's a leap of faith and trust on their part.

One incentive that I'm able to offer them is a six-week course in tropical agriculture in Costa Rica. I included it in the budget, knowing they would benefit from the technical skills. They seem eager to attend the course and experience Costa Rica.

Everything's lining up, and now it's time to get to the physical work. It's the middle of May, and we want to start school in September. All we have is an empty building without doors, windows, or partitions. We also have six acres of land covered with jungle and loaded with dangerous snakes.

I decide the first thing we need is a road from the main road to the school so trucks will be able to get in and deliver sand, gravel, and other building materials. I've never built a road before. Everything I've done to get to this point has been backdoor negotiation, writing and rewriting proposals, promises, broken promises, and, finally, agreement. Now I'm about to do the first tangible, physical act to make the school a reality, and it's building a road.

It's important to me that I do it but I need help. I grab my machete and go to see if Arturo or one of his brothers is around.

"Hey, Arturo, get your machete. Vamos." I'm on my motorcycle, and Arturo is just about to walk into his house.

"Where are we going, Jorge?"

"We're going to build a road." I know the natural spontaneity of the Belizean culture, and I'm sure he can't resist the challenge I just offered.

"Okay, let me get my machete." He stops to talk to his father on the porch, and he comes back with his machete and a file.

"Wait, you will need this." It's Don Salus and he hands us an ax.

"Good idea. Thank you."

"Where are we making a road, Jorge?" Arturo's laughing as he climbs on my motorcycle, and I can tell he's excited about the idea.

"We're going to build a road from the main road to the front door of the school so trucks can come in with building materials."

When we reach the school, we calculate out where the entrance will be and then how wide the road needs to be. Once we have a rough idea, we start cutting down everything in our way. We spend the afternoon clearing trees and bush to make a passable road that leads to the front door of the school. It's only fifty yards but overgrown with thick vegetation.

We kill a few bad snakes in the process and we see a lot more. After killing a couple of tommygoffs, Arturo looks around and says with a nervous laugh, "There are a lot of bad snakes here, Jorge." That day, I learn that a "bad" snake will not run like the harmless snakes that try to get away. Instead, they hold their ground, ready to fight. We have to be on our toes all the time.

At the end of the day, we have our road. It doesn't look very pretty but it will work for starters. There is a big mound of dirt separating our road from the main road, and that will have to be leveled. I'll ask Mr. Martinez from Trinidad if he can bring his tractor to knock that down. There are still a few stumps that have to be removed, but I decide to come back and work on that myself. Arturo and I have done the hard part and the rest is easy. Now we can start building the school.

53

Him or Me

In accordance with my grant requirements, I hire two carpenters—one from San Lazaro and one from Trinidad. I have to make sure both villages benefit equally from the project. Men from both communities come out and spend a day clearing the bush around the school with their machetes. San Lazaro is cleaning one half and Trinidad is cleaning the other half, and they're in competition to see who can clean the best. I go crazy trying to keep them from cutting down everything in sight. There are a few fruit trees and shade trees I want to save. In the end, we're able to save an avocado tree and a custard apple tree. Everything else is cut down.

In the tropics, when you cut down bush, you leave it lie until it dries, then you burn it. After a couple of weeks, we're ready to burn the fallen bush around the school. First, we have to make some fire paths so we don't burn down the school, the teacher's house, and the two trees I saved. I'm working by the teacher's house, clearing a wide path around the custard apple tree. Instead of a rake, I'm using a tree branch with some smaller branches on it when I hear leaves rustling behind me. I turn around just in time to see a huge snake coming at me. Reacting immediately, I jump out of the way just as he strikes out at me. He misses and goes into a coil ready to strike again, his body constantly moving. This is the biggest snake I've ever seen, and he's mad about something. My skinny, little branch feels too fragile to be a weapon. But I can't let him go either because sooner or later, we'll meet again. I back out of his way and run to get my machete. I see Manuel and tell him and Mr. Blanco to come and back me up. We go after the snake armed with machetes and Manuel's shotgun. But he's gone and we can't find him. Manuel suggests we go ahead and light the fire to force him out of hiding.

The bush burns hot and fast. We watch the same spot I last saw the snake, waiting for him to make a run for it. The fire burns out and still no sign of him. There is only one place he could have escaped—under the custard apple tree.

I'm walking around the tree with my machete, and Manuel is a few feet behind me with his shotgun. I take a couple of steps when Manuel says, "Don't move, Jorge." I look down and see the snake in-between my legs, camouflaged in the green grass. I had almost stepped on him. He isn't coiled. He's stretched out to his full length and very still but not dead. Manuel slowly puts the shotgun a few feet from his head and fires. Then I move as fast and as far as I can. I'm shaking because I almost let this damn snake get me twice. Once is excusable but not twice.

He's dead now. We pick him up carefully with the end of a machete half expecting him to come back to life. Manuel and Mr. Blanco measure him out at a little over six feet of one badass snake. It's a tommygoff. Mr. Blanco says it's the same kind of snake that killed his father, even the same size and color.

I'm nervous now so I stay on snake alert for the rest of the day, jumping at anything that moves within my vision. Manuel tells me I should get a cat because they're good for killing snakes. The next day, I go to the village and find someone who has kittens. We now have an official school cat.

54

The Green Truck

I had agreed earlier to go on a trip with Matt and some high school students he's working with. They planned a twenty-mile bike ride to visit the village of Progresso, which is popular for its saltwater lagoon and sandy beaches. He asked me to follow along on my motorcycle to keep him company and be there with fast transportation in case there were any emergencies.

To keep myself from getting bored, I drive ahead a few miles at a time and then double back. When we're five miles from the village, I drive ahead to the entrance and turn around.

The dirt road is rough so I'm only going about twenty miles an hour and staying in the middle of the road to avoid potholes. I'm just outside the village when I hear someone blowing their horn. I look in my rearview mirror and see a truck coming up fast, about a quarter mile behind me. I move over to my side of the road but he keeps his hand on the horn. *What's wrong with this guy? He has the whole road.*

By this time, I'm as far to the right as I can go without going off the road, and his hand is still on the horn. I can see him in my rearview mirror right behind me; his right bumper is just inches from my motorcycle. *This guy wants to run me over.* I can't speed up because the road's too rough, and if I slow down, he'll hit me. I turn to make eye contact, and he speeds up swerving in sharply to hit the front wheel of my bike. *I'm going down.* I look for a license plate but there is none, so I remember it's a green Chevy with wooden sideboards.

The bike goes one way and I go the other. After skidding to a stop on my forearms and elbows, I get up and inspect the damage to my motorcycle. The headlight's broken and the handle bar's twisted. Both my arms and elbows have a serious case of road rash and are bleeding. Because it's still early morning, I have my Levi jacket on, which protected me from getting hurt worse.

The truck is long gone and all I can see is a cloud of dust. He sped away as soon as I went down. I look around to see if there are any witnesses. There's a woman standing in front of a small bush house on the side of the road. I walk over, making myself as calm as possible. I know villagers tend to mind their own business, and I don't want to scare her off with any display of emotion.

"Excuse me, miss, did you see the truck that just passed?"

"Yes, suh, I mi si," she said, nodding her head.

"Do you know who was driving it?"

"No, suh, mi no know who di drive." She was shaking her head.

"Do you know who the truck belongs to?"

"Yes suh. Da de truck fi Mr. Zul." (name changed to protect the guilty)

"Does he live in the village?"

"Me no know where he di live." I can tell she doesn't want to say any more.

"Thank you, miss."

"Yes, suh."

I go back to my bike and pick it up. It starts right up, but I'll have to straighten out the steering before I can drive it. Matt and the kids are still on the road, but there's nothing I can do to warn them about this maniac.

About twenty minutes later, they ride up.

"Jorge, what happened? Did you wreck?"

"Some guy hit me on purpose. Did you see a green truck?"

"No, we didn't see anyone."

"He must have turned off on one of the cane roads then."

"You think he hit you on purpose?"

"I know he did." I explain to Matt exactly what had happened.

"What are you going to do?"

"Help me straighten out the bike, and then I'm going to report this guy to the police."

We get the bike as straight as we can and I drive into town to find the police station. There's one policeman, a Creole man whose name badge says Inspector Jones.

"I want to report a hit and run."

"Yes, suh. What exactly is the problem?" I can see him retreat into his position of authority.

"Some guy driving a truck hit me on purpose."

"Can you identify the driver?"

"No, but I know who the truck belongs to."

"Who is that, suh?"

"Mr. Zul. Do you know the man?"

"Yes, I know the family."

"I want him charged for assault with a deadly weapon." He smiles.

"We do not have such a law here."

"Well, he intentionally tried to hurt me using his truck as a weapon." I'm still angry.

"The most I can charge him with is careless driving and leaving the scene of an accident."

"But he did more than that."

"Maybe he did, but that is the law in Belize."

"Do you know where he lives?"

"Yes, suh. We can go there but you should go to the clinic first and get your injuries taken care of."

"No, I want to go there first."

"Okay, let me lock up the station and we can walk over there."

We walk through the streets with everyone looking at us. An angry gringo with bloody arms walking through the village with a cop is not a common sight. We come to a house on the north side of the village. There are several women, young and old, washing laundry outside. When they see us heading toward them, they begin to talk low amongst themselves.

"Good morning, ladies. We are looking for Mr. Zul. Is he at home?"

"No, he is not here." They look angry.

"Do you know where he is?"

"He took the bus to town this morning." They don't look at me, just the cop.

"Does he own a green truck?" They look at each other and the older one nods her head yes.

"Do you know where the truck is?"

"His nephew Miguel has the truck and he went to the cane field."

"Thank you."

We go back out to the road with the ladies watching us suspiciously. We stop there to decide our next move. While we're standing there, a group of teenage boys approach us.

"Inspector, we want to report this boy who tried to run us over in his truck. We want you to talk to him." They're upset and angry.

"What boy is that?"

"Miguel Zul."

"Tell me what happened."

"We were walking on the road and he came at us blowing his horn. We had to jump in the bush or he would have run us over."

"Was he driving a green truck?"

"Yes, suh. He was driving Mr. Zul's truck, the same man that lives right here."

"Do you want to come down to the police station and file a formal complaint?" They look at each other and I can tell they don't want to do it. I also know it will help my case if they do.

"Yes, why don't you file a complaint? I'm going to because he did the same thing to me on my motorcycle." They look at each other again.

"Yes, we will go later."

"Please do. Otherwise, this guy will get away with nothing happening to him."

"Yes, suh."

"Good, thank you."

The policeman and I walk back to the police station. The clinic's located directly across the street so I stop there to get my wounds cleaned up. The nurse scrubs them with soap and water, getting all the sand and gravel out of the cuts and applies some hydrogen peroxide. Then she wraps my forearms with bandages. I know I have to be careful of infection, which is common in the tropics.

I'm coming out of the clinic when the policeman meets me. He has a young boy with him. The kid is short, muscular, and around seventeen years old.

"Mr. George, this is Miguel Zul. He has something to say to you."

"Mr. George, it was an accident. I am sorry, suh." He's scared and pleading with me.

"No, that was no accident. You did it on purpose."

"Please, suh. I am sorry. I will pay for all the damage to your motorcycle."

"What the hell were you thinking?"

"Suh, I am sorry. Please believe me. If you will not press charges, I will pay for all damages."

"I am pressing charges. You should be punished for what you did." The policeman calls me over to one side.

"I advise you to take the payment he is offering. Otherwise, it may be hard to win for damages in court."

"But that means he gets off free."

"Well, at least he will pay something. If you go to court, you may not get anything."

"I see what you mean." I know I should take his advice, but it makes me mad to see him get away.

"All right, I'll take my bike in for an estimate on parts and repair and you'll pay for it."

"Yes, suh. Thank you, suh. You just give me the bill and I will take care of it."

Then Inspector Jones tells the boy to go wait in the police station and he stays to talk with me.

"You can give the bill to me if you have it by Wednesday. I have to go into Orange Walk Town, and I can meet you at the police station. Then you do not have to come all the way out here."

"Okay, I can do that. I'll meet you on Wednesday."

I leave them and go to find Matt and the students. They're at the beach swimming so we hang around for a couple of hours before heading back.

First thing Monday morning, I take my bike in for an estimate. The cost is over five hundred dollars for parts and repair. I have it listed out and signed on an official invoice. On Wednesday, I take it to Inspector Jones. He promises to get it to Miguel. I tell him I'll check on it over the weekend.

On Saturday, I drive my bike to Progresso and find Miguel's house. A woman comes out and angrily tells me that he's not there. I ask where he is and she tells me to go away. I'm determined to find him, so I ride around the village, asking people if they know where I can find Miguel Zul. Someone tells me he's at his brother's for some kind of celebration. I find the house and ask for him. He comes outside with five guys to talk to me.

"What do you want, gringo?" He's being cocky and I can tell he's drunk.

"Did you get the bill for my repairs?" I wasn't prepared for the attitude.

"I am not paying you anything." I want to grab him and choke the crap out of him, but I know I need to be careful. I'm on his turf, and he has his friends and relatives to back him up.

"But that was the agreement. I don't press charges and you pay for damages."

"It wasn't my fault you crashed your motorcycle." He's talking tough now.

"Okay, if that's the way you want to do it then we'll go to court." More people are in the yard now, and I'm starting to feel surrounded so I start backing out toward my bike.

"Get out of here, gringo."

"That's okay, Miguel. I'll see you in court."

I get on my bike and go to look for the policeman. The police station is locked up so I ask someone on the street if they know where he is.

"Excuse me, do you know where Inspector Jones is?"

"You will find him at Soli's shop. Today is his birthday and he is celebrating."

"Thank you."

I drive over a couple of streets to find the shop. Parking my bike, I go inside and find him drinking beer at the counter and talking to Soli.

"Hello, Inspector."

"Hello, Jorge." It's just after lunch, and I can tell he already has a good start on his beers.

"I just went to see Miguel about the bill, and he doesn't want to pay now. He said he wants to go to court."

"Then we shall take him to court. Come and have a beer with me. It is my birthday."

"All right, thank you." I'm ready for a beer after my confrontation with Miguel and friends. I figure I'll have one or two beers with him and then hit the road. I should have known better. He pulls out a hundred-dollar bill and tells Soli to keep them coming. We grab a table in the corner of her shop and sit down.

About four hours and a lot of beers later, I have a new best friend. I notice it's starting to get dark and remember I don't have a working headlight on my bike.

"I have to go, Norman."

"No, mon. Have one more beer. Di road still di dey."

"But I don't have a headlight, and I have to drive twenty miles just to get to Orange Walk and then ten more miles to San Lazaro all on a rough road." Not to mention how drunk I am.

"Just one more beer, my friend."

"All right, one more."

When I get on my bike, it's twilight and I'm a little worried about Miguel and his merry band of friends coming after me in the green truck. I look around to see if anyone's watching me leave, and besides a few kids playing soccer, I don't see anyone.

I start out fast to get as many miles out of the remaining light as I can. Right away, the flying bugs that come out at dusk become a problem, hitting me in the eyes and blinding me. The only protection I have are my sunglasses, but when I put them on, I can't see well. In fact, the only thing I can see is the outline of the road because it's made out of white marl. Everything outside the white road looks black. It's either poor vision, or bugs in my eyes. I figure if I just stay on the white and away from the dark outlines, I'll be all right with my sunglasses on. Lining both sides of the road are sugarcane fields and jungle.

For the first few miles, everything goes fine, and then I see a dark spot coming up in the road. I assume it's just a dark spot in the road and keep going. The next thing I know, I'm in the air landing upside down with the bike on top of me. The engine's racing and I smell gas spilling from the gas tank. I find the ignition switch and turn it off. Now I have to get the bike off of me.

I've hit a big pile of sugarcane that someone's dropped in the middle of the road. Looking around, I see headlights coming from the direction of Progresso.

It must be Miguel and the green truck. Panicked, I push the bike off and get up. I do a quick assessment. Besides a couple of scratches, I'm okay. My front brake cable has come off, and I quickly tie it in a loop and hang it around my neck so I won't lose it. The headlights are getting closer. I start the bike and take off. The bugs are not out anymore so I take off my sunglasses. I can see the road much better now and I increase my speed.

I make it to Orange Walk safely and stop in a bar to have another beer. I know the road to San Lazaro like the back of my hand, so I'm not worried about making it home, which I do around midnight.

55

Court

The laws in Belize were handed down from the British, and the prosecutor in a small court case like mine is the same arresting policeman. To go to court with Miguel is the responsibility of Inspector Jones. He has to prepare the case and present it to the judge. The only thing I have to do is show up.

I'm called to the witness stand and sworn in.

"Do you promise to tell the truth, the whole truth, and nothing but the truth, so help you God?"

"I do."

Inspector Jones puts me on the witness stand and asks me to explain what happened. I calmly begin to describe the incident and everything that happened.

"Mr. George, please speak slower, suh."

"Okay, sorry." I don't feel like I'm talking too fast, but I make an effort to talk slower.

"Please, suh, slow down. You are talking too fast." I start talking again even slower.

"Mr. George, the judge has to write down your words as you speak and you are going too fast."

"Oh okay, sorry. I'll speak slower." I didn't realize the judge is handwriting everything I say.

Once I slowly, explain my side of the story, they call Miguel to the stand. He says that I jumped off of my motorcycle, and he had nothing to do with it. The judge patiently listens and writes down everything that both of us say.

Inspector Jones does his best in questioning Miguel, but he's definitely no prosecutor.

After we both present our sides of the story, the judge takes a few minutes to review his notes and finds Miguel guilty of failing to stop at the scene of an accident and careless driving. His driver's license is suspended for one year, and he's ordered to pay me a hundred and fifty dollars. I turn to Inspector Jones.

"Why a hundred and fifty dollars? The damage is over five hundred dollars."

"This court can only award you that amount, and if you accept it, you cannot ask for more. If you want more, you will have to go to civil court and sue him. What would you like to do?"

"I'll take him to civil court and sue. I want him to pay for all the damages."

"Okay, that is your decision."

After court, I thank Inspector Jones, Norman, for his help.

"What do I have to do to take him to civil court?"

"You will have to get a lawyer for that, Mr. George."

"All right, well, thanks for all your help."

"That is nothing, suh."

There's only one lawyer in all of Orange Walk Town, and he only visits his office there one day a week, on Tuesdays. I explain the case to him and he agrees to take it.

"I will need a retainer fee."

"How much?"

"Twenty dollars is enough."

"Okay, here you go."

"I will contact you when we have a court date."

"Thank you."

After one month, I still haven't heard anything so I go back to check with the lawyer. His office is closed and his sign's been removed. His neighbors tell me he's gone and won't be back. He took my twenty dollars with him. I think about it for a while and decide I'm way too busy with the school to run around trying to find a lawyer and get a case going. As much as I hate to do it, I'll have to cut my losses and let it go.

56

Building a School

After a couple of months, the school is beginning to look like something. At least now we can see it from the road. I'm living in the teacher's house without doors or windows so I can keep an eye on our building materials. Every night, someone from the village comes over to keep me company. It's usually one of the Eck brothers: Arturo, Thomas, or Rodel. Although there are many things that can be stolen, nothing is ever taken.

Every day, I'm busy keeping the carpenters stocked with materials or working on other aspects of the school. We don't have architectural drawings, only plans that I drew with a pencil using a tape measure and a ruler. Besides adding doors, windows, and partitions, we're building real bathrooms with a septic tank, an enclosed veranda, storage shed, an outdoor classroom, nursery, and a water system.

I need to recruit a board of directors to act as the management of the school. I choose individuals based on their affiliation with the school. I have someone from our hosting villages, San Lazaro and Trinidad, the Catholic Mission, the ministry of education, Peace Corps, Rotary Club and, grudgingly, the ministry of agriculture. Even though the ministry of agriculture let me down, I still want and need their involvement.

I have to keep track of every penny I spend with receipts to back it up. I usually work from sunup to sundown and save the book work for the evenings. I've never been too good with numbers but I'm learning. The USAID expects monthly financial reports and I need to make sure I do it right.

Something comes up almost every day. Just when I think things are going fine, we discover a problem with our water supply. The property has a well with a hand pump. We quickly discover that after ten minutes of pumping water, it goes dry. We then have to wait another thirty minutes for it to fill up again. If we want to grow crops, we'll need a better water supply, and that means digging a deeper well. I convince the ministry of health to send out a team with their drilling outfit to look for another, more reliable water source. After two weeks and two dozen deep dry holes, we give up. Then right on schedule, an old timer from down the road stops by.

"Hi, Mr. Tillett. How are you?"

"Good, good. Thank you." He's checking out the progress on the school.

"So what do you think? How does it look?"

"Very good, Jorge. Very good."

"Thank you. We still have a lot to do."

"Oh yes, no true?"

"We're looking for a better water source, but we can't find one."

"Da only good wata ina this piece a land de right de wa unu got da well." (The only water on this piece of land is right where the well is.) He says this with authority.

"What? How do you know that?" We just spent two weeks looking everywhere for water.

"Cause when dem build da school, dem me look everywhere fu wata, and dat da only spot de could find."

"Well, the same thing just happened. Didn't you see them out here drilling the last couple of weeks?"

"Yes, a mi si dem, and a mi know dem people no goin find no wata." I notice a sense of satisfaction that his prediction came true.

I want to ask him, "*Why* didn't you tell us instead of watching us waste our time?"

Since we can't find another water source, I have to come up with a different strategy. I think the well will provide sufficient water if we have something to store it in. We need a pump that works slow enough to keep the well from going dry and consistent enough to keep an elevated storage tank filled with water. There are working windmills around and that may be the solution. The Mennonite community uses them, and most villages have nonfunctioning models displayed like antiques left over from earlier days. The problem is they don't make them anymore, and no one wants to give up something from their village history.

One day, I stop to eat some tacos in Orange Walk, and as I'm standing there, I notice the fins of a windmill stacked up behind a warehouse. I walk over and do a closer inspection. It's in a million pieces but it looks like everything's there. It belongs to the ministry of health, and after a few phone calls, they give permission for the school to use it. I get a cane truck and haul it away before they have a chance to change their mind.

The next day, I hire a Mennonite to put it up for us. He gets it up with a pump installed and it works perfectly. The next thing I do is get a galvanized water tank and elevate it to twenty feet on a cement platform that Manuel builds for me. It works, the windmill keeps the tank full, and we now have a good reliable source of water.

Things are beginning to take shape. We want to start school in September and that's only two months away. We still need to recruit students, but I figure Jose and Francisco can work on that when they get back from Costa Rica. I have plenty of other things to keep me busy.

57

Corruption at the Highest Levels

I've been working hard and it's showing. Last night, Mr. Eck told me my neck is getting thick. That's about as good a compliment as you'll get around here. Since I quit smoking two years earlier, I've put on forty pounds, from 150 to 190 pounds. I was pretty skinny to begin with but now my six-foot frame is filled out, and my overall health is better.

Getting the school ready requires a lot of physical as well as mental work. I spend many days with a shovel, mixing cement by hand and unloading blocks and lumber. I work closely with the carpenters to calculate the materials we need on a daily basis. I'm still doing my yoga and meditation every morning so I feel strong, healthy, and focused.

Working on the new school is officially my new Peace Corps assignment. Sometimes, it's stressful and things don't go as smooth as I expect them to. Once in a while, I go into town to relax and visit the other volunteers.

It's Sunday and Matt has invited me to his Belizean girlfriend's house to watch a football game. His girlfriend is from one of the wealthier families in town, and they're one of the few who have cable television. They also happen to be well-connected to the same political party that's currently in power, the People's United Party (PUP). It's also the same family the "grim reaper" stayed with while he set up some drug business with Victor.

We're in the house, relaxed, watching TV, when someone starts blowing their car horn. Instantly, people I didn't even know were in the house start moving outside. I look out the window and see a pickup truck with a camper shell backed into the driveway. Matt tells me to come with him. I follow, wondering what all the action's about.

We go outside, and there's an assembly line of men passing something from a dark storeroom to the back of the truck. It looks like they're planning on filling it and they're in a hurry. We get in line and start passing packages that weigh about a kilo (2.2 pounds) and are packed in green garbage bags.

"Matt, is this what I think it is?"

"Don't ask, Jorge. Don't ask, and don't act like you know anything." He's whispering.

Then, I notice the driver of the truck. I haven't seen him since the time he gave me a ride to San Lazaro and interviewed me. It is the honorable minister of energy and communication. He stands in the doorway of his truck, talking to the man of the house while we load his truck up with kilos. He doesn't seem to notice me, or, he doesn't care. I put my head down and keep a low profile once I recognize him. Afterward, he takes off with a full load of packed garbage bags. The workers disappear to wherever they came from, and we go back to watch our football game.

Now a minister in the government is a very powerful person. Some people say they are too powerful. They can do pretty much whatever they want and get away with it. The only problem is that Belize is too small to keep secrets, and eventually, people talk and word gets around. But ministers make up for their indiscretions by doing a few favors here and there. They can change the average person's life with the stroke of a pen or a verbal command that can mean the difference between ownership of land and dispossession. People have a short memory when the government gives their son or daughter a job or they get a piece of property they want. There are many rewards that can be had with the blessing of a government minister. There can also be consequences. Just as they can give jobs or land, they can also take them away.

I know things have been progressing with the drug trade. The runway for small planes is located just a couple of miles behind the school. I can tell they're busy with the amount of planes that land every day.

The Belize Defense Force goes out every so often with explosives and blows big holes in the runway. We hear the explosions from the school. Then we watch the soldiers pass by waving to us as they're leaving.

Whenever they blow up the runway, it's fixed the very next day. The minister of works, who happens to be the brother of the minister of energy and communication, sends out heavy-duty road machinery to repair the damage. There's hardly any interruption to planes landing and it's business as usual. It's like watching a bad comedy and it might be funny, if drugs and violence weren't involved.

58

Danger at Home

Victor with his natural leadership skills has become the chief drug lord. I'm no longer hanging out with him on a regular basis. We're both too busy. I'm busy with the school and he's busy with the drug business. Plus, he always has his "men" with him. They're armed, serious-looking guys, and I don't find them much fun to be around. We're still friends; we just don't do things together like we used too.

I do become friends with his right-hand man. Antonio is from El Salvador, and he's been fighting with a rifle since he was twelve years old. He has the scars and old bullet wounds to prove it. He has an imposing presence, bigger than most Belizeans and strong. He's a natural leader, like Victor, but younger with a quick temper. He's more likely to jump into a fight while Victor would rather walk the long way around if it meant avoiding bloodshed. Antonio and Arturo are in charge when Victor's not around. I'm still eating with the Eck's every night, and he is usually around when I go. He likes Arturo's sister, Socorro, who is also my ex-first baseman from the softball team. Antonio likes to practice his English with me.

I like Antonio and I feel like we're friends. I know he can be dangerous from hearing stories about his past and the gun he always carries. He accepts me because the Eck family lets me into their home and because I'm friends with Victor and Arturo. I know he can be a good friend to have around in times of trouble. A big part of his job is to protect Victor.

Rival gangs are establishing their turf, but that doesn't seem to bother Victor. He tells me, "There is enough for everyone, Jorge." New faces are appearing in the village almost daily, most of them aliens. They're guns for hire to the highest bidder. I have to be careful because these strangers don't know who I am or how I fit into the village. Most of these guys have survived brutal civil wars in Guatemala or El Salvador. Many of them are aware about American and CIA involvement in these wars. I can see and feel the angry stares from them when they see me walking around. A couple of times, I'm hassled, but as long as I'm in the village where everyone knows me, I feel safe.

It's already dark, past dinner time, and I'm late and in a hurry walking from my house to Arturo's for dinner, which is a distance of one hundred yards. There are three strangers standing on the corner, talking in front of Victor's house. As I approach, their attention turns toward me.

"Hey, gringo, where do you think you're going?" They're speaking Spanish, but I know they just challenged me and I don't like them.

"Hello." I keep walking, changing my direction slightly to make a wider path around them. I smile in a friendly way even though I'm angry that they're challenging me on my own turf.

"Gringo, we're talking to you." Now they block my way. I decide to bluff it out. All I have to do is get past them to safety at Arturo's or Victor's house less than fifty feet away.

"Okay, no problem." I'm forced to stop and they close in, circling me.

"Hello, my friends, is there a problem here?" It's Arturo and he's smiling, but it's a smile that says you're in my turf so watch your step. They look at Arturo who has come to stand beside me as he puts one hand on my shoulder and the other on his hip.

"We are talking to the gringo." One is still talking tough, but I can see the other two are already starting to back down. I'm definitely feeling better because now I have the upper hand. They just don't know it yet.

"Jorge is our friend." It's Antonio, and he's not smiling. He's come up a little ways behind them and to their blind side. One of his hands is behind his back and I know he has his gun out. They turn to look at Antonio. At the same time, Thomas and Don Salus come up on their right side. Now they're outnumbered and they start talking low among themselves. Victor steps out his front door and asks, "What's going on?" He directs his question to Arturo.

"We are talking to our friends here," he responds with a smile.

"Yes, we are leaving. We have made a mistake. We are sorry." It's one of the strangers.

"That's no problem. We wish you a good visit to our village, no true, Jorge?" Arturo looks at me and grips my shoulder reassuringly.

"Yes, have a good visit in San Lazaro." I'm smiling now. I agree with Arturo; there is no need to make enemies.

"We are looking for work. Do you have work here?" The leader of the three is directing his question at Victor, who ignores him and goes back into his house. *These guys are guns for hire, and someone must have directed them to Victor's house.*

"We have no work, but try the next village up the road. They might have something," Arturo responds for Victor in a friendly way and points up the road toward Trinidad.

The three men walk away and Antonio stays to watch them. I'm walking to the kitchen with Arturo, and he's laughing at the predicament I had gotten into.

"What happened, Jorge? Where did you meet your new friends?"

"They were right there on the corner when I was coming over."

"We know, Jorge, we were watching them. We saw the whole thing happen."

"What took you guys so long to get there?"

"Don't worry, we were not going to let them get you."

While I'm being teased by everyone, Victor comes over to make sure everything is okay.

"Are you all right, Jorge?" He's standing across the dinner table from me.

"Yes, I'm fine. I was just about to kick their butts when you guys showed up to save them." Everyone starts laughing.

"We saved those guys, no true, Jorge?" They're all laughing.

"Yes, you saved them." They're still laughing, but then Victor turns serious.

"Don't worry, Jorge. You have friends here. We will not let guys like that get you." He was reading my mind because I was worried.

"Thanks, I appreciate that."

At that point, Rodel hollers from the bathhouse. "Jorge, guess what I am doing." Then he laughs like a maniac.

Antonio is still on the street keeping watch when I go home. I feel better knowing he's there. Luckily this time, my friends were here to protect me, but what if they had not been there? I have to be careful. There are too many new faces in the village everyday now. Big money and big people are getting involved. Some days I see as many as a dozen small planes coming and going. I know people will start getting greedy and want more than their share and then there won't be "enough for everyone." Every day, I'm hearing stories about people killing each other over drugs and turf wars. It's not uncommon now to hear automatic weapons being fired on a daily basis. Sometimes they're close, too close.

59

The Mennonites

Roadblocks are being set up on a daily basis now by both the Belize Defense Force (BDF) and the drug dealers. The BDF have to work with the local police because according to the Belizean Constitution, they're not allowed to stop the public. Only the police can do that with the BDF as backup. We never know where or when a roadblock might be and they have them day and night.

The BDF stops are harder to get through, and sometimes I'm searched while guns are pointed at me. The ones set up by the drug dealers are easier. They know exactly who they're looking for. When the BDF set up a roadblock, it's because they have to make a show of force for the public. When the drug dealers do it, it's because someone has cheated them and they want their money or drugs back. They also want revenge and that means someone's life. But they know exactly who they want. Even though I know this, it doesn't help the brief moment of fear I feel when I turn a corner on my motorcycle and guns are pointing at me.

The drug wars between rival gangs are getting worse. I stay focused on getting the school ready, but all around me is violence and bloodshed. It's pretty easy to tell who's involved, and I do my best to stay away from them. They're the ones driving new trucks with bodyguards and guns.

Lately, I've been hearing stories that even some of the Mennonite farmers are growing the new crop. That's hard for me to believe, knowing the Mennonites that I've been working with. They seem wholesome in all ways.

In the process of rebuilding the school, I need to buy lumber on a regular basis. The closest sawmill is in a Mennonite community called Shipyard, located about twelve miles from the school. I go there every week for lumber and furniture.

Each week, I place my order ahead of time, and every time, I have to wait several hours while they mill the last of it. I still have enough Americanism in me to be on time even though I know they won't be.

While I wait, I pass the time talking with an old man who works at the mill. Benjamin is a leader in the community. He's around sixty years old and looks like a typical Mennonite dressed in overalls and a straw hat. One day, I asked him how they govern themselves since the Belize government does not usually interfere in their business. Is there crime? If there is, how do they handle it? He explains to me that their community of approximately six hundred is divided into smaller "camps," and each camp has a leader. Once a month, the leaders from all the camps meet and discuss any particular issues they may be dealing with. If there is a problem, they decide how to best deal with it, and their word is law for everyone who lives in the community.

I ask him, "What kind of issues do you have to deal with?" That's when he gets into the story that he's ashamed to tell me but tells me anyway.

"I shame fu tell yu, I shame fu tell yu." Most Mennonites speak Creole, Spanish, and English in addition to their first language, High German.

"Now that you have my interest, you have to tell me."

"Buoy, I shame fu true."

"Well, go ahead and tell me because we have at least an hour before this lumber's ready."

It seems this one family was giving them some unusual problems. The woman had about six kids right in a row, and now she's pregnant again. Some of the older women in the community were worried because this woman and her kids always looked sickly, and she seemed very depressed. With a little investigating, they discovered that they were not getting enough to eat.

Now as a rule of their society all members of a Mennonite community are entitled to paid employment. They take care of themselves before they hire any "outsiders." Everyone has a job. It might be in one of the lumber yards, farming, the grocery store, or working with livestock. The man of the house for this particular family worked in a shop, making furniture, and he was getting a regular paycheck. The problem was that the money wasn't making it home. He wasn't providing for his family, and there was no food in the house with six small children.

"Where were the paychecks going?"

"I shame fu tell yu. I shame fu tell yu." Benjamin's shaking his head while he says this.

"When this man got paid every week, he went to Orange Walk and spent all his money on cigarettes, booze, and whores."

"You mean he gave nothing to his family?" This guy sounds sick.

"Nothing, he gave nothing to his family, I shame fo tell yu."

"So what happened? What did you guys do?"

"We arranged for his paycheck to come to us."

"Then you paid the bills and made sure there was enough food for his family?"

"Yes, and we gave him a small allowance for his cigarettes after everything was paid."

"Did that work out all right?" I thought it was generous that they gave him anything at all.

"Yes, but then the women reported that the new baby was not healthy."

"What was wrong with it?"

"Buoy, I shame fo tell yu," he said, shaking his head again.

"Was he doing something to the baby?"

"That son of a bitch was drinking all the breast milk from his wife and not leaving enough for the baby."

"This guy is sick, Benjamin. What did you do then?"

"We had a very serious talk with him and told him if he did not stop drinking the baby's milk and start providing for his family, he will be excommunicated."

"Did that work?"

"Yes it worked, so far."

Benjamin says that's the worst problem they've ever encountered in their community.

He also tells me there's no violence or robberies within the community. However, they do have to watch out for outsiders. Sometimes, there are people who show up in their community that look like they're checking everything out for an opportunity to steal or rob. When that happens, they band together and approach the strangers to ask what their business is. If it's legitimate, they leave them alone but keep one eye on them.

Across the country, there are several Mennonite communities at different levels of religion and conservatism. They come to Belize from Canada, Mexico, or Bolivia. The communities they live in are identified by their geographic location. There are the Shipyard Mennonites, Spanish Lookout Mennonites, Barton Creek Mennonites, and the Blue Creek Mennonites.

I'm more familiar with the Shipyard Mennonites. They lean toward the higher end of the scale in conservatism. They all wear the same thing every day just like a uniform. For the men, it's overalls and straw cowboy hats. For the women, it's plain dresses, down to the floor and high around the neck, with an apron and a wide brim bonnet. The kids dress exactly the same and look like miniature adults.

They have a rule that allows them to travel with rubber wheels if the vehicle doesn't have an engine, like a horse and buggy. If it does have an engine, like a tractor, it has to have iron or steel wheels. Supposedly, this helps to separate them from the outside world and keeps them moving at a slower pace. The only problem with that theory is the fact that they're always hiring outsiders with trucks to take them and/or their wares someplace, usually to interact with the outside world. They're good farmers and are always selling whatever crops may be in season like peanuts or watermelon.

The other community of Mennonites that are close by are the Blue Creek Mennonites. They're about twenty-six miles from San Lazaro, close to the three corners where Belize's border meets Mexico and Guatemala. Blue Creek is the most liberal Mennonite community in the country. There is no rubber-wheel rule and no uniforms. In fact, I've seen Blue Creek Mennonite girls wearing shorts and driving motor scooters. Most of them are wealthy, and all of them have trucks, cars, and tractors. A few have airplanes and their own landing strips. Several Mennonite companies out of Blue Creek do road contracts for the Belize government with heavy equipment. The first hydroelectric plant in the country was established in Blue Creek. Their farmers are first rate, and they produce much of the country's rice and beans. These are also the Mennonites that are supposedly involved in the drug trade.

I find the Mennonites to be very resourceful people, and surrounding villages benefit from the services they provide. Mennonite communities are where we go for lumber, furniture, chickens, eggs, animal feed, a mechanic, welder, groceries, and hardware. If I need something, I can either find it with them or they'll make it for me. They seem to have a peaceful coexistence with all Belizeans who respect them for who they are. There are even some converts to their religion and a few intermarriages. The Mennonite gene pool desperately needs new blood. They tend to stick within their own community, and it's hard to find someone they're not related to, so it's not unusual to see first cousins marry.

I contract with a furniture maker to make all the chairs for the school, and I make friends with his sons. They're seventeen and nineteen years old and curious about the outside world. I talk to them while I'm waiting for their father to get my invoice together.

"What do you guys do for entertainment around here?" I wave my hand at the vast countryside.

"We go visit other families."

"What else do you do? Do you have girlfriends?" They look mischievously at each other.

"The girls here always stay home with their mothers."

"How will you meet anyone to get married?"

"Sometimes, the parents arrange the marriage, and sometimes you meet someone at church or when you're visiting."

"You guys marry your cousins?"

"Yes, that happens, but many parents don't allow that."

"Does your father allow it?"

"No, he will not allow it."

"Well, you better get out there and meet some girls."

"We are not in a hurry."

"Will you stay here your whole life and take over your father's furniture business?" Like most Mennonites in the furniture business, they're already missing half fingers from accidents with power saws that they run off generators.

"Yes, we will make furniture."

"So you don't do anything else for fun?"

"We like to drink beer, but don't tell our father."

"Who do you drink beer with?"

"Sometimes by ourselves, and sometimes we go to town with our older cousins."

"You go into the bars?"

"Sometimes, and sometimes we buy the beer and bring it back here to drink."

"But your father doesn't know?"

"No, he will be angry if he knows."

"Well, be careful. It's good to have fun when you're young, but your father is a good man and you should listen to him."

"Yes, we know." Then after whispering back and forth, they cautiously ask me, "Can you bring some beer for us when you come back?"

"Maybe, I don't want your father to get mad at me."

"He will not know."

"We'll see, maybe."

The next time I went to pick up some chairs, I took a six-pack for the boys. After that, we were best buddies.

60

Coming Together

Everything's pretty much in place for the school to open. The last thing I have to do is get the school registered with the government of Belize. The official document is returned to me in the mail, and it's signed and registered on July 4, 1984. We are now an accredited school recognized by the government of Belize and, to top it off, we became "official" on the Fourth of July. I may leave and be forgotten, but that date, that little piece of American history will be with the school forever.

I stop to reflect on what I'm doing and what I've done. I realize that back in the United States, in my own culture, as an American, I would have never been allowed to accomplish something like this without a college degree. Empowerment was the key for me. I know now that I can learn or do anything I want. It's an energizing and powerful feeling.

I took the lead, but the school has come together with everyone's support. I haven't had time to appreciate it or even feel proud. It's been all work and I'm still not done. Without students, it's just empty buildings. I have two years to get it up to speed before handing it over to the ministry of education. We decided it will be a two-year course. That means I'll be able to see the first graduating class.

Jose and Francisco are back from Costa Rica. We have legal documents to sign, curriculum-development workshops, teacher training, and meetings to attend. They know exactly what to do with the standard school stuff. I work with them to make sure we have more creative ideas on the curricula like appropriate technology and practical learning. Our goal, the big picture, is to teach students how to think, manage projects, and be resourceful with what they have. I find that I have to keep reminding people that this school is going to be different.

As soon as Jose and Francisco return, parents begin coming by to enroll their kids. There's still some uncertainty about the school, and people are very tentative at first. For one thing, we named ourselves the Belize Junior School of Agriculture, and we're not a four-year high school. It's not our goal to become another academic school. The students we're looking for are the ones who failed the national selection exam. We want to teach them how to be entrepreneurs with the land they have.

The Peace Corps assigns two volunteers as teachers, Margo and Steve. That gives us five teachers, counting myself. Our goal for the first year is to recruit fifty students, boys and girls. We set a deadline and we end up with twenty-five students, all boys. It's less than expected, and we had hoped to get some girls, but we'll take what we have. It looks like we'll have to prove ourselves.

A few days before school starts, we have an official inauguration with guests from the ministry of education. The village chairmen from Trinidad and San Lazaro are there. Victor's there with his entourage. Approximately two hundred people show up, mostly from surrounding villages. Myself and several others give speeches, and then we officially cut the ribbon and open the doors. Most of the comments are about the collaboration it took to get the school started. All the organizations involved are recognized. I say a few words to emphasize that this is not a regular academic school. It's a school of agriculture.

Even though we've opened, there's lots of work left to do around the school. It was only two months ago that Neb handed over the money. The doors and windows have been installed for both the school and the teacher's house. Partitions were made, an enclosed veranda was added. With the help of Peace Corps Volunteers and the Rotary Club, we painted both buildings inside and out. We have chairs, desks, and blackboards. We also have farm tools to work with.

The school and land look pretty bleak right now. It needs that lived-in look, and we still have more construction to do. We're in the middle of building real bathrooms (for the time being, we're using latrines) with toilets and showers. We also have plans for an outdoor classroom with a floor and roof but no sides. We still have to build a storage shed, nursery, pens for livestock, basketball court, soccer field, and more.

School begins at 7:30 am. We design the schedule so the first ninety minutes of each day is for practical work, and there are three work groups of students that rotate each week between landscaping, construction, and nursery.

The first day almost turns disastrous when the landscaping group tries to clear a small section of land behind the school. The boys kill a total of seven bad snakes with their machetes in the first few hours. After that, even the most macho among us (and these boys are macho) are a little nervous. We don't want to scare the students away on the first day, so Francisco has them take a break from clearing for a while. Damn snakes.

The students and teachers work hard clearing the land and building livestock pens and nurseries. I still have the carpenters working and we assign students to work with them. After the practical work, students go into the classroom for regular school stuff like math and English. We have to meet the requirements from the ministry of education in order to get accreditation. At the end of the day, when the students leave to go back to their communities, I know they're our role models. They're going to give us credibility and demonstrate that we're a real school.

In the morning, when students are arriving is when I feel proudest. That's also when I feel the most responsible for making this idea work. For that to happen, they have to be learning and believing in what we're doing. Sometimes I worry too much. I worry that they'll stop coming and I will have failed. I worry about the teachers. I know they're not sure about this whole thing either. I also worry that the work is too much because there's so much to do and we never stop. But they keep coming and we keep going. Together we're working to make the school a reality.

61

Back in the United States

Overall, the school is recognized as a big accomplishment by the Peace Corps and USAID. Peace Corps Belize nominates me for volunteer of the year. It's quite an honor, considering there are only three other nominations worldwide.

It's time to get ready for my home leave, which I postponed earlier to get the school open. I have six whole weeks of vacation time coming to me, and I'm looking forward to it. It will also be my first time home in three years to see my family and friends.

I'm met at the airport by my younger sister, Michelle. We go to my mother's house where they have a little welcoming party for me. Everybody's telling me how much they admire what I'm doing. They tell me that they could not live in a foreign country and be away from family and friends. Once again, I feel guilty for taking their praise because I'm doing exactly what I want to be doing.

I notice a change in my feelings toward my family. I feel more compassionate than I did when I left three years ago. At that time, it was more like, "get me out of here." Now I feel closer and I understand where we're each coming from. I still don't want to stay, but I'm comfortable and no longer feel desperate to get away. I'm able to understand them without being drawn into the drama.

Everyone's amazed at how big I've become physically, from 150 lbs. to 190. One of my friends asks me what kind of workout I've been using. I tell him it's all from using the working end of a shovel, pick, and posthole digger. I also haven't smoked a cigarette in over two years.

After the party, I'm getting ready for bed and I notice that I feel out of place. For the last three years, I've been living in a remote village with no running water and no electricity. My home in the village always has open windows with a fresh tropical breeze coming in at night to help me sleep. I don't hear the frogs, birds, and other night noises of the jungle that I've become accustomed to falling asleep to. Instead, I feel like I'm enclosed in a tight little space with bright lights and all kinds of strange noises.

It's after midnight, but I feel a need to go out and get some fresh air. The streets are empty. There are no groups of men to talk to and get the latest news. I hear a loud buzzing noise coming from all the street lights and the traffic from a nearby highway. A cop car comes up from behind and slows down. I feel vulnerable, like I'm not supposed to be out in the night, like I'm doing something wrong. I feel like I've lost my voice, my place in the universe. I turn around and go back to the house.

I didn't expect it but I'm having reverse culture shock. I recognize the symptoms from the information they gave us at our COS conference. The habits I've developed over the last year aren't necessary here. Every time I have to use the bathroom, I automatically check to see if I have matches for the candle before I remember there's electricity. Whenever I walk outside, I habitually keep one eye out for snakes. Driving anywhere and being on the freeway is almost too much for me, especially with all the traffic and big trucks. That's another thing—where have all the cars come from? There are about two or three times as many cars on the road as there was when I left.

I have a hard time being in stores and shopping malls. I feel like my senses are being overwhelmed and overstimulated with too many flashing colors, mirrors, and noise. Several times, I leave my shopping cart and walk out of a supermarket before I finish my shopping.

Another new thing is all the answering machines. When I left in 1981, people answered their phones. Now everyone has voice mail and no one answers their bloody phone. It is annoying to me and I'm surprised at how easily everyone accepts it. It seems very impersonal and I have a hard time speaking to a machine. I'm amazed at how much has changed and how much I've changed in three years.

But what affects me the most is the media. I finally figure out that that's the background mantra I'm always hearing wherever I go. It never stops. Each day, wherever I go, I hear the constant chatter, trying to sell me something or set a state of mind that takes over my consciousness and makes all my decisions based on what the latest crisis or style is. Even when it's background noise, it still has a powerful, almost magnetic energy. It's like the world's going to blow up in twenty seconds. I better hurry up and buy something I didn't even know I needed or worry about something happening on the other side of the world that I can't do anything about. The twelve-hour countdown for Armageddon begins each day with the morning news and gets to down to zero hour every evening and then it starts over again. Every day, 24/7, it's coming at me. I have to make a conscious effort to keep it out.

The hardest thing is trying to fit back in. I don't. I just came from someplace where I was somebody and now I'm just one of millions.

When I see friends and relatives, they ask me about my Peace Corps experience. They seem sincere, like they really want to know what I'm doing in Belize. But when I start describing my experience and what I'm doing with the school, I watch their eyes glaze over in about thirty seconds. No one seems to be able to relate to it or even care.

It's frustrating not to be able to share something that's been so meaningful for me and my growth as a person. In Belize, just about every place I go, people recognized me. I'm making a difference in people's lives. Hell, I can walk around Reno all day and never see anyone I know.

After weeks of trying to entertain myself and deal with my culture shock, I feel ready to go back. I know I have a lot of work waiting for me at the school and I want to get started on it. I realize I'm actually homesick for Belize, where I feel like I have a purpose in life. I can't wait to get back and get to work.

62

Home

"How was the White House?" I'm back in Belize City and I drop by the Peace Corps office just to let them know I'm still alive. A few of the volunteers hanging around the office immediately hit me with the question.

"What do you mean?"

"It says in the *Peace Corps Times* that you went to the White House for dinner."

"It does?" I pick up a copy of the Peace Corps Washington newsletter from the receptionist. Sure enough, it says I had gone with the three other nominees for Peace Corps Volunteer of the Year to the White House to have dinner with President and Mrs. Reagan.

At first, I feel a little upset that no one even bothered to tell me that I was invited to have dinner with the president of the United States. The article also explains that I wasn't selected as volunteer of the year; someone from Africa got that. That's fine with me; Africa should get it. I still would have enjoyed going for dinner as a nominee. But it's done; the dinner's over and there's nothing I can do about it now.

I have more exciting news waiting for me. The new school truck has arrived and is parked in the AID compound. This is exciting because if there's one thing a Peace Corps Volunteer covets, it's having a vehicle and being mobile. It's against all the regulations, but since this is officially a "project truck," and I'm the project leader, I get to drive it. There's even money in the budget for gas. It's a real change from the regular bus ride to drive a brand new, pure white, Ford F-150 supercab back to the village. I stop and show it off to Jose and Francisco on my way home. They're excited about the truck and catch me up on everything at the school. The main thing is all the students are still there and things are going fine. They killed a couple more snakes, but otherwise, things are fine.

I drive to the school, and I feel like a king driving through the villages in this nice, new truck. Nobody recognizes me because I'm not on my motorcycle. Normally, I would have to stop three or four times to talk with people on the streets. This time, I ride through without stopping. At the school, some of the natural plants and trees have grown a little. The place is starting to have that "lived-in" look. I feel like I'm home.

63

Plane Trouble

Polo and I are standing outside his house, watching the lights of a small plane fly over. It's about 7:00 p.m. and it's been dark for almost an hour. The plane's coming down low and going the length of the village and then turning around and doing it again. It's unusual because we normally don't see or hear these small planes after dark. After about the third time, it's obvious he wants to get our attention.

"What's that guy doing, Polo?"

"He wants someone to go shine their headlights on the runway so he can find it."

"Why don't you go?"

"My wife is afraid. She does not want me to go."

"Why doesn't he go back where he came from?"

"He needs gas. When they meet planes at the runway, they take gas to fill their tanks." This is something I didn't know.

"You mean he's going to run out of gas?"

"It looks so, Jorge."

I consider going out there with the truck, but I'm worried I might run into whoever's supposed to meet him arriving late. They might think I'm a rival gang. The police might even be there, and it wouldn't look good for the school truck to be involved in a drug bust. I start driving back toward the school, and I see Luty standing in his yard watching the plane. "Luty, what's going on?"

"Hola, Jorge."

"What do you think he wants?"

"He cannot find the runway, Jorge. He needs light."

"Why don't you take your truck and show him where it is?" I want someone to help this guy but not me.

"My wife is afraid. She does not want me to go." I've never seen these guys let their wives stop them from doing anything.

"What will happen if no one goes?"

"Maybe he will crash. I do not know, Jorge."

I start driving toward the school and home, which is the same direction as the runway. As soon as I get out of the village, he starts buzzing my truck. I can feel him pleading with me to go shine my lights on the runway. He's coming down very low now. It sounds like he's just inches above me. I resist my impulse to go to the runway. I drive to the school and stop. He turns and continues buzzing the village.

When I wake up in the morning, I get the news. Everyone's going to check out the plane wreck by August Pine Ridge, a village about ten miles up the road. One of the villagers tells me he witnessed the crash. He says the plane went up high and then came straight down very fast and crashed into the ground. I also hear that some people went to loot the plane. The pilot was probably carrying lots of cash to purchase his load. I wondered why he didn't try a crash landing, at least he might have had a chance. Maybe he wanted to make sure he died and took the cash with him.

A couple of days later, I'm having a beer with Arturo and Victor, and I ask about the plane.

"Victor, what happened with the plane crash the other day?"

"The plane was late, Jorge, and the people that were supposed to meet it got tired of waiting and left."

"So that's it? Nothing happens now?"

"No, they should not have left. Someone will have to pay for that."

"They say the pilot took the plane up and came straight down."

"Yes, that is what they say."

"I think I would have tried to land it. I don't think I would have given up like that."

"Come on, Jorge, let's drink another beer."

I don't ask how they'll "pay" for it and I never find out who was responsible. Victor knows, but he's not saying. It's hard to tell who might have paid because there are too many dead bodies found over the next couple of weeks to say who was responsible for what.

64

Relationships

Margo is one of the Peace Corps volunteers assigned to work at the school. She's not my type but she has a friend, Candy, who is. Candy's Peace Corps assignment is in the development of sports and physical education for the ministry of education. She's based in Belize City, but on weekends, she comes out on the bus and stays at the school. She and I hit it off right away, and after the first day, we're sleeping together. We get along well, but like most of my relationships with women, this is about sex. There's no interest with either of us to go any further than that. Normally, that is the ideal situation for me—no commitment just easygoing fun. But recently, I've been having this nagging thought in the back of my mind that maybe I need to look for a little more in a relationship.

I still see Maria around the village, and lately, she has been paying some attention to me. I seem to have developed this deep curiosity about family and everything that it means in her culture. I've been here for almost four years now, and it feels like I'm finally making a little headway with the women. Starting the school has increased my importance and status as a member of the community. I'm no longer seen as a visitor or short-time resident.

I start comparing my relationship with Candy to what it might be like if I was with Maria. Up to now, the majority of my relationships have been superficial. If I were to go for a village girl, just getting past the front door would be serious. The commitment that comes with it attracts me and scares me at the same time. From the first date, there's an expectation from her and her family. Since I'm a gringo, she would be taking a risk. Everyone would be watching to see what the white boy will do.

It's the way the culture works, but it's also the area I know least about. The men are expected to behave like men and take opportunities whenever they can. Sometimes they have marriage in mind and sometimes they don't. The women are expected to hold out until they find a man they feel will make the commitment and they're sure they can live with. It's definitely harder for the women. As a result, there are all these cultural courting rituals that take place with the girl's whole family watching out for her.

Once a girl gets married, she is married for life even if the man leaves her. According to her religion (Catholic), she is still married to him. Even if it is an "unofficial" marriage by eloping, many still see themselves as "married" for life.

Once a girl gets pregnant, she will have the baby unless she has a miscarriage or other complications. On rare occasions, this can be arranged with an herbal concoction from the local bush doctor.

I know my relationship with Candy is of no concern to a village girl. I'm a man and I'm doing what I should be doing. I can be someplace with Candy and see Maria, and she doesn't seem to be threatened or jealous. In fact, it seems to enhance our relationship. It's as if she's saying, *"That gringa is not good enough for you. I will treat you much better. I will show you devotion and commitment. I will treat you like a king, and I can be sexy about it too."*

Over the weekend, we decide to have a party at the school and I invite Maria. I've invited her out before, but this time she comes and brings her older sister with her. Candy's not there so I manage to get Maria by herself, and after a little resistance, I kiss her and she kisses me back. It's a hot, passionate kiss and I want to take it further. I feel all her resistances melt away as her body presses against mine. That's when her sister finds us and, doing her job, breaks us up.

After they leave, I think about what happened. Something is bothering me and I'm not sure what it is. When Maria left, I felt an unspoken commitment about taking our relationship a step further. It makes me feel cornered and threatened. I have the feeling that if her sister hadn't been there and we ended up in bed, that's where she would have stayed. I don't think she would have gone back home. We would be, as Chabby once told me, "married." I know I'm not ready for that. Even though I like her and she's incredibly beautiful, I'm not ready to be married.

This is new territory for me, and it feels like I'm walking into a mine field.

In my culture, I would be all about collecting on that commitment. But this is different because there is an expectation that I will marry her. I'm not ready for that kind of relationship. I'm too happy being free to choose who I want to be with and when I want to be with them.

65

Life Changes

As a new school, we're often invited to participate in school events, inaugurations, and other special ceremonies. Both Jose and I do our best to attend these because it gets our name out there. It's part of our strategy for building the school's reputation. Anytime we're invited to a public event, at least one of us goes.

We receive an invitation to a school function in Yo Creek. Their primary school is inaugurating a new storage shed. Inaugurations are something Belizeans love to do, and they usually attract a big crowd. I decide to go since Jose has other commitments.

As a rule, these events are a little boring. They always have way too many speeches while everyone waits in the hot sun. The best part is afterward because they always follow with something good to eat. Plus, you get to network with ministry officials and other teachers. That's the work part. The other incentive for going is the fact that Yo Creek is well-known for their pretty girls.

I arrive at the school, and I'm checking out the crowd for someone familiar to go talk with. Then I see her. I'm attracted to her right away and can't take my eyes off her. I know right away I want her. She's standing with a group of girls, and all of them are attractive, but she is beautiful.

Through the whole ceremony, I can't take my eyes off her. I like everything about her. She has high cheek bones, arching eyebrows, and slanted eyes that give her that exotic, oriental look. Her hair's jet black and that, combined with the gold jewelry she's wearing, contrast perfectly with her brown, glowing skin. Her lips are full and she's pretty from every angle. I especially like the way she holds herself. She looks proud, confident, and sure of herself. Her posture is straight and she holds her head high. *I've got to know this girl.*

After the ceremony, I start working my way toward the group she's with. One of the men closest to her is someone I've had a few beers with before. His name is Benito and he's chairman of the Yo Creek Village Council. I go over on the pretense of talking to him. He's friendly but he's not introducing me to anyone. Finally I ask him, "Are you related to all these beautiful women?"

"Oh yes, would you like to meet them?" He's smiling with pride as he notices my interest.

He then introduces me to his two daughters and to all the others who are his nieces. The one I'm interested in is one of his nieces and her name is Irma. She looks like she could be anywhere from eighteen to her early twenties.

I go out of my way to shake her hand when Benito introduces us. Her hand is warm and soft, and when I look into her eyes, I sense a strong presence. *This woman knows who she is.* But she doesn't seem the least bit interested in me and she turns to talk to her cousins and sisters. One of her cousins, Carla, takes an interest in me and steps up to shake my hand and introduce herself again. I figure I might be able to get closer to Irma through her and start a conversation. She invites me to a dance that's going to be in Yo Creek this coming weekend. I thank her, but I'm still trying to get some recognition from Irma. Once I see a girl I'm interested in, I can usually get some kind of indication that it's mutual, but she's giving me nothing. Of course, this makes it more interesting and challenging. I tell Carla I'll try and come to the dance. I say good-bye to my new best friend, Benito, and leave.

Two days later, I'm cruising through Yo Creek on my motorcycle, and I see a woman walking up the road on the right-hand side by herself. There's something about the way she walks that intrigues me, and somehow it seems familiar, like I've known her for a lifetime. As crazy as this sounds at that moment, I know, *"That woman, whoever she is, will have my children."* It's almost scary because I haven't seen her face, but somehow I know her.

When I go past, I turn to look. It's Irma, who, of course, doesn't even look at me. I feel shaky and excited because now I'm sure that something's going to happen between us. I know I'll have to work for this. At the same time, I feel a confidence and calmness. It's built into the courting rituals of the culture, and for the first time, I can see how it benefits both the man and the woman. It takes time and patience, and if it's going to happen, it will happen.

66

Irma

I decide to go to the dance in Yo Creek, and I'm unusually nervous about the possibility of meeting her there. For moral support, I invite Steve. He's the other volunteer working at the school, and he recently moved into the teacher's house with me.

I know a little bit about dating protocol in a village. It starts with meeting the girl's parents and visiting on a regular basis with a chaperone present. Basically, you've got to prove to the whole family and yourself that your intentions are honorable. It's not said but understood that marriage is the desired result. It's quite a commitment and one that scares the hell out of me. I decide I'm going to explore the possibilities of courting this girl and see how far I get. The hard part for me is getting into a social situation that offers an opportunity to get to know her better. I, at least, need to have a conversation with her.

When we get to the dance, I see Irma at a table with her family. It's not uncommon for a village girl to go to a dance with her parents and other family members. Carla, Irma's cousin, comes up to greet me and invites me to dance. While I'm dancing with her, I keep one eye on Irma.

After a few more dances, the band takes a break. I buy a beer and go over to say hello to Irma. She smiles and says hello. I ask her to dance and I'm expecting her to say no, which happens to me frequently at village dances. To my surprise, she says yes, and when the band comes back, we go out to dance.

I'm thinking about how to begin a conversation and start this whole process, but I feel tongue-tied and she looks so calm. *How can I start anything when I can't even talk to her?*

"What's your last name?"

"Novelo."

"My name is George."

"Yes, I know who you are."

"Is that your mother over there?"

"Yes, that is my mother, my grandmother, and my sisters."

"How old are you?"

"I am twenty years old."

"I'd like to visit you sometime. Is that okay?"

"If you want to visit, then visit." It's not an invitation, but it's not a no either.

"Where do you live?"

"I live down the road and to the back." Since roads in a village don't have names, it's hard for someone to describe where they live if you don't know one of the neighbors as a reference point. "Do you know where Benito, my uncle, lives?"

"No, but I can find it."

"I live next door to him." I notice her English is very good.

We stay on the dance floor for a few songs then I take her back to her table. I decide to wait until the dance is over and see if I can walk her home. I have a few more beers and talk with some friends. Steve's hooked up with one of Irma's cousins, and he wants to stay too. When the dance is over, I offer to walk her home so I can learn where she lives. She agrees and introduces me to her mother, who walks about twelve steps behind us the whole way. When we reach her house, I say good-bye and tell her that I'll come to visit her sometime. She smiles and says, "Okay." Again, I feel no commitment or strong encouragement.

I walk away feeling smitten. There's something about her that appeals to me in every way. It's spiritual and sexual at the same time but at a higher level. With everything she says and does, I sense a freedom about her that I've never experienced before. I can tell she doesn't care about impressing me or anyone else for that matter. There's a strong presence and sense of self about her.

Steve's been close by the whole time, talking and walking with Irma's cousin, Donni. In fact, it looks like he's made more progress than I have. They're having such a long conversation that I have to interrupt so we can go home. At least they seem to have something to talk about. Donni is one of Benito's daughters. Since she and Irma live right next door to each other, we make a deal to go visit them together.

In a village, when you go to visit someone, you don't normally knock on their door. You stand in the yard and "hail" them, meaning you yell out a greeting until someone comes out. One of Irma's sisters, Sandra, hears me and comes out on the front porch.

"Hi, is Irma home?"

"Yes, she is home." Then she stands there watching me.

"Can I talk to her?"

"Just a minute, I will see." She disappears for a minute, and I hear her calling Irma by her nickname, "Web." She comes back in a few minutes.

"She does not want to come out."

"She doesn't?"

"No."

"Oh, okay. Well, tell her I said hello." I'm kind of waiting for an explanation or excuse, but none's coming.

"Okay, I will tell her." She then stands there and watches me leave.

I'm crushed and I don't know what to think. I thought we had hit it off pretty good, and I've been thinking of her the whole week. Now she doesn't want to see me. I go down the street to Benito's house, and Steve's already inside the house visiting Donni. *What's going on? What does Steve have over me? If Donni can see him, why can't Irma see me? It can't be a cultural thing. Am I wrong in my feelings for her?*

I worry about it for a couple of days and finally decide that maybe she was having a bad day. I know there is something there, something between us, and I know she feels it too. I can't be wrong about this; it goes too deep for her not to feel it.

67

A Sign

Today, Jose and I have our usual meeting to talk about school business.

"Do you know this girl from Yo Creek, Irma Novelo?"

"Yes, I know her." Jose is from Yo Creek himself.

"What's she like?"

"She is a nice girl. I know she is different, more serious, not like the usual girls."

"Is she dating someone?"

"I don't think so but I am not sure, Jorge. Why, are you interested in her?"

"Yeah, I am, but I don't know much about her."

"She seems to be active in the community. I know at one time they were thinking about asking her to run for the village council."

"Yeah, she seems pretty sharp."

"Oh yes, mon, she is smart."

Who is this mysterious woman?

Christmas is coming, and it's been a long time since my one and only attempt at visiting Irma. I feel somewhat rejected especially since Steve is visiting Donni on a regular basis. That wasn't supposed to happen. He was just going to keep me company.

At first, I'm expecting him to become a conduit for Irma and me to communicate through. But every time he comes back from his visits to Donni, there's no word or indication she's interested in me.

Then it happens. Steve hands me an envelope after one of his visits with Donni. It's a regular Christmas card and she's signed it "Your friend, Irma." I know this is big. She would never send me a card unless she's interested. I buy one for her and I also sign it "From a friend." Then I send it with Steve to give to her. I wait up late for him to return, and when he finally gets back, I quiz him.

"Did you give the card to Irma?"

"Yes, I gave the card to Irma."

"You saw her?"

"Yeah, she came over to Donni's while I was there."

"Did she say anything?"

"About what?"

"About me, you clown."

"No, (laughing) she didn't say anything."

68

Christmas

Steve tells me there'll be a dance in Yo Creek on Christmas Eve, and he's going with Donni.

"Do you think you'll go?" he asks.

"I already promised Candy I would cook dinner for her on Christmas Eve."

"So you'll be in Belize City?"

"Yeah, it looks like it. Is Irma going to the dance?"

"As far as I know, she is."

"I may try to make it later."

I want to go to the dance, but I can't be in two places at once. There's something special about attending a Christmas Eve dance to see a girl you like. The problem is I can't easily get out of my dinner with Candy. I promised her and I owe her that much. Then I come up with a plan so I can be in both places. I decide I'll go to Belize City early, cook dinner, and leave in time to get back to Yo Creek. The dance doesn't start until 10:00 p.m. and will go until two or three in the morning. I tell Steve I'll see him at the dance.

Just as planned, I get to Belize City early and start putting my dinner together. I love having the opportunity to cook in a real kitchen. I don't skimp on expenses and cook a nice Italian dinner of lasagna, garlic bread, and a green salad. Candy comes home after work with a decent bottle of wine. She's in a romantic mood, and right away, I know I'm going to have trouble if I try to leave early. After eating and drinking my share of good wine, I realize I feel too tired to drive sixty-five miles. I end up spending the night and leave early in the morning.

Since I have to drive through Yo Creek on my way home, I decide to stop by Irma's and give her a gift. A week earlier, I had picked up a gold necklace in anticipation of seeing her at Christmas. When I get to her house, they tell me she's at Donni's. I go over to Donni's and this time she comes out. I give my gift to her and we talk for a while.

"How was the dance last night?"

"It was okay."

"I would like to come and visit you once in a while, if that's okay with you."

"Yes, I would like that."

"You would? That's great because I want to get to know you better."

"I want to know you too." It's amazing how just the slightest encouragement from her makes me feel like I'm the greatest thing in the world. I drive home singing the whole way.

When I get to the school, I find a Christmas card and a gift from Maria. Her gift is a set of sheets and pillowcases with lions on them. There's also a message that she wants to see me and that she's at her cousin's house in San Lazaro. I get a bucket of water and clean up a little. On my way to San Lazaro, I make a decision to tell her I'm not interested in a romantic relationship. We both need that out of the way to be able to move on. *Hopefully, we'll remain friends.*

I pull up to her cousin's house, and she comes out with a small duffel bag and gets in the truck. She sets her bag on the floorboard and scoots over next to me, putting her hand on my leg. My mind is still on Irma and I'm not ready for this.

"Hi Maria, what's going on? Where do you want to go?" She looks at me, smiles, and says, "I want to go with you."

Then I get it and it hits me like a ton of bricks. Her duffel bag, picking her up at her cousin's, the hand on my leg—she wants to go home with me.

Like I said, I'm just not ready for it. I know if I take her back to the school (home) with me, we'll be "married." After that, to make it right, I'll have to go and talk to her father. By tomorrow, everyone in the village will be saying, "George and Maria got married last night." I'll be on the front page of the sugarcane wireless, and worse, I'll be committed forever. No more Irma, no more Candy, no more anyone.

My mind's racing with all these thoughts as I start the truck and drive very slowly up the street. I stop at the corner. This is it, this is the big decision. If I go right, I'm taking her home with me and I'm "married." If I go left, I'm taking her back to her parents and losing my relationship with her forever.

I think for a moment with her sitting next to me, her head on my shoulder. I make a hard left. I stop in front of her house and look at her. She doesn't look back, and without saying a word, she gets out of the truck. Before she closes the door, I say "Good-bye, Maria." She doesn't acknowledge me. I know she's crying and I feel like an ass, but at the same time, I know it's better to do it now rather than later.

I drive home slowly, thinking about what I've done. *Did I do the right thing?* I like Maria but I can't make the commitment she wants. I like Candy with no commitments but still sleep with her. But she's from my culture so it's different. I know the rules. I like Irma, but I don't know if I love her. I'm not even sure what love is. There's this irresistible attraction to Irma that I can't seem to get over. Maybe I'm only interested in Irma because she's a challenge.

I feel bad about what I've done to Maria, and I know I'll probably never see her again. She offered herself to me, a very brave move in her culture, and I shut her down. *Jesus Christ, what's the matter with me?*

69

The Dream

I find my feelings toward Candy are changing. I don't feel right being with her when I'd rather be with Irma. I decide it's time we talk.

"I'm dating a girl from the village, and I probably won't be around much."

"You dumping me, LeBard?"

"I mean I want to spend more time with her."

"That's cool, my dance card is full. No problem if you want to be with your village girl."

"Irma."

"Okay, Irma. Go ahead and be with her. You know where to find me."

"Thanks, Candy. Thanks for understanding."

"Hey, we're still friends, right?"

"Right." I know there are plenty of guys waiting in line to date her.

Now I feel like it's time to step up my relationship with Irma, and the perfect opportunity comes along. Some girls from Yo Creek approach me about coaching their softball team, the same team that Irma happens to play first base for. I agree, and we start practice right away, which means I have to go to Yo Creek almost every day.

During practice, I focus on the team and improving their skills. I do my best to treat Irma as just another player. It's a fun group of girls and I'm happy to be coaching again. Being on the field, getting exercise, and making friends is what I like doing. Some of the girls start out the same as the team from San Lazaro. They ignore me, but now I know what to do. I focus on the girls who want to work with me and don't worry about the others. After practice, I always walk Irma home and stay for a little visit.

Our walks are sometimes silent and uncomfortable. I don't always know what to say to her. The usual "chitchat" doesn't seem appropriate, and I feel like I need to dig a little deeper. She's very honest and logical in her thinking. It seems to have the effect of grounding me when I'm around her. It's one of the things I'm attracted to, along with her quick wit and sense of humor.

This whole relationship is different from my usual mode of operation, which is *when can we start having sex?* The interest is there; it's just that sex is not my priority and that's unusual.

Her family is nice to me. Her father, Don Francisco, is away six days a week working on the new Western Highway that the government is building. I met him once before when he stopped me in town to ask about the school. He seems like a good man who takes care of his family.

I like her mother. She talks to me and, like most Belizeans, she is very direct when she wants to know something.

"What is your religion?" she asks.

"I'm Catholic but I'm not a practicing Catholic."

"So you don't go to church?"

"No, I don't agree with organized religion, but I don't have a problem with people who do go to church."

"That's because you are American."

"No, there are lots of Americans who go to church."

"I always tell my daughters they should go to church. But I cannot make them go; they have to want to go."

"That's true. I feel the same way."

I talk a little with two of Irma's six sisters, Sandra and Lilly. The rest are shy about using their English around me. She has one younger brother, Junior, and he's polite to me but no real conversation. Irma's English, on the other hand, is very good and she's not shy about using it. Her nickname is "Web," taken from the Mayan word "Webon," which means lazy.

"Are you lazy?" I ask.

"No, it's because I like to read, and sometimes when everyone else is working, I go hide someplace with a book."

"So they think that's being lazy?"

"Yes, they say I like to read too much."

We talk about things that are very much in the present. She asks me questions about my family but not about my past. I recognize the wisdom she has and that makes her sexy. I'm starting to like her more and more.

Once summer starts, we practice less and have more games on the weekends. Our team is good, and we come close to winning the district competition, losing to only one team. Our pitcher is chosen to go with the national team as a backup pitcher to the Pan Am Games. We all feel proud of that.

I'm visiting on a fairly regular basis by now. It's mostly friendly visits on the front porch with her whole family just a few feet away in the living room. Steve's still visiting Donni, and they seem to be getting serious.

For the last month, I haven't felt like partying and chasing women like I usually do. I know there's some kind of connection with Irma because when I'm with her, everything seems to make sense. At the same time, I'm confused about my true feelings toward her. *Am I going to marry her? Am I in love? Wouldn't I know it if I was in love? What is love?* This is such a new thing for me, I feel like I need help. *Who can I go to for help? What kind of help do I need?* I find myself curious about my father and my great grandfathers. How did they get to where I was conceived? What were their hopes and dreams for me? How does being at this point in my life relate to them? Somehow, the decisions I'm making is linked to them, and living or dead, I want their guidance. Sometimes I feel like I'm going crazy.

I'm having trouble with my meditation technique. It works best when I practice it with no effort. If I'm using effort, I know it's not working. After a particularly unsatisfying meditation, I fall asleep and have a dream.

I'm in a dark void, and I see a bright light coming up from what looks like a large rectangular hole in the darkness surrounding me. I can hear a female voice that gets louder and stronger the closer I get. I know the voice from somewhere in my past. I know she's playing a game and wants to lure me in. I'm apprehensive because I'm aware of the power behind the voice. At the same time, I'm secure because I know as long as I'm not playing the game she can't do anything to me.

When I reach the opening, I peer over the edge to see people walking around below me. Their eyes look glazed over, like zombies in a trance. They're in a large supermarket and they're all listening to the voice. As part of the game, the voice is constantly telling them what to do. I've played it before, and even though I can't remember how, I'm sure I can win. In fact, I'm so sure I can win I want to play.

I engage the voice, and immediately, we're communicating telepathically. She tells me that in order for me to come into the game I have to agree to her conditions. My strategy is to play dumb. I believe that if I pretend I don't know how to play, it will be easier to win.

To enter and play the game requires specific collateral that only she can provide, and I have to buy it from her. The only payment she'll accept from me is my "life force." Every time I need something from her, I have to pay for it with a little piece of my life force. The trick of the game is not to give up so much of my life force that I become a zombie like the others. I agree to her conditions, telling myself that I know how to win.

The first thing I need to come in to the game is a sexual identity. I choose to be a male and I'm in the game. I see two scoreboards light up, similar to the ones they have at basketball games. One is for her and the other is for me. My score is high and hers is zero. Each time I buy something with my life force, her score goes up and mine goes down. The next thing I need for my new identity is friends, and to have friends, I need to have "deceit." I buy it and BAM! The scoreboard flashes another big score for her.

I sense that each time I give up some of my life force, the memory of who I am gets weaker. It's still there faintly in the back of mind, but I have to hide it or she'll see it and somehow take it away. I tell myself, "I'll hide it where she can't find it, that's my power, my edge in the game. When it's the right time, I'll use it to win the game."

Now that I'm in the game, she's on me like a pit bull, telling me everything I need to be happy. I need women, cigarettes, booze, and drugs. Everything's there, available for me to buy, and I start going around the store like everyone else filling up my shopping cart. Before long, she's in charge and I've forgotten that I'm playing a game. I'm a zombie like everyone else, enjoying all the good things I can buy to occupy my time and my mind.

After a while, I come to a spot in the store that has furniture, and everyone has to pass through a turnstile. When I'm going through, I look up and see my reflection in a mirror. As soon as I see myself, I remember I'm in a game and I've forgotten how to win. I know I still have enough life force hidden deep within to win this game. As soon as I remember, the voice zeros in on me, intense like I'm in the crosshairs of a sniper ready to take my life. I get scared and pretend I don't remember so the voice will back off. I have to wait until the right time to use my knowledge to win. But how do I use it without her seeing it and taking it away from me? Then I wake up.

It's 3:00 a.m. I turn on my flashlight, find a paper and pen, and begin writing the dream. At first, I don't know what it means. I just know it's important and real. I go back to sleep, and in the morning, I take another look. I still feel the intensity of the dream and I focus on interpreting its meaning. It takes me a while but then I start to understand. The "voice" is the mantra of mass consciousness, always telling me to be like everyone else. I'm always hearing it in the back of my mind, especially when I try to meditate or make a decision. The "game" is life and the choices I make. My life force is the seed of my being and my power. The things I "need" to be happy are all my superficial needs and addictions that I put in front of my life force to avoid taking charge of knowing what is right for me.

The knowledge for winning the game is always with me. It's having the clarity and courage to take charge of who I am and what my truth is. Every time I want to take charge of my life, I resist by bringing in fear. Fear that I'll lose everything that I think I need to be happy, fear that I won't survive without those things. So I lie to myself and forget again, feeling safer to hold onto what I'm familiar with until I reach a turning point in my life.

Since I've been in Belize, I've learned how to take charge of my life and make it more meaningful. I know what I'm doing. I'm making the most important decision of my life. What could be more important than marriage and deciding to spend the rest of my life with someone? I'm going to marry this girl, and I've known it from the first time I saw her. What I'm asking is, *How do I give up my loneliness and boredom, something I'm so familiar with, for something I don't know?*

I realize I've been watching and studying family life for four years now. The entire time, I've been working on healing myself. The commitment to family and simple, honest living is very appealing to me. To have it, all I have to do is be willing to change my life as I know it. That's not easy for me to do. In fact, it scares me. For me to take charge and manifest a family into my life feels like the old me has to go away.

I know I've created the opportunity to have a richer life and someone to share it with. Irma has everything I desire in a woman. She's beautiful, honest, intelligent, and, best of all, she cares about me for who I really am. She's also good at challenging me to be the best I can be, which I need. But then all my self-doubts come up—*"Am I in love? Is this what I really want?"* Then I see Irma and she makes all my doubts and fears disappear. My confusion and fear are slowly being replaced with certainty.

We start going out more often. We have fun even though at least one of her sisters is always with us playing chaperone. We go to dances in town, soccer games, softball games, fairs, and anything else that happens to be going on. There's a big difference in our age. I'm thirty-five and she's twenty-one, but it doesn't seem to matter. Irma's very mature and, in many ways, more mature and logical than I am. She is not a person who will point a blaming finger at others and say her situation, or lack of one, is the fault of others. She knows that she's in charge of her life and what happens to her. It's a level of responsibility that connects with me. With that responsibility comes a sense of freedom that I've never experienced before. It's the freedom to feel however I want to feel. I've always resisted certain feelings because I've always been told they're "bad feelings" to have. Once I allow myself to have those feelings, they lose their power. If I want to feel angry or jealous, the power of those feelings immediately diminishes with the permission to feel however I want to feel without judgment.

We talk about our future and marriage, and we both agree that we belong together. We also talk about the beautiful children we want to have. When we tell her family, everyone's happy for us, but I also sense her mother's worried. Now according to tradition, I have to ask permission from her father.

I wait for the weekend when I know Don Francisco will be home.

"Don Francisco, can I talk to you for a minute?" I feel nervous.

"Yes, we can talk."

"I want to ask your permission to marry Irma."

"What does Irma say"? He says this like Irma might not know about my plans yet.

"She says yes."

"Well, if that is what she wants then it is okay with me." He doesn't display any emotion; he just wants to make sure it's what his daughter wants.

"Thank you, Don Francisco." We shake hands.

"You are welcome."

We set our wedding date for December 21, 1985. Around the same time, Steve and Donni set their wedding date for December 23.

70

Marriage

We're getting married. We have lots of planning and wedding preparations to take care of. One of the first things I do is let everyone back home know what I'm doing. I send out invitations and pictures. I don't expect anyone to come. I don't think anyone in my family has the money or time to make the trip.

One of my best friends surprises me and comes for the wedding. Jackson is someone I've known since high school. In fact, he was a high school English teacher and my homeroom teacher. At some point, we had formed a friendship and kept in touch with each other.

We have the wedding at the Yo Creek Catholic Church. Irma looks beautiful in a traditional white wedding gown, and I wear a suit that I have tailored for me. Following the wedding, we have a reception at the school. Over two hundred people from Belize attend, and Jackson, my sole representative from home.

The next day, Irma and I leave for our honeymoon. We rent a car in Mexico and drive up to Merida. From there, we go to Cancun and down the coast of the Yucatan Peninsula, stopping wherever we want along the way. We see some beautiful sights and get to know each other better. The whole time we were dating, we had a chaperone with us. Now it's just the two of us and that takes a little adjusting.

I'm still on the budget of a Peace Corps volunteer, so after a couple of weeks, it's back to work. Steve and Donni get married a few days after us. They move into Donni's parent's home, and Irma moves into the teacher's house with me. We have no electricity or running water like Yo Creek has. So much of our daily living is taking care of the little things that need to happen. It also means there's no TV or anything to distract us, and we spend more time with each other.

One of the first things we realize is that sometimes we have different priorities. That's understandable since we're from different cultures with completely different backgrounds, values, and beliefs. We quickly recognize the problem and make an agreement. We agree that even though something may not be a priority for one of us, we will understand if it's a priority for the other and respect that. Once we make that agreement, things go pretty smooth.

My favorite thing about her is her sense of humor. I appreciated that from the first time I met her. She has a great outlook on life, is always positive, and able to find the humor in just about everything. Nothing seems to get her spirits down.

Speaking of spirits, mine is getting a little worried. I only have about six months left in the Peace Corps and then I'll be unemployed. We have to decide what we're going to do. To be safe, I go ahead and apply for and receive my permanent residence card, which is the equivalent of a green card for Belize. We also go through the process of getting Irma's green card for the United States, which takes a lot more time and effort than I thought possible. Having our green cards gives us some flexibility for the future.

The most promising option is to return to the United States. This is something Irma's not too excited about but is willing to do. I want her to meet my family and friends. Financially, it's going to be difficult because I've been living on a volunteer's salary for the last five years. I have a little money that the Peace Corps puts aside for volunteers called a "readjustment" allowance. But I borrowed from it for our wedding and only have about three thousand dollars left. Not much of a start for newlyweds going back to basically nothing. We have no home, no car, no job, but we have my family. I've never asked them for help before, but now I'm expecting some, and I'm not sure how that will go.

71

Breakthrough

The second year of school is going well. I'm still getting pressure from everyone to go more academic and become a four-year school. The parents, the students, the teachers, and now the board of directors are all asking me to consider it. My argument is if we do that, then we become just another high school like everyone else. We would defeat the vision we had for the school. We've already added the academic classes we need for accreditation from the ministry of education. If we change, I worry that it won't be long before we're requiring our students to take the national selection exam for entrance. The easy thing to do would be to give in and become another high school. I find myself constantly reminding everyone of our original vision.

Sometimes I make myself step back and look at what we're doing. Everything we do is designed to live in harmony with the environment and make the most efficient use of our resources. We still have work groups that rotate on a weekly basis so that all students experience each aspect of having a farm. We now have crops growing, and we practice crop rotation so the soil is not overused. We follow "heavy-feeders" like corn and cabbage with "givers" like beans and other legumes, then "light-feeders" like lettuce and cilantro. Each morning, the students assigned to the nursery water the seed beds and plant new seedlings. Sometimes, they do grafting with fruit trees that we grow and sell to the public. The students assigned to landscaping work on keeping the school grounds neat and trim using the cut grass and green foliage in our composting. They also design a landscaping plan and plant ornamental shrubs and fruit trees in designated areas. Their plan includes companion-planting methods, plants that complement each other with their characteristics. The students in the livestock group take care of our broiler and layer chickens. They make sure they're fed and watered. They do the same with our pigs and our one cow. Sawdust from the local sawmill is used as litter in the pens and collected every six weeks for composting. Eventually, it will be added to the soil in our gardens to improve soil structure and health. Once a month, the local veterinarian comes out and teaches animal health. He shows them how to give injections and check for disease. The students in our construction group learn how to build livestock pens, working with cement and lumber. They also spend time helping the carpenters build outdoor classrooms using materials from the jungle nearby.

I'm proud of our students. They are strong and they're working hard to build this school. We make sure they're learning how to take the resources around them, the land, the water, the jungle, and make it work for them. Every day, I see improvements and feel our reputation in the community becoming stronger and gaining credibility. With that recognition comes increasing pressure to go academic.

Then we have what I consider a major breakthrough with our students. After a year and a half of working with them, we discover something that no one expected. All our students had failed the national selection exam, barring them from attending other schools. We assumed it was because, academically, they were underachievers and would never excel. We were wrong. From the academic work they're producing now, we can see that they're not dumb. They're smart, and some of them are very smart. Yet they had failed the selection exam. We have students in our school that only scored 7 percent on the exam. Now they're proving to us with their work that they can compete against anyone, at any level. The teachers and I decide to take a closer look. We have lots of questions. Are we going too easy on them? Are we accurate in our assessment? Are they somehow cheating? What's making them smarter?

As trained, experienced teachers, it doesn't take long for Jose and Francisco to figure it out. During our first year, Francisco, who is also the English teacher, noticed that every student in our school had very poor to nonexistent English skills in both speaking and writing. All of them relied on their first language, Spanish. As a result, he and Jose made a decision to double up on English by adding an extra course in literature, which Francisco taught. Francisco, being the task master that he is, had been merciless on them until they learned English. It's when they improved their English skills that they began to show potential and, in some cases, "excel" in academics.

Why had they done so poorly on the national selection exam? The exam is given in English. These kids are not academically challenged, they're language challenged. We realized that this is most likely the problem with the majority of students failing the national selection exam year after year. It's a no-brainer that no one has ever bothered or cared to investigate. I guess part of it comes down to the selection exam doing exactly what it is supposed to do in a country with few educational resources. It eliminates the underachievers and, in this case, the "language challenged."

With this discovery, I feel I have to reevaluate my position on going forward to become a high school. We schedule a meeting with the board of directors, and I agree to work toward making the school a four-year institution with a few conditions. The first condition is that we continue accepting students that don't pass the selection exam. The second condition is to keep the agriculture and resource management courses as a permanent part of our curriculum. I also request for our school to have a direct link to the Belize College of Agriculture. My hope is that we can channel students into the only tertiary institution in the country that focuses on agriculture.

72

Firefight

The violence from the drug wars have been increasing to the point where it's out of control. I've managed to avoid it so far, but it's just a matter of time before I get caught in the middle.

At school, we're recruiting for the third year. This time it looks like we're going to get more students enrolled, including some from Orange Walk Town. Six of our current students are already coming from town. I've arranged for a bus to bring them as far as the village of San Lazaro. The school is still a mile from there, so I take the truck every morning to pick them up.

It's 7:00 a.m.; school starts in thirty minutes. As usual, the Caribbean sun is already hot, and the air's heavy with humidity. I'm sweating from opening up the doors and windows for the school. The breeze coming through the open window of the truck feels good as I start driving. As I get closer to San Lazaro, I hear gunfire, but it's hard to tell which direction it's coming from. For the last year, it's been like this almost every day, and I'm used to hearing the popping noise of automatic weapons going off.

I go over the last small rise into the village and then I see it. It's a gun fight and it is happening right in front of me. Fifty yards from me, two men are firing automatic weapons at Victor's house. I can see Victor's men firing back. Bullets are flying everywhere and right there on the sidelines are my students. There are six of them standing there, frozen, in their school uniforms of light brown shirts and dark brown pants.

They're staring at a dead man who's lying in the fetal position twenty feet in front of them. What's left of him is bleeding out the top of his head into an expanding pool of dark fluid. His body seems to shrink in the few seconds I stare at him. I see his gun on the ground where it fell, close to his limp hand. I smell fear and death as the picture of the dead man puts everything else out of my mind for a split second. Without even knowing it, I've come to a complete stop. *I've got to get those kids.* Stepping on the gas, I pull the truck between the students and the gunmen still firing. I yell at them through the open passenger window, "get in the bloody truck and keep down!" I'm pumping pure adrenaline and I'm scared. I'm also angry and amazed that these kids don't have the sense to duck or get under cover some place.

I put the truck in reverse and burn rubber into the elementary school yard to turn around. The two men firing at Victor's house turn and start running for a tall cane field across the street, toward the direction I need to go. Some of Victor's men are running in front of us after the escaping men, shooting as they go. To my right, Victor's standing in his front yard, holding an Uzi in firing position. He sees me and gives a little nod as if to assure me that we will not be harmed. In the meantime, shots are still being fired. Then one of his open jeeps with four of his men armed to the teeth roars past me. They're heading in the direction of the cane field where the two men have disappeared. I know I have to get out of here, but at the same time, I'm trying to stay out of the way of bullets and gunmen.

I speed back toward the school and nearly run head-on into Victor's men as their jeep careens around a corner from the cane field. They're still looking for the two men, pumped up and ready for action. Their guns point dangerously in our direction for a split second and then away.

I floor the gas pedal, worried now that the two men running for their lives might jump out of the cane field to hijack our truck. After we make it back to the school safely, everyone calms down a little. Except for me. Once the adrenaline wears off, I feel shaky and weak. I let the realization sink in that we came very close to getting killed. *I only have two months to go before I go home. I've made it this far now; I want to finish my time and go home safe.*

I'm not too worried about the two men who got away. Unfortunately, Victor's men are good at what they do, and they'll find them before they get too far. Just the same, we bring all the students inside and lock the doors. We have a general meeting and explain that there were some men fighting with guns, but it's all over now and there's no threat to us. We take time to answer some questions and then send everyone to their classes.

It's hard to focus on schoolwork for the rest of the day. All the kids keep talking about the gunfight and the dead man. The six students find themselves very popular, and at every break, there's a crowd surrounding them asking questions. "What happened? What'd the dead man look like? Who shot him? Why didn't you run or hide (my question)?" They said it all happened so fast that they froze and couldn't move.

I'm not exactly sure what happened. Later, I find out that it was a rival gang. The "alien gang" attacked him at his home, but he had been ready for them, and they never stood a chance. Three men are dead—one in the streets, two in the cane fields, and the score is three-zip. I know it won't stay that way.

Two days after the fire fight in San Lazaro, Victor and I are sitting under a coconut tree in his backyard, having a discussion.

"What happened, Victor? Why were those guys after you?"

"Did you get scared, Jorge?" He says this and laughs. In his eyes, the fact that he survived this attack made him more macho.

"Hell, yes. It scared the crap out of me." He laughs again.

"No need to be afraid, Jorge, we had those guys."

"Why were they after you? What happened?"

"I will tell you. About two weeks ago, Sergio (leader of the alien gang) sent me a note. The note said, 'I need $10,000 by next week.'"

"That's all it said? Did he sign it?

"Yes, he signed his name."

"Was it a loan he wanted? Did he want you to loan him the ten thousand dollars?"

"The note did not say it was a loan. I read it like he wanted me to give him the money, and I would not get it back."

"Damn, did you give it to him?"

"No, but I thought about it. I had two thousand dollars in my pocket, so I sent it to him with a note that said, 'This is what I have and you are welcome to it.'"

"So you were giving him two thousand dollars just because he asked for money from you?"

"Yes, I sent it, thinking maybe he was in trouble and needed some help."

"What did he say? Did he thank you for it or say anything?"

"No, Jorge, he sent me another note that said, 'Pay me $10,000 by Sunday or I will come after you.'"

"You're kidding. Did he send back the two thousand dollars you sent the first time?"

"No, he did not send anything back, Jorge." He laughs and shakes his head.

"Damn, he was really putting pressure on you. Why do you think he did that?"

"Yes, I had to consider what he was doing. I think he wanted all the groups (he never said gangs) to pay him to do business like he is the big boss."

"That's what it sounds like. What did you do?"

"I talked to Antonio and Arturo. They did not think I should send him anything."

"What did they want you to do?"

"Antonio said if I sent this man anything else, he will not respect me, and he will not stop asking for money."

"So basically you would end up working for him if you sent the money?"

"Yes, Jorge, if I did not stand up to him, my own men would also lose respect for me."

"So you decided to fight."

"Yes, he said he would come after me if he did not receive anything by Sunday so we waited."

"So that was his men that came?"

"Yes, I did not know who he would send or when they would come, but I knew they would come. I told Antonio to be prepared."

The Monday morning after the Sunday deadline is when all hell broke loose. Victor's mother-in-law, Mrs. Eck, was walking up to his house, when three armed men called from the road and told her, "Tell Victor to come out." She went inside and told Victor that men with guns were waiting for him outside. He looked out the window and saw members of the gang that sent him the note.

After first making his family lie on the floor, he grabbed his gun and ran out the back door. His men were set up in a bunkhouse directly behind his house and they were ready. He only had to make the prearranged attack signal, and six of his men, led by Antonio and Arturo, came out ready for a fight. They ran around to the front and the men in the road began firing at them. Victor's father, who lives across the street, heard the first gunshots and came out with his weapon, creating a dangerous crossfire. That's about the same time I pulled up in the truck to get the students. The outnumbered men from the rival gang never had a chance. With all the shots that were fired, it's a miracle our students did not get hit.

Someone called the police from the community phone in the village. They arrived two hours later after everything was over. Victor's men were nowhere in sight, but he did have a dead man on the road in front of his house. He quietly slipped the police a few hundred dollars. Then he told them the story that his night watchman had killed this man while he was trying to break into his house to rob his family. He showed the police a license for the watchman's gun and that satisfied them. As far as they were concerned, it was a case of self-defense and the case was closed.

73

More Trouble

The problem for Victor now becomes much more serious. Within one day, he receives word from the rival gang that they've declared war, and they'll get him and/or his family one way or another. He can handle himself, but now he's worried about his wife and kids. Things have gotten out of control and there's way too much violence.

I stop in front of Victor's house to let off the same students that I had rescued a few days earlier. He motions for me to join him under a coconut tree by the side of his house. Sitting in the shade, drinking a beer, Victor tells me that even his men are hard to control now. They're feeling anxious and pressuring him to go and attack the other gang before they're attacked again. He resists because he knows the violence has gotten out of hand.

He has decided to leave. He'll take the money he's made dealing drugs and make a new start. He'll give up his country, his land, and birth place. He says, "I don't want to fight anymore, Jorge. I don't want my family to be in danger." At this moment, I see Victor as I remember him before drugs came on the scene. We were best friends at one time, and now I am seeing him as a father and a husband concerned about how the consequences of his decisions will affect his family.

I'm not sure what he means or where he might go. But four days after the fire fight, Victor and his immediate family, including his father and mother, are gone. They disappear overnight. Nobody knows where they went.

When I pass by his house, I can see it's deserted. Some men are hanging out in front, talking in small groups. I know that Simon, who works for Victor, will know what's going on. He's married to the sister of Victor's wife and, as part of the family, he should be able to tell me more about what happened.

"Simon, what happened? Where is Victor?"

"He left, Jorge."

"What do you mean he left? Is he gone for good? Where is his family?"

"They all left, even his mother and father went with him."

"Where did they go?"

"Maybe they went to Mexico, nobody knows."

"What about Arturo and Antonio?"

"They went with him."

"Is this because the other gang threatened him?"

"Yes, Jorge. He was worried about Maria and Roberto (his children). He did not want them to be in danger."

"Is he gone forever? Will he come back?"

"I think he is gone for a long time, Jorge. He is selling his house and his land."

"What about his men? What will they do now?" He has armed men that are now unemployed.

"He called us together last night and gave us a bonus."

"What about his drug business?"

"I think me and Javier will take over. I still have to think about it. My wife does not want me to."

"So will his men work for you and Javier now?"

"Maybe."

His men are not the only ones he paid off. Before Victor left, he made a deal with two Belize Defense Force soldiers. For ten thousand dollars, they were supposed to pick up and assassinate the two leaders of the rival gang that had declared war on him and his family.

He also left them one of his cars as a bonus. The soldiers go to find the men he wanted killed and tell them they are under arrest for selling drugs. The men recognize Victor's car and resist arrest, but the soldiers convince them and their family that they confiscated the car as part of their drug-bust operation. The men are handcuffed and put in the backseat of the car. The soldiers drive to a deserted spot outside of Orange Walk Town, where they shoot and kill both men. The bodies are found inside the car with their hands still handcuffed behind their backs.

The two soldiers are picked up and charged with murder. They use some of their ten thousand dollars to get a good lawyer and are acquitted of all charges using a "drug sting" defense. Before long, they're free men and go back to their life in the defense force.

The saddest thing is that these two soldiers made a mistake and picked up the wrong guys. They didn't get the leaders of the gang as they were supposed to. They murdered the two younger brothers of the gang leader's wife. They were members of the gang, but they were not the ones that had threatened Victor and his family. Now the gang leader, plus the wife's family, is ready for war. Someone will have to pay.

Shortly after the two men were murdered, I run into their father, Don Pablo, in Orange Walk Town. I had just come back from a trip to Belize City. It's late and I'm hungry so I stop at a restaurant to eat dinner. I'm drinking a beer and looking at the menu when someone sits down at my table. I look up and see Don Pablo. He's drunk and his eyes are red and swollen. In the past, we've talked a few times about the school, but otherwise, I don't know him very well. He's an "alien" living in San Lazaro, and he's a very big man, about six foot six and 250 pounds. He's one of the guys Victor warned me not to turn my back on, and I believed him. I can tell this guy's been on the business end of some rough times.

Right now, he seems like a big teddy bear. He's sobbing and I truly feel his pain. Two of his sons have just been found murdered earlier in the morning. I know about it from the sugarcane wireless, but I act surprised when he tells me. He's been at the coroners to identify the bodies. He may have even witnessed their autopsy. In Belize, they have a morbid law that requires someone, usually a family member, to witness the autopsy. He's very drunk and is speaking quietly and deliberately. I think he just needs someone to talk to.

"Jorge, they murdered my sons." He speaks in Spanish, and his big sad eyes are looking right at me.

"Who murdered your sons, Don Pablo?"

"Victor. They were in his car." For a minute, he looks mean, and then the sadness comes back into his eyes.

"Don Pablo, I am so sorry."

"They were too young to die. They were my *sons*."

"How old were they, Don Pablo?"

"Rigoberto was seventeen and Fidel was nineteen." He sobs as he says their names.

"I am so sorry, Don Pablo."

"I will get Victor and I will get his family." He looks mean again. I would not want this guy mad at me.

"Don Pablo, you should take some time and take care of your family."

"Yes, I have to be with my wife and kids."

"Is there anything I can do?"

He shakes his head. "Nobody can do anything. They are dead."

"Do you need a ride anyplace, Don Pablo?"

"No, I am going now to find my wife. Good-bye, Jorge."

"Good-bye, Don Pablo."

The whole thing is very sad and it makes me lose my appetite. All this killing and cruelty was because of drugs, money, and greed. What a bloody mess.

74

Graduation

I'm coming to my last few weeks in Belize and things are going fine. The school's popularity is increasing, and we're getting more students all the time. The ministry of education promises to take over after I leave and the Peace Corps promises to help with volunteers. I've successfully completed the biggest and most important project of my life. The school's a functioning, accredited institution and I'm very proud of it.

The Peace Corps uses it as an example of what one person can do. USAID uses it as an example of what can be done with collaboration and financial support. Both San Lazaro and Trinidad are benefitting from the school even beyond what I had outlined in my grant proposal. Both villages have vendors that come to the school to sell food. Both villages have begun providing bus service to the school, which is growing as the school grows. We are creating income-generating projects exactly as we had envisioned.

We have our first graduating class on June 9, 1986. Twenty-three students made it out of the original twenty-five. Since we just decided to extend to be a four year school, we decided to go ahead with the graduation. Some of these students will transfer into a high school in town, and the others will go back to their communities. Their parents and invited guests fill the school as we have our first official graduation. We have guest speakers and ministry officials make their comments and pledge support. We look, and feel, like a real school.

The principal and I give the welcome and opening remarks. I'm very proud as I recognize the accomplishments of our graduating students. I thank them for all the work they did to make our school a reality. I tell them they will always be remembered as the first graduating class, and they should be proud of that. They made the school what it is today.

After that, we have more speakers and then the chief education officer gives out the diplomas. It's a perfect end to my two years of managing the school. I'm now confident that the school will continue on under the ministry of education. I feel like a weight has been lifted from my shoulders. I also feel sad that I'll no longer be a part of something that I put my blood, sweat, and tears into.

Jose has my name put on the school and it reads, "The Belize High School of Agriculture founded July 4, 1984 by George LeBard." I could not have been prouder. When I reflect on what I've accomplished with the school, I'm glad I extended my stay to five years as a volunteer. Nothing else could give me the satisfaction I feel when I see students showing up for school every morning.

I remember when I first arrived in Belize. At that time, I was struggling to survive. Then just three months after taking that first big step to change my life, I was empowered. I told myself at that time that my journey here would be like going back to school, to a university, for that degree I never got. The journey took a little longer than I expected, but I've learned so much more than I could have ever learned in an institution of higher learning.

I also recognize that for the last five years, I've been studying family. I've fallen in love with the values of family that I've witnessed here in village life. I've learned to accept the dreams and hopes, along with the realities and hardships. I've experienced the closeness along with the unconditional love and acceptance. It is a powerful force that validates my needs and desires as a human being. I've met my wife and I'm going to be a father. I have a family—my family.

I'm also worried. I now have someone besides myself to take care of and another one on the way. The fact that I'm going back to live with my mother is a reality check.

Everything I own can fit into a small backpack. Here, I've been an important person who had an impact on the education system of a country. But back home in my own culture I know if I'm not careful, I'll be swallowed up in the masses and become another social security number punching a clock.

I do have one big advantage. I'm going back with strength and confidence that I didn't have before. I know what I can do now, and I know I can succeed at whatever I want to do.

I'm also concerned about how Irma will do. She's a village girl, born and raised. She has been surrounded her entire life by people who love her and care deeply for who she is. *Will she be okay living in a culture that surrounds itself with strangers and not the family environment she's so used to?* As the time draws closer, we have several conversations about it.

"How do you feel about moving?"

"I try not to think about it too much. I know everything will be okay."

"Are you going to miss your family?"

"Yes, I worry about that sometimes."

"Do you ever feel afraid?"

"I worry sometimes that your family and friends will not like me. But I know you will be there."

"My family and friends will love you. I worry about what I'll do for work. In the U.S., I won't be the important person that I am here."

"You will still be important and I will get along with my mother-in-law and everything will be fine."

There are times I think about staying. I've been gone for five years, and I'm uncertain about what waits for us. Yet it's time to leave. For the last two years, everything I've done has been for the school, and I'm physically and mentally tired. I've also noticed that whenever a major decision has to be made, the board of directors looks to me for answers. I know that as long as I'm here, no one else will take over the management and make decisions. For the growth of the school, it's better that I leave.

I'm also stressed by the increasing violence since Victor left the country. It's ironic that he helped to start the drug culture and violence around us, but when he was here, he also kept the violence down and somewhat under control. I can feel things heating up and getting even more violent. Many of the men who worked for Victor are now unemployed and armed with automatic weapons. I can feel the tension in the community. There are too many dangerous, desperate men running around with automatic weapons.

75

Letter Home

June 1, 1986

Dear Dan,

I hope this letter finds you and yours well. This may surprise you, but after five years, I'm finally coming home. I have our plane tickets in my hand and we leave June 18. We fly into Reno and, at least to start, we'll stay with my mom and stepfather until I get a job and a little money to get our own place.

I have some good news. I'm going to be a father. Irma is three months pregnant. She gets motion sickness easily right now so the ride home is going to be a little rough on her. I'm excited for you to meet her. I think once you get to know each other, you'll be friends. I'm also looking forward to getting to know your new family better.

We've been friends since high school, and we've both been through some changes in our lives. I don't expect to come home and fit right back into everything. I know things are different, and I'll have to make up for some lost time. I don't even know if I can cook in a big kitchen anymore. But I'm fairly young and healthy, and it's not too late to start over.

I don't want to get sentimental here, but I'd feel better if I'm able to share some of the last five years with someone from home. Once I get there, things may seem different, and I might not feel like sharing as much. So you're the lucky guy that gets to hear my story. I've changed a little over the last five years. If you remember how I was when I first left, you know I wasn't doing too well. When I got here five years ago, I was running away. I was scared about what I was doing to myself with drugs and drinking. I ran away to save myself and to heal myself. The Peace Corps was good for me, and Belize was good to me. I found what I came for.

I put myself in a situation where I had to learn how to walk, talk, and eat all over again. I find it a little amusing that I picked a foreign country for my "rehab." Not only was the language and culture different, but it was also hot and humid, with lots of insects and snakes. Plus, I somehow managed to end up right in the middle of a drug war. Although I didn't see it at first, all these things played a role in helping me grow and become a man. I know now that I can go through anything if I'm willing to take the risk for what I want.

Eventually, I realized that healing means owning your problems. You can't fix it if you don't know it's broken. I always believed that chasing women, drinking, and one-night stands was a good life. Here, starting over, I was able to change my lifestyle. I no longer identify myself with who my friends are, how many girls I have, or what is currently popular. I thought I needed all those things to be happy.

The truth is I was lonely, bored, and angry. Drinking, drugs, and women kept me company and helped me forget. When I got to the point where I wanted more out of my life, those things didn't work anymore. I could not have both, simple as that. I wanted my own family, with real values and relationships. That doesn't mean that everything's perfect after that. There are problems and consequences in whatever we do and every relationship we have. It means that's what I want out of life. It's taking care of me at all levels of mind, body, and soul and that's healing for me. Being here, I've learned to be responsible and take action for what I want. I know now that anything less than that is deceiving and lying to myself.

Last, but definitely not least, finding meaning for my life is rewarding. Discovering how I learn opened up the universe to me. Once I got that, once I understood it, there was, or is, nothing I can't do. I'm not the first person to build a school or turn around a self-destructive life to a productive one, and I know I won't be the last. But I did it. I gave up a life of boredom and anger. I had a vision, a dream, and I took action and made it happen. Because of that, I know what my life force, my truth feels like. I also know the confidence and strength it brings with it.

These are just a few of the things I experienced while I was here. I wish I could share everything that's happened, but that would take about ten years and be a book by the time I'm done. I think going through these experiences by myself was part of the growth process for me. I had to learn it by myself, for myself.

I know all this must be hard to understand, and you're probably thinking I've been out in the sun too long. But in short, the last five years has been a life-changing experience, culminating with my marriage just six months ago. Irma's a beautiful, humorous, and wise woman. I know I'll spend many years with her and have lots of children.

I wish I could say I'm looking forward to coming home. But right now, I'm feeling sad about leaving the place that's been my home, my education, and my healing place for the last five years. I think once I get there, I'll feel better. I'll give you a call, and maybe we can get together with our families for dinner or something.

Your friend,
Jorge

76

Holdup on the Way Home

In just three days, we're leaving for the United States, and the only way to get U.S. dollars is to go to the Central Bank for permission. Most of my Peace Corps savings will be mailed to us once we reach my mother's house. In the meantime, we have five hundred dollars US and our plane tickets. Everything is lined up, and we're counting down the days to when our lives are going to change.

Irma and I are on our way home from the Central Bank in Belize City. It's around four o'clock in the afternoon when we pass through Yo Creek and pick up a policeman hitchhiking to San Lazaro. He tells us he's going to investigate a reported murder.

"Did you say someone's been murdered in San Lazaro?"

"Yes, suh, a murder has been reported there." The policeman is young and trying to be professional.

"I live in San Lazaro. Do you know the name of the person?" I'm almost afraid to know.

"Yes, suh, he is a Mr. Pablo Garcia."

Pablo and his family are friends of ours. He's young, around twenty-six years old, and single. Two of Pablo's brothers attend the school, and his sisters come every day to sell food to the students. The policeman doesn't know any of the details yet, so I have to wait until we reach San Lazaro to find out what happened.

Once we arrive, I see the usual small groups of people on the street. Women are crying, kids are trying to get a peek at the body, and Pablo lies dead on the ground. I see his father, who comes over to talk to the policeman. Without getting out of the truck, I look for someone who can tell me what has happened. I find Thomas who tells me the story.

"Thomas, what happened to Pablo?"

"Hi, Jorge. Boy Pablo dead, mon," he says, shaking his head with worry.

"I know, but what happened? Who killed him?" Thomas is a Spanish man, but he likes to speak Creole.

"Buoy eh look like Tino kill him, Jorge." Tino's a Salvadorian and former gunman of Victor's.

"Why? Why did he kill him?"

"Buoy eh looks like they want di same girl. You know that girl she works at di bar." Recently, a bar had been established in the village, the first real bar in San Lazaro.

"Yeah, I know who you're talking about."

"Bad news, Jorge." Thomas takes a deep breath.

"Where is Tino? Did they catch him?"

"No, mon. He have his gun. He just walk away. No one can stop him." He shrugged his shoulders.

"So they don't know where he is?"

"No, mon. He gone. He di hide back a bush, Jorge."

Turns out that Tino, who is around nineteen years old, liked the same girl as Pablo. Tino gets drunk at the bar and starts pressuring her to sleep with him. She tells him she's in love with Pablo and to leave her alone, or Pablo will come and punish him. So Tino goes home and gets his machine gun. Then he goes back to the bar and points it at the girl, telling her to send her son to get Pablo.

The little boy, about eleven and unaware of the danger, goes to tell Pablo that his mother wants to see him. As Pablo's walking up the path to the bar, Tino steps out from behind the door and yells at him to take out his gun and fight like a man. Pablo has no gun, but that doesn't stop Tino from shooting him, seventeen times. Once he's sure Pablo's dead, Tino calmly walks away, pointing his gun in the direction of anyone who gets too close, and disappears into the bush.

We leave the crowd and go home to the school. I'm preoccupied thinking about poor Pablo as I drive the rest of the way to the school. Irma goes into the house to start some dinner, and I go out to feed the school animals before dark. After feeding the chickens, I walk over to feed the pigs. Out of the corner of my eye, I see someone come out of the bush very close to where I am. Looking up, I see Tino coming toward me, and he's carrying his gun. I quickly evaluate my situation. I'm too far from my house and the school. He's too close; there's nothing I can do but bluff it out. Playing dumb and letting him believe I don't know what has happened seems to be my best option right now. But here I am, face-to-face with a guy who has just murdered a friend in cold blood. I feel angry but mostly scared for my life.

He wants to talk to me and motions for me to come closer. His eyes look hooded and dazed, like he's high on something more than alcohol.

"Hello, Tino." I know he's dangerous right now, and I have to be his friend because everyone else is looking for him and wants to kill him.

"Mr. Jorge, I need five hundred dollars." I had just come from the Central Bank, and I have exactly five hundred dollars, but there is no way he could know that. That is a lot of money to me right now, and there is no way I'm giving it to him without a fight.

"Tino, I don't have five hundred dollars." He looks disappointed, desperate.

"I will sell you my gun for five hundred dollars." He shows me his weapon, which is some kind of automatic rifle.

"Tino, I'm sorry, man, but I don't have any money."

"This is a very good gun." He doesn't want to take no for an answer.

"Tino, I don't want any problems." He looks at me, and I know I just said the wrong thing.

"What problems? Why are you talking about problems? Who said anything about problems?" Now he's getting defensive and I don't like the look in his eyes.

"No, mon, sorry. I should not have said that. I just mean I can't buy your gun. I don't have any money." He starts to calm down.

He's still irritated that I mentioned "problems," and he starts walking away, muttering obscenities under his breath.

For a split second, I think about tackling him. I'm bigger than him. But if he manages to get away before anyone can get here to help me, he will definitely kill me. The problem is I'm not completely convinced he's not going to do that anyway. The other problem is there is no one around that can come and help me if I do tackle him. So I let him go or, to be more exact, stay out of his way. I keep a close eye on him, ready to jump for cover, until he walks out around the school and into the road. The last time I see him, he's walking right down the middle of the road like he owns it. Just a mile away in the opposite direction is the police and Pablo's family, who I know would love to get their hands on him.

I decide to take Irma and go into San Lazaro for the policeman, but when I get there, he's already left. I go to the community phone and call the Orange Walk Police Station. By this time, I'm still feeling the adrenaline rush from being so close to Tino and the danger of losing my life. I tell the police that this killer just left my house twenty minutes earlier, and if they hurry, they might catch him walking down the road.

The police arrive at my house an hour later. There are ten of them crammed into an open Land Rover with shotguns and revolvers pointed in every direction, including at me. I go out to talk to them, scared for my life the second time that day. Clearly, the first cop on the scene had reported that they were dealing with an automatic weapon. They're pumped up now, thinking they might find Tino waiting for them to shoot it out, and they know they're outgunned. I tell them which way he went, and they pile back into the Land Rover and head in the right direction with their guns pointed everywhere but where they should be.

They don't get Tino; they couldn't find him. The next day someone stops by to tell me that Tino sent word that he's not done killing. He's angry because someone called the police, and he says he's going to kill them for that. I know this culture, and when someone comes directly to you with a vague message, it is generally intended for you. It does not make me feel too good. My name's not mentioned, but everyone knows I'm the one who called the police.

We only have two days to go. I don't want to make it this far and get murdered on the last day for something stupid. We decide to spend our last couple of nights with Irma's family in Yo Creek. If Tino does decide to come after me, he'll have to find me. It's a good opportunity for Irma to say good-bye to everyone. I also say all of my farewells to my friends over a few beers. There is lots of crying and well-wishing on both sides.

The night before we're leaving, I go for a walk in the village. I'm feeling melancholy thinking about my future and wondering if I'll ever see Belize again. I guess it's not all bad. I won't have to worry about renegade killers, death threats, drug wars, and poisonous snakes. Then again, it might be boring without all those things I'm used to.

I pass by some young boys playing a pickup game of soccer in someone's yard. One of them sees me and shouts out "King George." Then the other boys chime in, "King George, King George." It makes me think of four other young boys from long ago who declared themselves kings. We thought we were immortal, ready to stand together and take on the world to rule our own destiny. We had a lot of dreams for ourselves in those days. We felt like there was nothing we couldn't do. We would fight off the bad guys, win the most beautiful girl, and live a good life. We were kings. But somewhere along the way, the realities of life made us forget we were kings, and we lost our way. I remember now and I won't forget again.

Epilogue

Irma and I returned to Reno, Nevada, where we both experienced culture shock. After three months of working odd jobs, I was offered a job in Belize with the Peace Corps. I gladly accepted, and we loaded everything we owned in a used car and drove back through Mexico. I went on staff with the Peace Corps as associate Peace Corps director in charge of volunteer training, the environmental education program, and staff operations. We built a nice home in Yo Creek, the same village that Irma was born and raised in. Our sons—Sean, 23; Alan, 21; and Ryan, 19—were all born in Belize.

In 1998, after seventeen years of living in Belize, we finally made the move back to the United States to reconnect with family and friends. Irma and I both got involved in social services work. I run a hunger relief organization and she works for a community foundation. Part of her work as the "Hispanic community liaison" overlaps with my work so we often work together. This year, we will be married for twenty-five great years, and we're looking forward to another twenty-five. We try to get down to Belize at least every other year; eventually, we plan to retire there.

The School

The Belize High School of Agriculture is doing well. We had transferred many of the first twenty-five students to high schools in town. All of them made the top ten academically and one graduated as valedictorian. These were students who had not passed the national selection exam. The original principal and vice principal are still with the school after twenty-five years. Of all the decisions I made in the planning and development of the school, selecting those two teachers was the best thing I could have done. They have kept the original vision alive, keeping the agriculture components, and they're still accepting students that fail the national selection exam. The enrollment is at capacity, with over two hundred students, and growing as the school's facilities grow. Over five hundred students have graduated since we opened the school in 1984 to twenty-five students. Many have gone on to excel in higher education. There is writing on the wall as you enter the school. It says, "The Belize High School of Agriculture, founded in 1984 by George LeBard."

Victor

Victor lived in Mexico for a while before moving to the United States. There, he was busted in a drug sting and did two and half years in a North Carolina prison. In prison, he found religion. He is now living somewhere in the United States as the pastor of a church.

Arturo

Arturo returned to San Lazaro. He is happily married with kids and is a successful cane farmer.

Maria

Maria got married and had four children before dying of cancer in her early forties. Before she died, we had become friends again.

Tino

The only reason I mention Tino is because he was my number one concern when Irma and I returned to Belize three months later. He had threatened to kill me and I wanted to know where he was. He was never captured by the police. Shortly after killing Sebastian, he went to hide out in the village of San Felipe. He used his gun to bully his way around until someone shot and killed him.

The Other Kings

After finishing my tour with Peace Corps, I returned home. A short time later, I was contacted by my mother. Fred, the original King, was in town living with his mother. He was dying and sent a message that he wanted to see me. The other two Kings were gone long ago. Hugh died in a motorcycle accident, and the last I heard, Teddy had wasted his mind sniffing glue. Now Fred's heart was blown out by too much heroin. He had two open-heart surgeries over the years, but there was nothing more they could do for him. I went to visit and recognized immediately, that he was still looking for the same freedom, still rebelling. I couldn't tell him about the freedom I had found. He didn't want to hear it. He wanted to get back together as friends like old times drinking, doing drugs, and looking for chicks. We talked for a while, and when his mother wasn't looking, I took him to the nearest liquor store so he could pick up some beer. I left promising to keep in touch.

Two months later, I attended the funeral of Fred's nineteen-year-old son, who died from a heroin overdose. One month after that, Fred's heart gave out, and he died at his mother's house. He died in his sleep, in the same room we used to sneak out of when we were kids.

The Kings were my first real friends, and I will always remember the allegiance and loyalty we shared. They were my family on the streets, and they became more important to me than my blood family. Their friendship meant survival.

After Fred's death, I worried that his life, our lives, our dreams, that we had as children would become meaningless, lost as each one of us passes. As the only King left, I won't let that happen. I want to realize those dreams we had as children and take back the power to create our own reality.

MEMORIES

After clearing the jungle away—1984

Recruiting 1st year students—1984

Sugar cane fire

Doing the books—1984

My wedding day—December 1985

Students in the field—2010

The Belize High School of Agriculture—2010

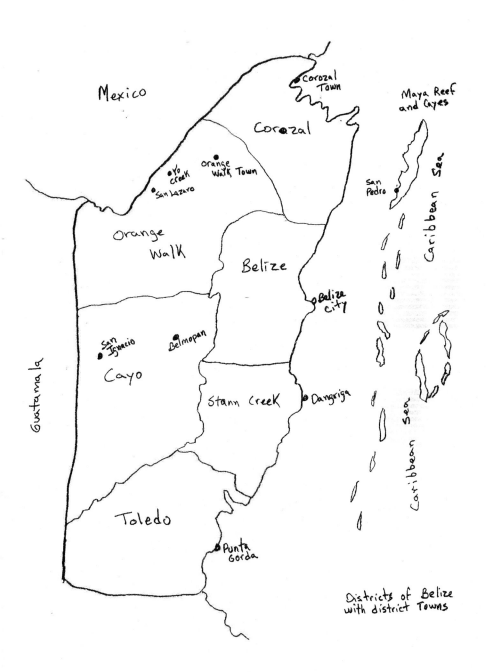

Map of Belize